The Christmas Book

CHRISTMAS LIST

Joan — £100 Ford
Fred — bicycle
Peg — doll's house
Bill —

GIVE A FORD £100 SALOON THIS YEAR!

The eternal problem of gift-selection, of hitting on something really appropriate, acceptable, useful, something concerning the value of which there can be no doubt, is solved. Whether the recipient has or has not other cars, the FORD £100 Saloon will be equally gratifying and welcome.

Smart and trim, inside and out, non-fatiguing to handle, compact in overall dimensions (for the negotiation of dense traffic, ease of parking, inexpensiveness of garage), it is an honest, "full" four-seater, with plenty of head, leg and elbow-room for all occupants. No other car of comparable performance costs so little, on insurance, taxation, fuel, lubricants, tyres or — in time to come — replacements or repairs. The Local Ford Dealer will delight to give you a really demonstrative run, to prove what sort of gift it is, one that will create pride of ownership almost equalling the genuine, lasting gratitude such a handsome present must inspire. He can deliver the £100 Ford Saloon, Taxed and Insured, on an Initial Payment of £25. 18-month and 24-month transactions can be arranged with slightly higher initial payments. Literature on Request: All Prices at Works.

"There is no comparison! More miles per gallon is good: Fewer pence per mile is better!"

FORD MOTOR COMPANY LIMITED, DAGENHAM, ESSEX. LONDON SHOWROOMS: 88 REGENT STREET, W.1

The Christmas Book

**The Best of Good Housekeeping
at Christmas
1922 – 1962**

Compiled by
Brian Braithwaite
Noëlle Walsh

EBURY PRESS
LONDON

Published by Ebury Press
an imprint of the Random Century Group Ltd
Random Century House
20 Vauxhall Bridge Road
London SW1V 2SA

First Impression 1988
Second Impression 1989
Third Impression 1990

ISBN 0 85223 756 1

Printed and bound in Great Britain
by Butler & Tanner Limited, Frome and London

CONTENTS

FOREWORD

EDITORIAL VIEWPOINT

The highlight of Good Housekeeping during the forty Christmases between 1922 and 1962, was undoubtedly the pages of festive fare. No matter how many times a Christmas cake may have been baked, a turkey stuffed, mince pies prepared, there was an insatiable appetite for new and exciting ways of treating the traditional favourites. Of course, the war years gave a different perspective to Christmas and in particular, to the food. It was then that the Good Housekeeping Institute, founded in 1924, came into its own, providing recipes for baking an eggless cake or, more drastic, substituting traditional fare with potatoes (page 136). Whetting the appetite for the depletions of rationing, patriotic slogans abounded as readers were urged: 'Don't forget – every time you use a potato in place of bread, you're helping to save British lives'.

Christmas was a time for celebrating family life so there were plenty of ideas for children's games (page 22), new outfits for the younger set (page 104) and stories to keep them amused (page 74). In fact, the main ingredient of Good Housekeeping, particularly during the war years when spirits needed lifting and minds distracting, was fiction. GH was one of the main vehicles of the day for publicising the work of writers who went on to become household names; writers such as W. Somerset Maugham whose short story, Louise, you can read on page 30, and A. J. Cronin whose poignant story, Christmas for Agnes (page 94) will arouse as much compassion – and anger – today as it no doubt did in 1933.

The names of non-fiction writers, too, are like a literary hall of fame: Rebecca West (In the Absence of a Possible Husband, What is a Girl to Do? page 18), Lady Violet Bonham Carter (Relations, Weighed in the Balance and Found Sometimes Wanted, Sometimes Not! page 44, and The Voice of the Young Women page 50), Beverley Nichols (Christmas and the Gardener page 106).

By the close of the forties, tired of the bleak austerity of post-war Britain, colour was introduced on a large scale. The big-name writers disappeared, lured away by the burgeoning book publishing industry, and GH drew in on itself, printing great tracts of fiction – most of it of the light, romantic type. As the housing industry geared itself up once more to rebuild homes destroyed by the blitz, the home became the central theme of the magazine. Articles on architecture, house prices and decoration ideas proliferated as did recipes and products for the kitchen.

Fashion in the fifties was less frivolous than in the previous decades, due partly to the continued rationing and partly to the attention being given to other areas of everyday life. There was less interest in looking outward to Europe and beyond, an understandable reaction to the trauma of the forties. But the magazines of the fifties are a real reflection of what life was like for the ordinary woman and man, retrenching and gaining strength before the excitement of the sixties.

NOËLLE WALSH

ADVERTISING VIEWPOINT

Christmas has always been a bonanza time for advertisers – both for the seasonal surge in buying and selling and for the flightier indulgences of yuletide creativity. While not reflecting the reckless overspend of the contemporary television age, with its credit card extravagances and high juvenile expectations, the decades covered in this book are redolent with Christmas presents and offers for adults and children – from the humblest toy from Hamleys to the breathless excitement experienced on Christmas morning by the recipient of a Hoover vacuum cleaner. This latter gift was trumpeted in the earliest issues of Good Housekeeping and was still being received with ecstatic gratitude in the 1950's. The illusion that the lady of the house would emit shrieks of delight at the sight of household goods to lighten her work-load was heavily extolled in the pre-war copies of the magazine. In 1924 the children were presenting Mother with a Whirlwind Suction Sweeper and only the following year she could get knocked out by the gift of the Johnson's Floor Polishing Outfit at the reckless price of 22/6d. Her gift value leapt in 1928 to 43/- as the family decided that the apogee of her yuletide happiness would be an Acme Wringer.

The Big Stores always presented themselves as the mecca of childish thrills and delights. Hamleys, then as now, was an obvious choice but the specialists in the Christmas Bazaar were Selfridges and the now-defunct Gamages. The latter's half page advertisements were show-pieces of condensation and enthusiastic information. The centrepiece was their Christmas Bazaar, from the Enchanted Castle to Toyland by the Sea. Each year they offered free their bumper Christmas gift book. Never modest, in 1924 they were claiming that 'nothing so charming or so colossal has ever been staged at Christmas-time in London Town'. And it is intriguing to read that 'The Chimpanzee's Orchestra will perform'.

The first-ever Christmas issue of Good Housekeeping, in 1922, carried a full page advertisement for Mackintosh's toffee which was a fascinating early example of philanthropy and commercialism at work hand in hand. By purchasing a tin of Mackintosh's toffee the reader would be sending a "Holly Bag" of toffee to some hundred thousand underprivileged children – a representative sample of whom were shown pathetically watching through the railings at the rich kids with their own toffee-laden Father Christmas.

Christmas memories are stirred by the recollection of Christmas pleasures past – Harbutt's Plasticene, Hornby trains, Fit-Bits and Meccano (for real boys). Other products light the memory: Tom Smith crackers, Ingersoll pocket watches, Big Ben alarm clocks, Wills's Gold Flake, Grants Morella Cherry Brandy (Welcome Always – Keep it Handy) Rose's Lime Juice as a hangover cure, the war-time Ministry of Food standing on its head to give us ersatz recipes. In these pages is the ghost of Christmas past, alluring us with yuletide goodies before the days of wide-spread colour advertising.

BRIAN BRAITHWAITE

1922

Make it a Xmas de Luxe for those who otherwise would have to look on

Messrs. John Mackintosh & Sons, Ltd.

invite the readers of "Good Housekeeping" to share the pleasure of a great **Christmas Gift** to over **100 000 poor kiddies**

The Editor of "Good Housekeeping" has nominated The National Children's Home to distribute "Holly Bags" for "Good Housekeeping" readers.

All "Happiness Coupons" should be posted or handed to your confectioner before or not later than December 16th. Holly Bags for coupons received later will be sent as New Year Gifts.

No Holly Bags can be sent to individuals; no "Happiness Coupons" can be acknowledged — a general acknowledgment will be published early in January.

Copies of this advertisement will be sent free on request to church officials, etc., willing to assist various charities by supporting the Happiness for Everyone scheme.

Happiness for Everyone!

How you can help to make the wish come true

IMAGINE the bitter disappointment of waking up on Christmas morning and finding yourself forgotten—on the very morning when most people are surrounded by tokens of goodwill expressing the Christmas spirit . . . on the happiest morning of the year.

Your children's stockings will be crammed with good things. Some children's stockings will be provided for less generously.

To bring happiness to over one hundred thousand poor kiddies we are distributing on your behalf Holly Bags of Mackintosh's Toffee-de-Luxe.

All you have to do to share in this scheme is (1) Buy one lb. of Mackintosh's Toffee-de-Luxe. (2) Fill in the "Happiness Coupon" printed below. (3) Hand the coupon to your confectioner or post it to "Happiness Scheme," John Mackintosh & Sons, Ltd., Toffee Town, Halifax.

We will then put aside for distribution as your gift, one Holly Bag. And for every lb. of Mackintosh's Toffee-de-Luxe you buy we will give on your behalf one Holly Bag provided that you comply with these simple conditions.

Happiness for everyone . . . let the poor kiddies share the delights of the toffee *you* will choose for your own children's stockings, and help to make the wish come true.

A reduced facsimile of the Holly Bag. Your name as the donor will be written on the Christmas Card which accompanies it.

Mackintosh's

Toffee-de-Luxe

The purchase of 1-lb. of any of the following varieties of Mackintosh's Toffee-de-Luxe will entitle you to make a free gift:

Egg and Cream-de-Luxe, Mint-de-Luxe, Cocoanut-de-Luxe, De-Luxe Assortment, Almond Toffee-de-Luxe, Café-de-Luxe, Toffee-de-Luxe, Chocolate Toffee-de-Luxe, Almond Chocolate Toffee-de-Luxe, Assorted Chocolate Toffee-de-Luxe

NOTE TO CONFECTIONERS.—You are invited to co-operate by sending coupons handed to you over the counter to John Mackintosh & Sons, Ltd., Halifax, in weekly batches. All postage costs incurred will be refunded promptly.

HAPPINESS COUPON

I have to-day purchased......lb(s). of Mackintosh's Toffee-de-Luxe. Please distribute on my behalf ....Holly Bag(s).

Name ....

Address ....

Shopkeeper's Name........................

Address ....

*TO BE SIGNED BY SHOPKEEPER

G.H.

POST THIS COUPON IN AN UNSEALED ENVELOPE WITH $\frac{1}{2}$d. STAMP.

Post to "Happiness Scheme," John Mackintosh & Sons, Ltd., Toffee Town, Halifax, or hand to the Confectioner who sells you Mackintosh Toffee-de-Luxe.

FASHIONS

Drapery is Closely Allied to the Waistlines of Our Frocks—Sleeves Are Long and Close-fitting—and Skirts Break Out Exuberantly into Flounces

BY ANNA VAN CAMPEN STEWART

1922

At the moment the smart hat is small, and that to the right, of copper velvet, has a cocarde of copper-coloured feathers with copper fringe

To look ingenuous appears to be the sole object of the little hat below. It is made of black velvet and trimmed with green and silver ribbon

EVELYN VARON

The large capeline of velvet is too picturesque to be completely ousted by the small hat, and below it is expressed in copper-coloured velvet with plumage of the same rich colour forming a second "brim"

GERMAINE-PAGE

GERMAINE-PAGE

"GOOD HOUSEKEEPING" OFFICE,
2 RUE DE LA PAIX, PARIS.

First there is a long slender cloak of black velvet—it may be brown or dark green—collared, cuffed, and bordered at the hem with brown fox, mink, or sable. This cloak is usually very slightly draped at the hips—a fold or two, no more. Then there is a tube-like jacket of caracul, broadtail, or some short fur above a skirt which flares sharply in some fashion. A three-quarter coat of black broadcloth, straight almost its length, is banded with black phoque and finished with a flaring ruffle of cloth, the narrow underskirt showing for several inches below.

Fur capes have disappeared from the pesage at Longchamps, women wearing loose cloaks of fur instead. Mink is most favoured at the moment—the pelts placed crosswise at the shoulders and hem and lengthwise between. Capes of fabric, except for evening wear, are seldom seen this season, although a number of pretty models were shown in the collections. An exception was a slender black velvet cape, worn at Longchamps, which was collared and edged down the fronts with ermine.

Evening cloaks are made of soft velvet—rose, blue, green, red, orange, or black, collared preferably with chinchilla or sable. A beautiful cloak worn at a recent *première*, at the Gymnase, was of black velvet with a deep collar and yoke of sable pelts posed crosswise, the

THE mid-season fashions so far have only accentuated, as it were, the silhouette of the August collections. Where there was one puff below the waistline in August there are ten now. Where there were ten straight, short, loosely belted jackets in August there are now fifty. At the races one sees but little else—but that little is significant.

1922

velvet being fulled on to the fur yoke. Other cloaks are of rich brocade in metal and colours or of plain velvet lined with silver tissue.

Just now there are many frocks of silver lace about—brilliant silver lace over underslips of bright-coloured velvet, the colour showing prettily through the open, glittering mesh. Elderly women are wearing low-cut corsages under over-dresses of silver lace which veil the shoulders most effectively. Recently at a *première* a woman with beautiful grey hair appeared in such a gown—the silver lace veiling her shoulders above a black velvet slip which was cut straight across under the arms.

About her neck she wore one of the short ropes of pearls which are now so much the fashion, while a slender chain of diamonds weighted with a monocle strayed down over the brilliant lace corsage, and straps of brilliants, supporting the velvet underslip, gleamed through the lace at the shoulders. With

diamonds in her wonderful hair she was a very exquisite figure—and she knew it!

Jean Patou shows a collection of mid-season frocks which are charming—fur-trimmed belted jackets over one-piece frocks with, often, corsages of gold or silver, evening frocks of silver lace over tinted underslips, and several frocks of crêpe de Chine with an odd puff on the side at the hip and shallow folds of drapery falling below. The slender, slightly draped frock with the great *chou* at the hip presents a most fascinating silhouette.

Another Patou model of great beauty is a simple creation of silver brocade—the design only slightly indicated. The straight corsage is attached to a skirt which is quite flat in the back and rather wide and flaring toward the front —the flaring section being embroidered decoratively and not too elaborately with vivid blue beads.

Molyneux also shows the circular

Another of the unusual girdle effects Paris is busy producing appears in a rust-red velvet frock above, in which tiny flounces are masquerading as sleeves

Grey wool tricot is used for the little frock to the left, and the hat worn with it is of grey felt trimmed with rust and brown feathers. Lanvin makes the suit below of black cloth and trims it with ermine

A black velvet jacket trimmed with ermine is worn over a grey cloth frock in the suit to the right below, and shows the loosely belted effect now in vogue. One of the new furs—phoque—makes the collar and cuffs of the suit to the right. Note the simplicity of the short jacket and plain ankle-length skirt

LANVIN

1922

CALLOT

Callot introduces the high waistline into a frock of brown wool fabric banded with brown fur. Novelty lurks in the queer little puffs that finish the sleeves of the black velvet and kolinsky cloak to left above

Drapery invades even our suits this winter and adds grace to the slender line of a black cloth model trimmed with kolinsky. To the right, a frock of black velours de laine boasts a positive landscape of Chinese embroidery for its girdle

Reminiscent of a less hurried age are the two demure-looking flounces in the frock below. It is made of green velvet and buckled in artless fashion on the left hip

effect in skirts in several of his new models, where shallow godets fall all about below the closely fitted hips. These circular skirts are attached, as a rule, to a long straight corsage with long, close sleeves cuffed in some fashion at the wrists. However, many of the new Molyneux skirts are quite straight and narrow.

Everywhere now in Paris we see slender frocks of beaded velvet of every colour. The favourite is a grey or *grisbeige* velvet of wonderful softness —a most exquisite colour—beaded with tiny crystal tubes. But the colours vary. A frock of amber velvet is beaded with topaz, emerald green velvet is beaded with silver, and a black velvet frock is beaded with opaque crystal tubes combined with silver. They are all lovely.

New evening shoes are of metal brocade or of gold or silver cloth buckled with brilliants. Evening shoes of velvet are sometimes made to match the

gown, but these are seen less often. A new model for the street is a low shoe with a single barrette, with a flat buckle or ornament at each end of the leather strap. The high boot, so much talked about of late, is not yet worn in Paris. Some of the models shown are rather eccentric and will not be accepted by the smart Parisienne, whose taste bars always the bizarre.

At present the smart hat is a small cloche of felt, trimmed most scantily if at all. Often the only trimming is the narrow grosgrain ribbon which binds the edge and the two great pearl pins which are thrust through the front of the crown.

With the new close sleeves a moderately high gauntlet glove is worn—the flaring cuff lined with white or coloured kid or silk. Moiré is the silk usually employed for this purpose. Some new models show coloured embroidery on the back, but the plain glove is, as always, in better taste.

The Children's Time

By

Muriel Wrinch

Decorations by Elizabeth Montgomery

1923

CHRISTMAS is coming! And the hearts of little folks all over the world are beginning to beat fast in anticipation of Christmas joys. True, the celebration of Christmas is not so elaborate an affair as it was, nor in England does the Christmas season last for so long as, to the delight of small people, it lasts upon the Continent; but the children of this country still say, with the writer of the *Hue and Cry after Christmas*—"But is old, old Christmas gone? Nothing but the hair of his good grey old head and beard left? *Well, I will have that, seeing that I cannot have more of him.*"

They still hold on to the hair of the good grey old head, and countless little people in England pretend breathlessly to be asleep on the night of Christmas Eve, afraid even to peep from one wakeful eye in case Father Christmas, entering in his long red cloak, may vanish up the chimney as suddenly as he came.

But that does not prevent a night wakeful from excitement, and many a happy baby is worn out with fatigue by the time she appears at the breakfast-table on Christmas morning. It is my purpose in this article to suggest means by which Christmas Day may be made as happy and healthy a day as it should be.

I know one little girl who was given a Children's Annual each year for Christmas, who always rose and examined the presents on the chair beside her bed and in her stocking by candle-light at four o'clock in the morning. Though this little person was always most conscientiously asleep at the time when Father Christmas might be expected to arrive, by breakfast-time on Christmas Day she had always exhausted all the pictures in the new book! Quite a lot of English babies do not enjoy their Christmas Day as much as they should on account of the wakeful night of excitement which precedes it.

A mother of two little girls aged three and five, who appreciated the danger of over-excitement and fatigue, used to avoid this by never allowing Christmas Day to come so near as *to-morrow*. I mean, when Christmas was really only

"Saint Francis and Saint Benedight,
Bless this house from wicked wight;
From the night-mare and the goblin,
That is hight good-fellow Robin;
Keep it from a'l evil spirits,
Fairies, weezels, rats and ferrets:
From curfew time
To the next prime."

Children's Old Christmas Song.

three days off, the children thought it was four; when one day off, according to the children it was two. Thus when Christmas morning eventually did arrive, the two children woke up to it as a delightful surprise. This is a doubtful expedient from the point of view of the principle of truthfulness, which should be at the bottom of all our dealings with children, though not

"This wonderful Saint Nicholas"

from the point of view of efficiency. It seems to me that the continental way of celebrating Christmas as a season rather than as a one-day festival for children is much to be preferred to our own. The Christmas season begins about a month before December 25th. Suddenly, about the time of the first Sunday in Advent, Father Christmas will appear, with his cheery face shining and his beard sparkling with frost. And, of course, he doesn't forget his bag, nor his

writing tablet to record the list of presents, although first many inquiries have to be made as to Jacques' progress during the year and Marie's conduct at school! And many are the reassurances that have to be made on the part of the children as to good intentions for the coming year! And then this wonderful Saint Nicholas—Santa Claus—will shake out his big bag, filled with nuts and apples and oranges, upon the floor, and by the time the scramble for these treasures is over he has disappeared in his sledge into the night air.

Sometimes during this season delightful cakes appear for tea. Special honeycakes—effigies of the Virgin and Saint Joseph and Saint Nicholas—come to the table in French Flanders. Saint Nicholas is always the favourite, for he is the patron saint of children, and never does he fail to appear in honey-cake form on November 6th, Saint Nicholas's Day, though in the Low Countries he is always dressed as a bishop, complete with his mitre.

Farther south, Saint Nicholas gets himself made of raspberry-coloured sugar. Very sticky he is, and apt to get himself covered with looking-glass print when hot, eager little hands carry him home in a piece of newspaper from the sweetstuff shop!

And thus Christmas-time extends over a month, and no one under twelve gets unduly excited on one day nor depressed and unhappy when Christmas is over, for no one knows quite when Saint Nicholas with his presents will appear, nor when he has gone to get ready for next year.

Again, in England we might make more of a feature of the many old legends suitable to tell to children. I always think that Christmas in the old English country house, so charmingly described by Washington Irving, must have been a time of legends and old fairy-tales. One by one the company would tell a tale—"there were the usual proportion of old uncles and aunts, comfortably married dames, superannuated spinsters, blooming country cousins, half-fledged striplings, and bright-eyed boarding-school hoydens. At one end of the hall was a group of the young folks,

1923

some nearly grown up, others of a more tender and budding age, fully engrossed by a merry game; and a profusion of wooden horses, penny trumpets, and tattered dolls, about the floor, showed traces of little fairy beings, who having frolicked through a happy day had been carried off to slumber through a peaceful night."

Perhaps before they went they had been soothed by the old Canadian tale which your child and every other child in the world should know—the story of How the Robin got his Red Breast.

It is thus that the tale runs:—I write it in full and in my own words, for I do not know where the legend is to be found—

As Christ was hanging on the Cross, His arms outstretched as though to bless, yet secured by the nails driven through them by unbelievers, His head so mockingly crowned with thorns by those who derided Him, a little robin flew down and perched upon the Cross. As he saw the calm, kindly eyes and the pierced hands, the robin's heart burst with love and worship for the suffering Christ, and he longed to pull out the cruel nails driven so fast into the wood of the Cross, but his little beak was powerless to do this. All he could do for the dying Saviour was to pluck one thorn from the crown which the Jews had set upon His head. And as he flew down and pulled the one thorn away, a drop of blood from the brow of Christ fell upon the robin's breast, dyeing it a deep carmine for ever. To-day all robins have a red breast in memory of the one of their number who tried to help in his own small way the Lover of children and of animals.

Many old stories which could be adapted for Christmas have been handed down in the mythologies of various countries, and there are the merry tales of Jack Frost and Father Christmas and Christmas fairies which every mother will know how to tell, and which even the most grown-up amongst us will never completely forget. And I still maintain, old-fashioned a belief though it may be, that the Bible stories are the most suitable of all for children at Christmas. The psycho-analysts, it is true, speak wisely of the puzzling effect which the mystical element which appears in all these Christmas Bible stories may have upon the childish mind, but from the common-sense point of view, there seems to me little to harm a child, and very much to benefit him, in such a simple and appealing story as that of the shepherds watching upon the lonely hills. These stories, after all, were expressions of faith of a very simple people, whose minds were far more attuned to the mind of the child than are many grown-up minds of to-day.

The stories, too, have, most of them, great illustrative value. Charming little pictures of the shepherds, or the little inn in which there was no room, may be drawn by quite baby children, and Christmas afternoon will be a happy, quiet time if they are entertained in this way.

The reader will notice that I am laying great stress upon Christmas Day being a *quiet* day. This is a point of great importance, for it is quite certain that little children are not fitted to stand the strain of a day hectic with the excitement of many presents, all given at once so that the child does not know which to play with first, and heavy meals in which seasonable Christmas food is deemed of more importance than the child's digestion.

In many countries abroad the children have a little service all to themselves on Christmas Eve, and in church stands the Christmas-tree, decked with candles and tinsel and gold tissue, from which presents are taken and given to the children. This blending of the religious element with the everyday is of very definite psychological value in preventing over-excitement, upon the danger of which I have laid so much

stress in this article. In English homes—although, of course, the custom of the Christmas-tree in church has quite died out—there is no reason why the nursery should not be invested with very much the same atmosphere on Christmas Eve; old Christmas carols may be sung and old stories told, calculated to send the child peacefully to bed.

.   .   .   .   .

And the presents themselves—

My article in the last Christmas number of GOOD HOUSEKEEPING dealt fully with the question of the selection of suitable toys for children, and therefore I will only sum up quite shortly a few of the important points to bear in mind in selecting children's Christmas presents.

One very big, fundamental point is the necessity for *simplicity* in the choice of a toy. A little girl who has not been spoiled by the gift of expensive toys really prefers a rag doll she can cuddle to an expensive wax one only brought out for use upon special occasions. A small boy prefers an engine of which he can understand the mechanism to the more elaborate affair in which he only has to turn a screw to start the whole lot of carriages in motion.

Another point is *safety*. Babies' soft toys should be made of real flannel, not cheap cotton flannelette which rubs off in flakes, so that most of it, with the dust and dirt it picks up, is swallowed in the end by the child. Bright colours which come off are, of course, to be avoided,

---

Our Guarantee

All advertisements appearing in GOOD HOUSEKEEPING are absolutely guaranteed. If you purchase goods advertised in GOOD HOUSEKEEPING and they do not justify the claims made for them, your money will be promptly refunded by the advertisers or by us. This applies equally to purchases made through your retailer or direct from the advertiser. You can, therefore, purchase all goods advertised in GOOD HOUSEKEEPING with a feeling of absolute security. The only condition is that in making purchases the reader shall always state that the advertisement was seen in GOOD HOUSEKEEPING.

If you have any cause for complaint against our advertisers, please communicate with us immediately, giving all the facts relating to the transaction.

---

rubber toys with the colours well burnt in being easily procurable nowadays.

And toys which allow scope for *creative ability* on the part of the child are the best toys of all. Every child should have at some time or other in his career, a box of simple wooden bricks with which he can make anything he pleases. Later on the boxes of bricks specially designed to make one particular object, instructions for building which are given with the box, may be a valuable toy, teaching the child to work from printed instructions, which is quite a wholesome discipline later on, but at first his toys should be of the kind which give him the opportunity to work his own will upon them. They should be toys, also, in which his imagination is frequently called upon. The child who can transform a house of wooden bricks into a fairy castle is a child in whom the play spirit has not been lost, and a child to whom every day is Christmas Day because his toys are ever new and always full of delightful possibilities.

1922

GIFT
DEPARTMENTS.

Toilet,
Perfumery,
Fancy,
Leather,
Silver,
Art,
Stationery,
Book.

"-yet
more
presents
from
Boots"

EVERYBODY now-a-days seems to "go to Boots" for Christmas Gifts, for their Gift Depts. contain suitable presents for everyone at prices everyone can afford. Boots certainly spare no efforts to make Christmas shopping profitable and enjoyable for the public. This year their display of beautiful and useful articles is better than ever, and there is no difficulty in acquiring appropriate presents at little expense.

Go to Boots for YOUR Christmas Gifts.

At our Regent Street premises there is one of the most charming of Cafés in which dainty Luncheons and Teas are served at Popular Prices.

Carriage paid in the United Kingdom on all orders for goods value 20/- or over not exceeding 11 lbs. in weight.

Carriage paid in the United Kingdom on all orders for goods value 20/- or over not exceeding 11 lbs. in weight.

CHIEF LONDON BRANCHES:

182 REGENT STREET, W.1., & 112-118 EDGWARE ROAD., W.2.

Over 640 branches throughout the Country.   Boots Pure Drug Co. Ltd.

Cakes for

The tea table on the 25th looks festive with Santa Claus presiding over "the cake."

1923

Ye Olde Yule Time

Is the season for happiness and good will, and there is no better way of spreading cheer and fellowship than by providing perfectly planned meals. All the recipes and methods given here have been carefully tested, and we are always willing to help you with personal advice. Write, enclosing a stamped envelope for the reply, to the Cookery Department, GOOD HOUSEKEEPING, 1 Amen Corner, London, E.C.4

A S Christmas approaches. our minds turn instinctively to sweet things. Cakes, pies, puddings, and sweetmeats— all seem to fit in with the spirit of the season. A good supply of cakes is a real asset at this time of year, as they are always at hand for the frequent occasions when holiday hospitality can be shown by the serving of light and impromptu refreshments.

As all fruit cakes inprove with keeping, the wise housewife will make them in good time and not wait until the rush of the holiday season is upon her. Recipes for Christmas cakes are legion, and almost every household has its own favoured one, passed down probably from one generation to another. For those who have not inherited such a recipe, or who would like to try something different, the following recipe will be found both good and reliable:

A Christmas Cake

½ lb. butter	½ lb. currants
½ lb. margarine	½ lb. sultanas
1 lb. castor sugar	¼ lb. orange and lemon peel
1 lb. flour	¼ lb. citron peel
6 eggs	¼ lb. sweet almonds
2 tablespoonfuls treacle	½ teaspoonful ground cinnamon
1 glass sherry or rum	
Grated rind of 1 lemon	½ nutmeg, grated

First prepare the cake-tin. choosing one 7 inches in diameter, or two of a smaller size. Grease it first with salad oil or unsalted butter, and then line it smoothly with two folds of thick white paper. The band of paper lining the sides should stand about 2 inches above the rim at the top.

Next, prepare the fruit. Wash and dry the currants, and roll them in a little flour. Pick the sultanas and rub them on the top of a sieve with a little

dry flour. Shred the peel finely, and blanch and shred the almonds. Mix the fruit together and leave it in readiness

Christmas Snowballs

in a basin. To mix the cake, put the butter and margarine (or all butter, if preferred,) into a large warm basin, sieve the sugar on the top, and beat them together with the hand or with a large wooden spoon until of a soft, creamy consistency. Sieve the flour and add it alternately with the eggs, treacle, and milk, beating the mixture well after each addition. When the mixture has been well beaten, add the spices, grated lemon-rind, and the prepared fruit last of all.

Turn into the prepared tin, and bake in a moderate oven (275° F.) about 3 hours. Test when ready by running a hot skewer or knitting-needle into the centre; it should come out dry. Leave the cake in the tin for a few minutes, then turn out and cool on a sieve

or wire stand. When quite cold, wrap in paper and keep in a tin box for a week at least before cutting.

Almond Paste and Icing

A Christmas cake is not complete without a layer of almond paste and a coating of white icing or frosting on the top: *To Make Almond Paste*, take ½ lb. ground almonds, ¼ lb. castor sugar, ¼ lb. icing sugar, 1 dessertspoonful lemon-juice, about 2 yolks of eggs, and 1 tablespoonful rum or other flavouring. Put the ground almonds into a basin, and sieve the two kinds of sugar on the top. Add the flavouring and enough yolk of egg to bind all together. Knead with the hand until smooth.

Put this on the top of the cake and smooth over with a wet palette knife. Or, if preferred, the cake may be split and half the almond paste put as a layer in the centre. The almond paste should be allowed to dry for a day or two before the white icing is put on.

White Icing: In the November issue directions were given for making Boiled Icing, but here is a recipe for Royal Icing, which is rather harder in character: To 1 lb. icing sugar add 1 dessertspoonful lemon-juice and from 2 to 3 whites of eggs. Sieve the sugar and put it into a basin with the lemon-juice. Add the white of egg by degrees, beating well with a clean wooden spoon. When the icing is of the right consistency, the spoon should stand vertically in it without falling. Spread this icing over the cake with a palette knife, coating first the top and then the sides, or the top only may be iced and the sides covered with a paper frill or ribbon. Leave the icing to dry before decorating the cake.

O F   C O O K E R Y

Christmas

By

The   Director

FLORENCE B. JACK, M.C.A.

Whatever ingenuity you have, in the m.king of Christmas cakes you will find ample scope to exercise it

1923

Decorating the Cake

The ornamentation of the Christmas cake provides ample scope for one's ingenuity. This may be simple or elaborate in character according to one's talent and the time at disposal, and a walk round the confectioners' shops will always furnish the novice with many new ideas.

If the cake has to be finished off quickly, preserved fruits, crystallised flowers, bonbons, or marzipan sweets will make a pretty and effective decoration. Small sprigs of artificial flowers, holly, or leaves, can also be utilised. When time permits, however, pretty designs in icing may be piped on the cake by means of a forcing-bag and tubes of different patterns, or "A Merry Christmas" or other suitable greeting may be written on, in a contrasting colour.

The Little House Cake

This suggests something of a novelty, which means very little more work than any other form of cake decoration. Make a round cake in the ordinary way, and when putting on the almond paste mould it into a point to form the roof, keeping back a small portion to make a chimney-pot. Then make the white icing, and colour a small amount of it brown with fine chocolate powder. Spread this on the roof and roughen it over with a fork. Next coat the sides of the cake with white icing and let this harden. With a little melted chocolate and small paint-brush outline the bricks of the house and paint in the doors and windows. Colour any remaining icing with sufficient chocolate to make it stone-colour and, by means of a forcing-bag and tubes, pipe round the edge of the roof with this to form eaves, put a narrow piping round the door and windows, and indicate the door-handle. A small Father Christmas may be placed close to the chimney, and a few little dolls and animals will add life to the foreground.

Christmas Snowballs

These will delight the kiddies and the older folk too. Unlike the fruit cakes, they should be made fresh and not more than two or three days before they are

Tiny oranges and green leaves decorate this cake

required. Any white cake mixture will do, or you may use the following formula: 1 egg, its weight in butter, flour, and castor sugar, 1 tablespoonful of milk, flavouring to taste, and ½ teaspoonful of baking-powder. Put the butter into a warm basin, sieve the sugar on the top, and beat the two together with a wooden spoon until of a soft, creamy consistency. Add the egg and half the flour (sieved), beat well until thoroughly mixed. Then add the remainder of the flour and the milk, and beat again until the mixture is light and full of air-bubbles. Add vanilla or any other flavouring preferred, and just before using, stir in the baking-powder.

Have ready some small, round-bottomed cake-tins, greased, and dusted out with a mixture of flour and sugar. Half fill them with the mixture, and bake in a good oven (375° F.) about 15 minutes, or until lightly browned and firm to the touch. Turn out of the tins to cool. If necessary, cut a slice off the top of the cakes to make them level, and put two together with some tart jelly between, thus forming a ball.

Or, the little cakes may be slightly hollowed out, and the cavity filled with some rich custard or thick cream before putting them together.

Cover the balls with some plain white icing, holding them on a fork or skewer while doing so. Then roll in desiccated coconut and castor sugar mixed. Allow the snowballs to dry, and serve them garnished with sprigs of holly.

Suggestions for Decoration

1. Coat the cake with pale pink icing and decorate the top with marzipan fruits.

2. Coat the top of the cake only with white icing, and when quite dry decorate with small sprigs of artificial holly. Put a Father Christmas or a robin in the centre, and tie round with a piece of white and a piece of scarlet ribbon, making a good bow at the side.

3. Colour the icing yellow and flavour with lemon. Coat the cake with this and decorate with crystallised orange slices and small green leaves.

4. Coat the cake with white icing, and with a forcing-bag and small pipe write "A Merry Christmas" across the top. Pipe the sides of the cake with more of the icing and decorate with silver dragées.

5. Make a coffee icing, cover the cake with this, and decorate with crystallised violets and leaves and stalks of angelica.

1923

In the Absence of A Possible Husband

What

By Rebecca West

THE other day I read in an American magazine an admirable article by one Margery Swett, with the briskly practical title, "In the Absence of a Possible Husband What is a Girl to Do?" In it the writer deplores the lack of husbands available for educated women in the United States and sets down her concern at the situation with a lively frankness which gives a measure of how much we have gained by the feminist movement. In the old days it was the custom to jeer at "old maids." Even so kindly a soul as Charles Dickens found it hard to write about a woman who had reached middle life unmarried without representing her as a bony creature knobbed physically and mentally with eccentricities. While public opinion was in this state every woman of spirit felt bound to challenge it in the extremest way possible: to declare that not only were old maids far from ridiculous, they were even enviable, since they were free from the companionship of the sex that were idiotic enough to laugh at them. This naturally led, the argument being heated, to the statement that of course a woman was better off without husband and children. This statement was not true. Now that society has stopped jeering at the old maid we can afford to admit it, and own that if a woman wants to have her full ration of life she ought to have a husband and children.

A husband as good as herself, that is. It is an entirely necessary condition, though it has to be construed very broadly. He need not be as good as she is mentally. It is possible that clever women talking together decide that there is a lot too much of this nonsense about intellect in the modern man. What really matters is that he should be good-looking and have good manners and be a pleasant companion and have a strong sense of duty towards his home. Decidedly, his home must come before anything else for him. And—yes, he must be religious. It doesn't matter so much for a woman,

but it's nice for a man to go to church. . . . But though a husband may be entirely different from his wife, given to action while she is contemplative, or intellectual while she is practical, his qualities added together must come to about the same sum of human value as his wife's. They must have the same standards of morals and manners, the same conception of God, and the same intention of loyalty to these ideals. For the advantages of marriage, like the advantages of foreign travel, are strictly dependent on the condition of the place you go to being better than the place you start. A resident of Camberwell, going to spend a winter in Rome, gains a treasure of experience. But a resident of Rome, coming to spend a winter in Camberwell, stands to gain little but that extremely problematic spiritual treasure which is said to come from endurance of adversity, but which may be safely presumed not to do so, in view of the later life of Charles the Second, who of all English monarchs had in his youth the most thorough experience of adversity.

The trouble to-day is that many women have either no opportunities of marriage at all, or opportunities that are obviously much more likely to lead from Rome to Camberwell than from Camberwell to Rome. I am appalled by the number of women I see who ought to get married, who want to get married, who do not get married, and always for the same reason: that there are no men in their environment who are suitable husbands. There is nothing wrong with these women. But they either do not know any men, or the men they know are not of sufficient horse-power to make it worth while marrying them. Now, Margery Swett in her article on the similar conditions that have arisen in the United States ascribes this state of affairs to equalities of education between the sexes. It appears that in America many more young women go on to the higher stages of education than young men; there may be as many or more male students on the rolls of

the universities, but this is mainly because of the men who take purely technical courses; there is a growing surplus of women who have studied those things which make culture a part of their being, and which makes them discontented with the companionship of men who are not as cultured as themselves. If this were true, then the higher education of women would be disconcertingly expensive.

But, in England at least, it does not seem to be true. The type of woman who finds it most difficult to get a suitable husband is the type which is least touched by the higher education. This has been brought home to me several times during the spate of female unemployment that has followed the winding-up of the Ministries, when girls have come to see me to ask me how they may become journalists. They have usually brought work with them, which has showed that though they had ability they had not quite enough to give them a safe passage into journalism, since to hold down a job in a profession where there is free competition between man and woman a woman must have at least a hundred and fifty per cent. more ability than a man. (This is not altogether, though it often is partly, due to sex jealousy. It is more often due to an attempt to keep society rightways up and do the best for everybody by giving the jobs as far as possible to those who have families dependent on them. It is a highly crude attempt to do what can only be done by complicated readjustments of the economic system; it is cruel to the single woman, and mocking as well as cruel to the woman who has to keep a family. But one might as well admit the good intention that lies behind this imbecility.) Now though these young women were endeavouring to force their way into a profession for which they had no special aptitude, there was one vocation for which they were all obviously well-fitted. They would all have made exceedingly good wives and mothers. They were attractive and

I am appalled by the number of women who ought to get married, who want to get married, who do not get married, and always for the same reason : that there are no men in their environment who are suitable husbands

1923

Is a Girl To Do?

Illustrations by Stuart Hay

healthy; they had pleasant manners; they were, as their efforts to face this problem of their unemployment showed, persons of character. They were, when one talked to them, rather dear, secretly serious people with a desire to lay hold on life and do something with it, even if it was quite difficult and cost them a lot. They would have taken up the vocation of marriage with a reverent romanticism. They would have shouldered its realities with the pluckiest sense of duty. And, in fact, they had all obviously considered doing so and had not felt averse to it. For when I asked them, "Why don't you get married?" they answered with a dreary promptness, as if they were used to answering that question in their minds, either that they didn't know any men at all or that they didn't want to marry any of the men they did know. "A lot of white rabbits are all that's left," one said tartly. Now none of these women had been to a university. They were all ordinary middle-class girls. There was nothing of caviare about them; they were, if one must look for a dietetic equivalent, spring chicken followed by cherry tart and cream. One was alarmed to think that there were not enough people of wholesome tastes to appreciate this simple and straightforward pleasantness.

It may be objected that these young women, by their mere desire to be journalists, showed themselves unattractively inkstained with intellectuality, and that the feminists are to blame for their plight because this habit of thinking which they encourage in their sex is in itself unattractive. But take the case, to which this objection does not apply, of the dancing instructress. The dancing instructress is one of the two tragic figures of our time which perhaps show most perfectly and completely what

happens to the women who obey the anti-feminist teaching and devote themselves to the specifically feminine activities and let men have a free and uncontrolled hand in running the world. The other figure was the Belgian mother, as she arrived at Charing Cross station in the early days of the war. There she was, broad-built, motherly, inarticulate. Men had said to her, "You be a good wife and mother, feed and care for your man, bear and rear your children, don't bother about politics or anything of that sort, and we'll see to it that all's well with you." She had taken them at their word. And there she was; homeless, seared by the unholy sights of war, deprived of her man, searching for her scattered children, uncertain where to house them when she found them.

Not so acutely tragic, but still chronically tragic, is the dancing instructress. There she is, successfully devoted to being part of the decoration of life. Men have said to her, "Be beautiful and graceful, and we'll see to it that all's well with you." And there she is. . . . Oh, the sad army of dancing instructresses, all with the grace that one has been given to understand

---

White Rabbits!

When I asked them, " Why don't you get married ? " they answered either that they didn't know any men at all or that they didn't want to marry any of the men they did know. " A lot of white rabbits are all that's left," one said tartly

---

was practically a guarantee of the heroineship of a fairy tale, spending their lives propelling young men round the floor and saying "One-two-three-four" with a gathering air of exasperation. Ask them, if you will, how they enjoy their work, whether they like the man they have to teach. "Can you imagine," I heard one say bitterly, "a really nice man troubling to learn dancing? He wouldn't bother. . . ."

From that petulant cry of discontent, that wistful reference to a type more virile than the one encountered, one may deduce the reason why most marriages that come the way of the modern woman seem more like a journey from Rome to Camberwell than the desirable reverse. The trouble is that we have reached a point in history where conditions are, so far as this matter is concerned, disconcertingly different from those which fixed the primitive psychological types of humanity. Or rather they are disconcertingly different from those which fixed the primitive psychological type of the male, and disconcertingly similar to those which fixed the primitive psychological type of the female. Woman's life has changed remarkably little through the ages. The main business has always been, as it is now, to be a wife and mother. (There is nothing contrary to feminist doctrine in this. All that the feminist objects to is that she should be a fool or be made to look a fool while doing so.) The physical conditions of this business have altered only infinitesimally since the beginning of man; a new-born baby born to prehistoric parents on Salisbury Plain when Church Parade was held round Stonehenge must have looked the same and presented the same problems to its mother as a new-born baby born to-day to a bankclerk and his wife in Surbiton. *(continued overleaf)*

What is a Girl to Do?

The psychological conditions of the business have varied as little; a wife's and mother's primary task was then and now to make a series of skilful adaptations to the needs of dependent personalities so that out of the relationships of the many there comes a whole in the form of a united family. The outward change in the world, the increase in safety, infringes less on the fundamental unchangeability of woman's life than one would think. The streets are safer for her to walk in, she can travel here and there without danger; but that is only a slight shifting of the boundaries. Because of her preciousness to the race she was even in her primitive state kept to the safe spots round the camp; so security is no new and softening experience to her. It may be said that bringing up children is a much safer business than it was, but that is a masculine delusion. We have certainly fewer children to bring up, and more resources to call on if anything goes wrong with them; but the amount of mental and physical energy lavished by women on motherhood must remain constant through the ages. For one thing, as the number of children in a family decreases, the value of the individual child increases: the life of a child means infinitely more to its modern mother, who has only one or two others or perhaps none, than the life of a child meant to its primitive mother, who could rely on an annual baby. And it would, perhaps, be arguable that even from the purely physical point of view it is hardly

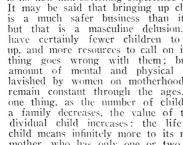

1923

easier for many modern mothers to bring up a modern baby now than under primitive conditions. Bad it was for little Johnny to wander out of the clearing and try to make a playmate of the hyena, or to perish of famine when a bad winter struck the country; but it is just as bad for the little Johnnies of to-day to suffer from chronic poisoning from the polluted air of the cities, as the enormous death-rate from respiring diseases prove that they do. And it is just as bad for Johnny's mother when she has to fend for herself because Johnny's father is unemployed as it would be if he had been lamed out hunting.

But this fundamental unchangeability of the most important issues of life which keep women much the same through the ages does not exist in the case of men. The primary condition which shaped the primitive type of man which corresponded to the primitive type of woman was the necessity to contend instantly with unmastered forces and dangerous enemies. This condition has, for large numbers of men, disappeared save for its intermittent recurrence in the form of war. It disappears almost entirely in the case of the middle-class town-dweller. Johnny's mother through the ages waits for Johnny's father to bring in something on which she can feed Johnny. So far as her emotions are concerned it does not matter whether what he brings in was caught by watching behind a bush till the moon rose and the bucks came down to drink or by sitting on a high stool at Barclay's Bank; in both cases it is whether he succeeds or fails from the

point of view of Johnny's nutrition that shapes her emotions, and consequently shapes her. But it makes the most tremendous difference to Johnny's father whether he has been hunting or banking. That is what shapes him. He therefore is highly variable, and is varying all the time farther and farther away from the primitive type. To the primitive type of woman therefore he is unsatisfying and irritating, and she often feels a positive terror at the idea of embarking on the primitive adventures of life with him.

We probably see this problem at its worst to-day, when the war has swallowed all the most virile types of this generation. We have no reason, too, to suppose that the state of society which has produced these conditions will last for ever. The industrial revolution which put this tame urban life on its legs dates only from the middle of the eighteenth century: only a blink on the eyes of Time. It may well be that some shift in the earth's circumstances will make it possible for man to have the leisure and means to develop some civilised activities that would compensate for the lack of his primitive pursuits as the routine of modern life does not. And in the meantime it is always possible for those women who do not get married to reflect that, while an unmarried man has no particular value because of his state, an unmarried woman has. The modern State could not exist for five minutes without the services of the unattached women who are free to work as teachers and nurses. In the absence of a possible husband a girl can always prop up civilisation.

Fig. 1

1923

EXERCISE *and* HOME HYGIENE

Ward off Lines and Improve the Expression by
Controlling the Muscles of the Face

By Nora Mullane

Fig. 2

Fig. 3

Fig. 4

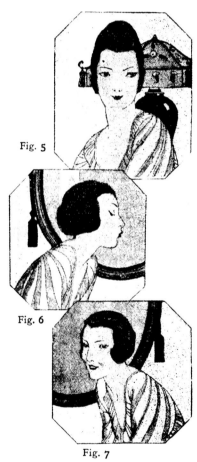

Fig. 5

Fig. 6

Fig. 7

sciously indulged in and which could be remedied if the afflicted persons only knew how. This article treats of exercises for the muscles of the face to overcome these defects. They are called Movements of Expression, are not difficult, and are applied on gymnastic principles. After learning to control the action of the muscles of the face, you cannot fail to see a marked improvement in the general appearance. The muscles become more flexible; the lines (when any are present) appear softer and the skin clearer. This method is the best remedy I know to correct facial defects acquired through faulty habits, and the best way to ward off traces of age. In other words, it will make us "wear our age well."

Take a sitting position in front of a mirror to make sure that the movements are correctly made, and practise each exercise from four to eight times.

Exercise 1
Raise and lower the eyebrows without wrinkling the forehead, as in figure 1.

Exercise 2
Move the brows inward and outward; contract and expand the muscles of the upper part of the face.

If this and the foregoing exercise prove difficult at first, use the finger-tips to move in the right direction until you gain muscular control.

Exercise 3
Drop the upper lids heavily over the eyes as if going to sleep, as in figure 3; raise them energetically.

Exercise 4
Raise and lower the lower lids, giving the eyes a searching or inquisitive appearance, as in figure 4.

Exercise 5
Raise and lower the muscles of the nose.

Exercise 6
Expand the nostrils as for conscious breathing.

Exercise 7
Raise and lower the muscles at the upper corners of the mouth, as in figure 5.

Exercise 8
Contract the lips as for whistling, as in figure 6, and stretch them for exaggerated laughter, as in figure 7.

WHILE we are carefully studying exercises for other portions of the body, we must not forget the most important part of all—the face. We admit that activity of the body lends brightness to the face and makes one appear young. Still, there are unmistakable signs of age that appear even with a healthy, active body, such as lines, crows-feet, double chins, soft and flabby muscles, and set expressions which are often the result of mannerisms and faulty habits uncon-

1924

It is wonderful to be chosen as the Christmas Fairy who gives away the toys from the tree

Christmas Parties & Games

By Muriel Wrinch

National Froebel Union Higher Certificate

IN writing of children's parties, I am thinking all the time of the real, old-fashioned children's parties, not of that function for miniature grown-ups where small boys in long trousers and black coats tend to collect in small groups and stand staring round-eyed at little girls in starched white frocks. At my party no one will have heard of etiquette. There will be a Christmas-tree and merry games, acting and music and small presents. There will be no conjuror specially hired from town, and no expensive gifts, for I am catering for *children,* and children are made happy by the simplest of entertainments and the most inexpensive of presents, if these are chosen with thought and understanding.

The most difficult moment at a children's party is generally at the beginning, when small children, very conscious of their best clothes, are apt to feel extremely shy. In a delightful book, *The Child's House,* published this year, there is a charming account of a children's party. Vanessa, the little heroine of the book, went through all the agonies of this initial period. " The party was still in the provisional shape when they arrived. There were great spaces of bare floor, it seemed to Vanessa, in a room that she would not have otherwise considered large. Round the walls a row of petrified children

ONE of the most fascinating things about children is their individuality. No two children are ever alike. For all that, there are certain laws governing their physical needs and general training that many parents do not know. Many of these Muriel Wrinch discusses month by month in her articles. But if you need additional advice, write to the Children's Department, " Good Housekeeping," 153 Queen Victoria Street, London, E.C.4, stating exactly what you want to know and enclosing a stamped addressed envelope for the reply

extended in a decorative fringe. Other little girls made circles, skirts and sashes standing out stiffly behind them as if to ward off an attack. No matter from what aspect Vanessa viewed these circles, it always seemed that a backward prospect was presented to her. This was awful, she was not going to know how to behave herself. Hector had remained in the hall with a number of wild boys who refused to have anything to do with the party once they had arrived, and considered that they held that part of the house against the others who were tame and party-rid."

If you wish to spare children the discomfort of those first few moments of awkward shyness arrange to have something going on from the moment the first few guests arrive. A simple skip

round the room in time to music, each child falling in as he enters the room, is often enough to break the spell; the child simply has no time to feel self-conscious. When there are enough children a game should immediately be started. " Blind Man's Buff " or " Hunt the Slipper " are great games to play before tea. All the children know these games, and can join in at once, while if there are any late comers they can be included without stopping the fun. The delight of knowing what to do takes away all embarrassment on the part of a sensitive child.

Tea should be fairly early, so that there is plenty of time for the Christmas-tree afterwards, but beware of fixing tea-time so early that it comes before party shyness has worn off. Let the children play together at least twenty minutes or half an hour beforehand, and then there will be plenty of chatter over the cakes instead of shy awkward pauses.

The tea table can be made gay with lengths of silver tinsel threaded in and out of the plates. Small cardboard Father Christmases, such as can be bought for a few pence each in the toy shops, make a bright splash of colour on the white cloth. Tiny silk or paper flags stuck into some of the cakes, and a few candles at intervals along the middle of the (Continued) table, well out of reach of small fingers,— and protected with coloured paper shades, make good and cheap decoration. A handful of silver dust from the Christmas bazaar makes a shine on the table-cloth which children love.

Wise hostesses will consider carefully the question of crackers. Crackers there must be a-plenty, but let them not all contain caps. One cracker containing a cap is enough for each child. At many parties one sees many discarded bonnets and crowns stamped underfoot because there are not enough heads to fit them! This introduces an element of disorder that may have a pronounced effect on the children's behaviour. At most parties two or three children, wildly excited, vociferous and hot, may be seen spoiling the fun of all the rest. Wise hostesses will arrange their parties with an eye to eliminating all possible causes of disorder. They will not provide too many crackers, nor too much rich food, and games will be so organised that quiet games alternate with noisy ones.

As to the tea itself, it is easy to provide simple dishes which give delight to little ones and which have no ill-effects afterwards. Bread and butter served in rolls make a change. Sponge cakes made from the usual mixture, but with a few drops of cochineal or vegetable colouring matter added, are hailed with delight. "Poached eggs" made with apricots surrounded by whipped cream on a slice of sponge cake will never go out of favour. It is also a good plan to have several plates of small iced sponge cakes with the name of a child upon each in coloured icing. This is a great treat, for children always love to have their individuality recognised. For the middle of the table, a "fairy tale" cake—such as the one described in the cookery section of GOOD HOUSEKEEPING last Christmas—is a very great attraction. This cake, too, may be made of sponge mixture, for fruit cake does not agree with many small children.

A few "disappearing teaspoons" will cause much laughter at tea-time. These can be obtained from most toy-shops for a few pence. They look like ordinary metal spoons, but when they are used for stirring they disappear, for they are made of some soluble material. If a disappearing teaspoon is placed in every fifth saucer everyone will be able to see the miracle taking place. The element of "magic" is introduced, and so long as no very small nor particularly sensitive child is made the victim of the joke everyone enjoys it.

After tea come games and the Christmas-tree. It is a good plan to play a few quiet games while the Christmas-tree is being lit up. This keeps the children all in one room so that no one catches a glimpse of the tree until everything is ready. Also, the children are able to rest a little before the next excitement occurs. "Twenty Questions," "How When and Where," "The Animal Game" are well known to most children, and great favourites. A Five Senses competition also comes in here quite well. Each competitor is given a card upon which the marks he wins are recorded and he is given five tests. The child with the most marks wins a prize. The sight test is well-known—a tray bearing ten or twenty small objects is placed on a table and each child after looking at it for one minute has to write down the names of the objects he can remember. The hearing test is great fun. The children are blindfolded and six or eight familiar noises are made—the fire is poked, water is poured into a glass, a pipe is tapped on the grate, some tissue-paper is rustled. The touch test, the smell test, and the taste test can be readily made up. With very small children the taste test might be omitted. "Bob Apple" is another game which

little boys love. It is extremely difficult to catch an apple in the mouth, and the attempts to do so cause much laughter.

A simple entertainment in which a dwarf figure appears can be carried out with a pair of curtains and the co-operation of two adults. A small high table should be placed in front of the curtains. One performer wears shoes and stockings on her hands and places these on the table, putting out her face between the curtains but keeping her legs well concealed. The other performer stands behind her entirely concealed, but puts her hands and arms out between the curtains just above the other's forearms. The dwarf thus made, who may wear a long white beard and a top hat, can give a very amusing entertainment of step-dancing, and the children who cannot imagine how this is done are greatly thrilled.

But all these delights are eclipsed by the joys of the Christmas-tree. The glittering branches loaded with tiny parcels and bright ornaments and the tiny coloured candles delight every child. There are certain elementary points to remember in decorating. Hang all heavy parcels on lower branches. These branches are usually the strongest and can bear heavy parcels without bending. Remember, too, to place the candles at the *ends* of the branches where they are not likely to set the higher branches alight and where they will show their light to the greatest advantage. A jug of water should be kept handy, so that if any accident does occur, the flames may be quickly extinguished. Of course, it is hardly necessary to say that *never* should a candle be placed anywhere near a present. A sudden draught may cause the flame to blow in the direction of the parcel, and then somebody's present may be no more.

In choosing presents, it is not enough to buy a selection of small toys and hang them on the branches in the hope that each child will receive a present he likes. It is absolutely essential to buy a present for each child, carefully chosen according to his or her taste. Small puzzles can be bought at ninepence each and much please little boys and girls of eight and nine. Picture blocks fitted into a small box please the six-year-old. Then there are "sets" of materials for handwork—a set for making paper flowers or an embroidery set pleases most little girls of eleven and twelve. A conductor's set outfit is a good present for a seven-year-old boy. Toy trumpets, whistles, and mouth organs are always popular. As far as possible, toys with which the child can really *do* something should be given from the Christmas-tree. We are apt to choose toys for their pretty appearance, but it is wise to rely for decoration upon ornaments and tinsel and to choose toys which are welcome and useful to the child after the Christmas party is over.

It is a good idea to do up all the toys in thick wrappings of white crinkled paper. These may be touched here and there with gum and sprinkled with silver dust and they will look like snowballs amongst the branches. A little label bearing the child's name should be affixed to each parcel and then each one is sure of receiving the right present.

A tiny child may act as the Christmas fairy to give away the toys. She may be dressed in any simple party dress, with the skirt puffed out by many petticoats of sheer white muslin. A tinsel fringe may be tacked all round the hem of the little frock and both petticoats and frock should be caught up slightly higher at the back than at the front to give the right tilt. A pair of little wings can be made by covering wire hoops, bent to the right shape, with sheer muslin painted in water

colours. The wand is made by covering a long bamboo stick with silver paper and placing a silver Christmas star at the top. A tinier star in the fairy's hair makes a pretty hair ornament.

After the children have had time to examine their little presents the party may end with a few musical games. "Roger de Coverley" still holds the time-honoured place and "Musical Chairs" will always be popular.

When the children are dressing to go home, it is a good plan to have a needle and thread at hand in order to tack up any frills that may be torn on little girls' frocks. Small children always appreciate being "mended" before they go home, for then there are no reproaches about accidents to meet from mother or nurse, and memories of the Christmas party are entirely bright and happy.

1924

1923

Ladies are literally flocking
to us for our Winter

STOCKINETTE FROCKS

Here we show
three out of a
variety of
thirty.

"ROWAN"

A new Frock in
Winter - weight
all wool Stockin-
ette, silk design
to tone, neck-
band and turn-
back cuffs of
artificial silk to
match. Colours:
Almond. putty,
beaver. tan. mid
grey, helio saxe.
tabac primrose,
and white.

43/6

"Rowan"

A Charming
ARTIFICIAL SILK JUMPER
at an attractive price.

"DAFFODIL"

Artificial silk,
fancy weave.
adaptable collar
buttoned high to
throat or V style,
finished at waist
with wide welt-
ing which gives
a pouched effect.
Shades stocked:
Ivory. black,
silver, lemon,
beige. navy.
tan sable.
mid grey and
other new
colours

25/9

"Daffodil"

"Montreux"

"HYDRANGEA"

A new cross-over style in
quiet effects. with braid of
self-colour round neck down
to waist line and with three
rows of contrast Russia
braid throughout; a per-
fectly-fitting style with
pull-through bel and braided
buckle - - - **45/6**

Colours: Almond green, putty. saxe. grey, navy, rust.
black tabac, café, nigger, and tan.

"ANEMONE"

New design, in medium
weight best quality Stockin-
ette, guaranteed perfect
shape. full on hips fancy design in two tones partly lock-
stitching, partly Russia braid,
pull through belt
with braid-
covered buckle **39/6**

---

*WRITE FOR
FREE COPY
of our
CATALOGUES
from following
Departments:*

*Ladies' Frocks and
Wraps*
Girls' School Outfits
Tiny Tots' Clothing
Boys' School Kit
Ladies' Jumpers
*Underclothing and
Shoes*

**ORDERS
BY POST**

State length and
second choice of
colour preferred,
and permit us to
send you

**A Selection
on Approval**

In the first trans-
action, a London
reference should
be given. If a
remittance accom-
panies an order,
we refund money
in full in the event
of the goods not
meeting with
approval

"Olive"

"BONZO"

Boys' or Girls'
Winter Woollies
of brushed artificial
silk in white, sky.
pink. jade. and
primrose. Price
for 22 in. chest,
rising 10d. every
2 in. up to 32 in.
chest.

Special price

5/11

(Postage paid)

"Bonzo"

"OLIVE"

House or Golf Coat or Under-wrap. all-wool
Shetland-knit. warm and delightfully cosy.
Colours: Putty, pink, saxe navy,
grey amethyst, black sky bottle,
and reseda. Special price **4/11**

Postage 4d.

Also in superior qualities in above shades,
at **10/6** and upwards.

" I am so very grateful for your helpful letter and have already ordered the B.V.C. and other things you so clearly explain about. Your magazine is a perfect boon to people stranded like I am in the depths of the country, yet trying to keep a little in touch with things! I wouldn't part with a copy for gold!!"
Mrs. C., *Enniskillen.*

" In the October edition of your wonderful magazine an Electric Motor is shown — please let me know where one can be bought, together with the necessary attachment. " In your April edition woodcut pictures are shown — please tell me where same can be bought. " Your little book is a treasure."
V. K. A., *South Africa.*

"Thank you so much for your very kind reply to my letter and the tabulated duties for the servants which will be most useful. I fear it must have given you a lot of work and trouble. I am most grateful for it. When next in town I shall be very glad to avail myself of your kind invitation to 'see the Good Housekeeping Institute and get further help on real good housekeeping. I have ordered the book you so kindly mentioned and do hope it will prove just what I want."
G. B., *Dover.*

" I should add that I have made use of other departments of Good Housekeeping before and found them most helpful and reliable. The advertisements, too, have been most valuable to us in reconstructing and fitting our home. I am constantly recommending the products to friends because I have proved the value of the magazine, over and over again."
Mrs. B., *Redruth.*

"We have just returned from India. I am interested in building and fitting out a home and my wife is interested in making it. We have been much struck by the excellence of Good Housekeeping as regards both our objects. In accordance with the notice on page 34, June Number, I venture to send you some questions."
Colonel C., *Broadstairs.*

...Do you know that Good Housekeeping Institute will solve your many household problems for you?

...Do you know that Good Housekeeping's Department of Furnishings and Decorations will completely decorate or rearrange your home under expert direction?

...Do you know that Good Housekeeping's Fashion Department will help you solve your dress problems—showing you: what to wear, how to make, where to buy?

...Do you know that the Good Housekeeping Shopping Service will secure you many bargains and save you much time?

...And do you know that everything advertised in Good Housekeeping is guaranteed?

1924

" Thank you so much for all I have learnt from the various articles. I have looked forward to your magazine eagerly every month ever since I got the first copy."
Miss D., *St. Helen's.*

" My sister finds many delightful recipes and household hints in your magazine of which we have not missed getting one since you started it." Miss F., *St. Andrew's.*

" I am having great satisfaction from some rubber stair covering recommended to me by you some time ago, and also from a study whose colours I took from one of the articles by Mr. John Gloag. Now would you be so good as to advise me about a vacuum cleaner."
Mrs. G., *Croydon.*

" Very many thanks for your letter of October 4th which is most helpful, and I am sure that from it together with the upholstering article in the November Good Housekeeping I shall become quite a successful upholsteress!! If one starts on small pieces as you suggest and works up to greater things, I do not think I have an unconquerable task before me. It is most kind of you to offer to procure the necessary tools and materials for me.
" All the articles you publish from time to time in Good Housekeeping on making a home nice, interest me very much, and I am sure that many other women situated as I am, somewhere out in the ' blue ' in various parts of the world, are also grateful for the help your magazine gives them."
Mrs. P., *Northern Rhodesia.*

" Your splendidly helpful article on Floor Coverings contains just the idea I needed, for I am wanting just such coverings. Will you kindly tell me where I may get the Chinese Mats, Dutch Mats and Coconut Fibre Matting. Enclosed stamped addressed envelope."
Miss A. A. H., *Morecambe.*

" Very many thanks for the detailed information and instructions *re* paint for concrete floors, etc. I find Good Housekeeping of immense interest and use to me." Mrs. H., *Newbury.*

By FRANK SWINNERTON

Having rent the veil that shields the face of Suburbia in several unforgettable novels, Frank Swinnerton here examines a queer characteristic common to all—from Pekinese to Peeresses

1924

Every Family has its — CARM

EVERY family has its Carmichaels. Most families have several of them. They are as universal as clever children. And yet as far as I know they have never been publicly named and classified until this moment. It was not I who first called the species "Carmichael," or observed the full enormity of the vast body of Carmichaels who infest the earth; but I have long gladly described Carmichaels as Carmichaels, and shall continue to do so. The word came into being in this way. Friends of mine who wished to talk with impunity before their children of what Dick Deadeye called "a certain intimate relation" hit upon the alias of "Mrs. Carmichael." Having so named her, and having discussed between themselves various Mrs. Carmichael's characteristics, they looked about the world, and found innumerable other Carmichaels dwelling in it. And, indeed, the explanation of "Carmichaelism" being once made, we perceive ourselves to be completely surrounded by Carmichaels of the first order. They fill our homes, they fill our businesses, our streets, our omnibuses and shopping-stores, they owe us money, they distress us in all sorts of indescribable ways. Members of the

inventors' family, making political speeches of "progressive tendency," have gone so far as to beg the nation not to let itself be "Carmichaeled by the Government." As for common life, one finds Carmichaels by the score in all varieties of circumstance, from the slum

"Go," said the callous daughter, to her ill-mannered son, "and get a pail of water. We'll throw it over her"

to the Cabinet, from the bench to the Bar, the forecastle to the Royal Academy, and beyond even the Royal Academy.

The first, and essential, feature of the Carmichael is the gift of being pathetic. Cats and dogs can be Carmichaels.

Cats that mope when they are left, and cause us to stay at home because they will miss us, are Carmichaels. Dogs that by their glee at the sight of our hats and walking-sticks make us take them inconveniently upon journeys which we would rather make alone are Carmichaels. Children who dissolve into tears at a hasty word, or who believe themselves to be misunderstood, or who cannot play by themselves, are Carmichaels. Older people whose feelings are easily wounded, who successfully wear a strained expression when we meet them after a short absence, during which we have written no letters, or when we part with them upon an excursion of pleasure to which they are not bidden, so that we are filled by the knowledge of their deprivation with shame and self-reproach, are Carmichaels. All parents whose sons and daughters dare not marry for fear of the gap they would leave at home are Carmichaels. Grandparents who show us that they feel rather neglected but that of course they are nobody at all, sniff, are Carmichaels. In fact, all those living creatures who make us feel absolutely and brutally selfish are Carmichaels.

Carmichaels may be meddlers and sensationalists. They may drink or

One Carmichael protested against the behaviour of one of her grandchildren. Her daughter was obdurate, and made it clear that she did not think her son's deportment was any business of his grandmother's

1924

Illustrations by Bert Thomas

$\mathcal{MICHAELS}$ — *Woe to them!*

suffer from paralysis or melancholia; but they are not Carmichaels in virtue of these habits or infirmities. They may lie, they may be hypocritical, they may feign illness—I knew one Carmichael who had an extraordinary gift for losing all control of her limbs in such an emergency, as the late George Grossmith is said to have done in the part of Ko-Ko; but these aspects of character in themselves are not prima facie evidence of Carmichaelism. They are what scientific people (especially weather experts) would call "secondaries," but the true Carmichael goes farther back than such manifest ailments and deceptions. The real Carmichaels can be known by their moral effects upon us, and by no other test. Nobody is a Carmichael unless he or she makes us feel inhumanly cruel and vilely selfish.

It must be realised that Carmichaels thrive and fatten upon the tender-hearted only. Really rugged egotists and bluff manly fellows with rude health and obtuse intellects are not conscious of them. It is the pedestrian who cannot escape the beggar, while his rich brother, the motorist, sails past unmolested. In the same way, only the sensitive can be Carmichaeled. But which of us is not sensitive in relation to those we love? Which of us in the Anglo-Saxon civilisation, based as it is upon conscience and the opinion of others (these two terms being often interchangeable), cannot be Car-

michaeled? Few indeed. Our hearts are easily lacerated. Shame, with us, is a potent force. We stand and deliver more readily to the appealing mother at the kerb than to the importunate hustler who looks strong enough to trounce us if we refuse his demand for alms.

When they returned with such restorative water as had been threatened, the fainting Carmichael had disappeared

I have heard of one Carmichael who called upon the hardest-hearted and most resolute of her daughters, protested against the behaviour of one of her grandchildren, and proceeded to deliver a lament upon the subject. Her

daughter was obdurate, and made it clear that she did not think her son's deportment was any business of his grandmother's. The Carmichael became violently distressed at such cruelty to herself, and showed signs of fainting. The hard-hearted daughter remained unmoved. The Carmichael rose, staggered. . . . Still her daughter was inflexible. With pathetic dignity the Carmichael proposed, as her counsels were not needed, to leave the house for ever. She was not begged to remain. She left the house, but as soon as she was beyond the front door the horror of the

(continued overleaf)

Carmichaels

scene in which she had just played a part had such an effect upon her that she sank weakly to the doorstep, and lost consciousness. Her brutal daughter, witnessing the scene through the coloured glass which formed the upper half of the front door, and dissembling her tremors, opened the door. A faint groan came from the Carmichael, who lay otherwise perfectly still, with her eyes closed. "Go," said the callous daughter loudly to her ill-mannered son. "Go and get a pail of water. That is the best thing for people who have fainted. Go and get a pail of water. We'll throw it over her." And with that the daughter and her son retired to the house. When they returned in two minutes' time, with such a pail of restorative water as had been threatened, the fainting Carmichael had disappeared.

But not all of this Carmichael's daughters are so cruel. The others are of gentler disposition. With them the conviction of sin (for, after all, this wicked daughter of whom I have told the above true story had been married very young, and had been subjected to the mental debauchery of a stern and methodical husband, a Civil Servant) was constant. The second, it is true, married; but for years was harrowed by weekly visits from her mother and by subjection to her own sympathetic dread of giving pain. As for the third, the youngest, marriage for her was out of the question. She was a pretty and intelligent and healthy girl; and in the course of a number of years she could have married any one of several agreeable young men who sought her company. But the thought of what the loss of her would mean to a delicate and sensitive elderly lady, whose heart became unmanageable at any suggestion that she might be left alone with her husband, deprived of a daughter's care, kept this girl single. She had in full measure the sense of wickedness which Carmichaels create in those they love. Desiring another kind of life than the one she led at home, she knew that in even conceiving such desire she was revealed as selfish to the core. Not only that. It was clear to this girl that if she married—even though it be for love, and to sacrifice herself to a husband—the knowledge of her mother's suffering would spoil any happiness the marriage might bring. Accordingly, she remained unmarried, cherishing the Carmichael, and struggling to quell the eagerness for other life which from time to time the Devil aroused in her heart. Until one evening this abandoned girl lost all sense of propriety. At the age of twenty-eight or twenty-nine she suddenly and hysterically fled from her parents' house. The Devil had won. But she had been Carmichaeled for so many years that she arrived at the home of one of her sisters in a state of incoherence and collapse. She was ill. She was oppressed with all the consciousness of guilt which we suppose a murderess to feel.

Nevertheless, she had escaped. She had broken the bonds of Carmichaelism. She never returned to her old home. For weeks conscience struggled in her breast with selfishness, and selfishness won. She took a situation, she found her mind and nature growing and flowering, she at length married, she achieved happiness. Nobody, seeing her now the loving and devoted wife of a poor man and the absorbed mother of a small and delightful family, could realise the wickedness of her selfish flight. Not even the fact that she several times a year has her mother staying in the house (presumably to quieten a still uneasy conscience, as I can think of no other reason) will palliate the horrible fact. The Carmichael, deserted, was a piteous figure. She had never been so ill, so pathetic, so bereft of love. All the illnesses of a medical dictionary attacked her simultaneously, and her husband would really have called in the doctor if she had not assured him that she was past all medical aid. But she is still alive, ten years after her bereavement, and her Carmichaeling talents are being surreptitiously exercised upon a younger generation.

The best of people have at times a touch of the Carmichael in them; and I must not be thought unmindful of the mother or father who genuinely suffers from the loss of a loved child. If we are forsaken, or dread that we may be forgotten, we do—all of us—strive to make ourselves more interesting to the beloved. For the time we are sick persons engrossed in our own ego. A cat will pluck the sleeve of one who plays with a puppy, a dog will lick a hand and whine for unaccorded notice, a child will make an appeal—in face of the admired exhibition of a younger child—which only a hard heart could ignore. How much more, then, a grown-up person, one who has a thousand endangered links with her child, and one who has proved the short memory and heedlessness of other humans, may feel a ghastly sense of loneliness or of being ignored! It is a disloyalty, a failure of confidence in the beloved, but how natural! It is only human—it is only canine and feline—to feel slight jealousy —jealousy that is no jealousy of an individual, no basely-motived hostility, although it arises from perhaps a similar cause. The cause of all jealousy is the feeling of powerlessness or inferiority. As jealousy arises when somebody does something that we should like to be able to do, and suspect ourselves of being unable to do, so this fear comes from conviction that love for ourselves is incompatible with love for the highly superior being who has won our darling's heart. We touch her sleeve, as does the cat; we do whatever is the human equivalent for licking his hand as the dog does; we strive to remind him or her of our existence, our claim to love, to attention. We soften our tone, as lovers grow gentle. Having gained momentary notice, we expatiate upon our own doings and our own helplessness. Ever so little, we yield to the temptation to appeal for sympathy. We do not beg—no! A wistful note, a glance, a pressure—so slight as hardly to wound our self-esteem—and the pathetic approach is made. Pity is what we crave. Pity—it is Carmichaelism, to be controlled! The poison is working in our systems. It is natural; it is pathetic; but we ought not to ask for pity. What we want is love, freely given. If we cannot keep it by fair means, let us not seek to keep it by foul! There is the world of difference between love and pity, for all that the poet said; and if we are wise and proud we shall be silent for the sake of the loved one's happiness rather than noisy and appealing for the sake of our own. What if he or she does forget us for a time. Will the tide of love not return? Then let our dearest ones come back to us as freely as they go, to love and understanding and not to the reproach of loneliness and neglect. For us the duty is clear. It is to hold our heads high. Death to the Carmichaelistic tendencies of our fainting hearts!

Christmas Day in the Dust-bin

1924

CHRISTMAS MORNING . . . . . and the dirt and dust snugly embedded deep down in the drawing-room carpet was dreaming of its Christmas dinner.

But . . . . . the Children's present to Mother was a "Whirlwind" Suction Sweeper. Of course, she said, it was "really and truly" just what she wanted. But she had to be shown how wonderful it was—at once. So, immediately after breakfast, it was given a trial trip over the drawing-room carpet. In three minutes it looked as though Mother had been given a new carpet as well as a "Whirlwind." And that complacent dust had a rude awakening. It was out of the carpet and in the dust-bin before it had time to realise what had happened.

Dust and dirt will spend not only Christmas but *every* day in the dust-bin instead of in carpets when "Whirlwind" comes into a home, for "Whirlwind's" watch-word is "Dust-bins for the Dust." No matter how deep dust lies in a carpet, nor how long it has been there, "Whirlwind" swallows every scrap in the depths of its bag. Its soft, revolving brush flicks up the surface litter—its powerful suction does the cleaning. "Whirlwind" is *not* electric. It doesn't run up housekeeping bills. All the attention it needs is a monthly sip of oil. It is as easy to push as a broom—as simple to understand as a flat-iron.

The WHIRLWIND Suction Sweeper.

£4.19.6

Complete—
No Extras—
No Further
Instalments

A HOME WITHOUT A WHIRLWIND IS A HOME FOR DUST

Louise

By W. SOMERSET MAUGHAM

"The Most Selfish Woman I Ever Knew"

1925

I COULD never understand why Louise bothered with me. She disliked me and I knew that behind my back, in that gentle way of hers, she seldom lost the opportunity of saying a disagreeable thing about me. She had too much delicacy ever to make a direct statement, but with a hint and a sigh and a little flutter of her beautiful hands she was able to make her meaning plain. She was a mistress of cold praise.

It is true that we had known one another, almost intimately, for five and twenty years, but it was impossible for me to believe that she could be affected by the claims of old association. She thought me a coarse, brutal, cynical and vulgar fellow. I was puzzled at her not taking the obvious course and dropping me. She was constantly asking me to lunch and dine and she invited me often to spend a week-end at her house in the country.

At last I thought that I had discovered her motive. She had an uneasy suspicion that I did not believe in her; and she could not rest till I acknowledged myself mistaken and defeated.

I knew Louise before she married. She was then a frail, delicate girl with large and melancholy eyes. Her father and mother worshipped her with an anxious adoration, for some illness, scarlet fever, I think, had left her with a weak heart and she had to take the greatest care of herself. When Tom Maitland asked her to marry him they opposed the marriage, for they were convinced that she was much too delicate for that strenuous state. But they were poor and Tom Maitland was rich. He promised to do everything in the world for Louise and finally they entrusted her to him as a sacred charge.

Tom Maitland was a big, husky fellow, very good-looking and a fine athlete. He doted on Louise. With her weak heart he could not hope to keep her with him long and he made up his mind to do everything he could to make her few years on earth happy. He gave up the games he excelled in, not because she wished him to—she was glad that he should play golf and hunt—but because, by a coincidence, she had a heart attack whenever he proposed to leave her for a day.

If they had a difference of opinion she yielded to him at once, for she was the most submissive wife a man could have, but her heart failed her and she would be laid up, sweet and uncomplaining, for a week. He could not be such a brute as to cross her. Then they would have quite a little tussle about which should give way to the other and it was only with difficulty that at last he persuaded her to have her own way.

Once, seeing her walk eight miles on an expedition that she particularly wanted to make, I suggested to him that she was stronger than one would have thought. He shook his head.

"No, no, she's dreadfully delicate. She's been to all the best heart specialists in the world and they say that her life hangs on a thread. But she has an unconquerable spirit."

Tom Maitland told her that I had remarked on her endurance.

"I shall pay for it to-morrow," she said to me in her plaintive way. "I shall be at death's door."

"I sometimes think that you're quite strong enough to do the things you really want to," I murmured.

I am afraid she did not like my reply, for though she gave me a pathetic little smile I saw no amusement in her large blue eyes.

"You can't very well expect me to fall down dead just to please you," she retorted.

Louise outlived her husband. He caught his death of cold one day when they were sailing and Louise needed all the rugs there were to keep her warm. He left her a comfortable fortune and a daughter.

Louise was inconsolable. It was wonderful that she managed to survive the shock. Her friends expected her speedily to follow her poor husband to the grave. They redoubled their attentions towards her. They would not let her stir a finger; they insisted on doing everything in the world to save her trouble. She was entirely lost without a man to take care of her, she said, and she did not know how with her delicate health she was going to bring up her dear Iris.

Her friends asked her why she did not marry again. Oh, with her heart it was out of the question, though of course she knew that dear Tom would have wished her to, and perhaps it would be the best thing for Iris if she did; but who would be bothered with a wretched invalid like herself?

A year after Tom's death she allowed George Hobhouse to lead her to the altar. He was a fine, upstanding fellow and he was not at all badly off. I never saw a man so grateful as he for the privilege of being allowed to take care of this frail little thing.

"I shan't live to trouble you long," she said.

He was a soldier and an ambitious one, but he resigned his commission. Louise's health forced her to spend the winter at Monte Carlo and the summer at Deauville. He hesitated a little at throwing up his career, and Louise at first would not hear of it; but at last she yielded, and he prepared himself to make his wife's last few years as happy as might be.

"It can't be very long now," she said. "I'll try not to be troublesome."

For the next two or three years Louise managed, notwithstanding her weak heart, to go to all the most lively parties, beautifully dressed, to gamble very heavily, to dance and even to flirt with tall, slim young men. But George Hobhouse had not the stamina of Louise's first husband and I fancied that he had to brace himself now and then with a stiff drink or two for his day's work as Louise's second husband. Then came the war. He rejoined his regiment and three months later was killed.

Though it was a great shock to Louise, at that moment she felt that she must submerge her private feelings; and if she had a heart attack nobody heard of it; but she said that she must distract her mind, so she turned her villa at Monte Carlo into a hospital for convalescent officers. Her friends told her that she would never survive the strain.

"Of course it will kill me," she said. "I know that. But what does it matter? I must do my bit."

It didn't kill her. I thought she was having the time of her life. I know that there was no convalescent home in France which was more popular. I met her in Paris once; she had gone there on business connected with the hospital; she was lunching with a tall and very handsome young Frenchman, and she told me that the officers were too charming to her. They knew how delicate she was and they wouldn't let her do a thing. They took care of her, well—as though they were all her husbands.

"Poor George, who would ever have thought that I with my heart should outlive him?" She sighed.

"And poor Tom," I said.

She gave me her plaintive smile and her beautiful eyes filled with tears. "You always speak as though you grudged me the few years that I can expect to live."

"By the way, your heart's much better, isn't it?"

"It'll never be better. I saw a specialist this morning and he said I must be prepared for the worst."

"Oh, well, you've been prepared for that for nearly twenty years now, haven't you?" I answered.

When the war came to an end Louise settled in London. She was now a woman of over forty, thin and frail still, with large eyes and pale cheeks, but she did not look a day more than twenty-five. Iris, who had been at school and was now grown up, came to live with her.

"She'll take care of me," said Louise. "Of course it'll be hard on her to live with such a great invalid as I am, but it can only be for such a little while. I'm sure she won't mind."

Iris was a charming girl. She had been brought up with the knowledge that

1925

Notwithstanding her weak heart, Louise managed to go to lively parties and flirt with young men

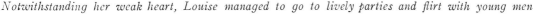

her mother's health was precarious; and though Louise told her now that she would not hear of her sacrificing herself for a tiresome invalid, the girl would not listen to reason. No professional nurse could have been more devoted.

"I can't get her to enjoy herself," said Louise. "Heaven knows I never want anyone to put himself out on my account."

And Iris, when I remonstrated with her, said: "Poor dear mother, she wants me to go and stay with friends and to go to parties, but the moment I go off anywhere she has one of her heart attacks, so I much prefer to stay at home."

But presently she fell in love. A young friend of mine, a very good lad, asked her to marry him and she consented. I liked the child and was glad that at last she had the chance of having a life of her own. She had never seemed to suspect that such a thing was possible. But one day the young man came to me in great distress and told me that his marriage was indefinitely postponed. Iris felt that she could not abandon her mother. Of course it was really no business of mine, but I made the opportunity to go and see Louise. She was always glad to receive her friends at tea-time, and now that she was older she cultivated the society of painters and writers.

"Well, I hear that Iris is not going to be married," I said.

"I don't know about that. She's not going to be married quite so soon as I could have wished. I've begged Iris on my bended knees not to consider me, but she absolutely refuses to leave me."

"Don't you think it's rather hard on her?"

"Dreadfully! Of course it can only be for a few months, but I hate the thought of anyone sacrificing himself for me."

"My dear Louise, you've buried two husbands; I can't see the least reason why you should not bury at least two more."

"Oh, I know, I know what you've always thought of me. You've never believed that I had anything the matter with me, have you?"

I looked at her full and square. "Never. I think you've carried out for twenty-five years a stupendous bluff. I think you're the most selfish and monstrous woman I have ever known. You ruined the lives of those two wretched men you married and now you're going to ruin the life of your daughter."

I should not have been surprised if Louise had had a heart attack. I fully expected her to fly into a passion. She merely gave me a gentle smile.

"My poor friend, one of these days you'll be so dreadfully sorry you said that to me."

"Have you quite determined that Iris shall not marry this boy?"

"I've begged her to marry him. Of course it'll kill me, but I want her to marry him."

"Did you tell her that?"

"She made me."

"As if anyone ever made you do anything that you were not yourself quite determined to do."

"She can marry her young man tomorrow if she likes. If it kills me, it kills me."

"Well, let's risk it, shall we?"

"Haven't you got any compassion for me?"

"One can't pity anyone who amuses one as much as you amuse me," I answered.

A faint spot of colour appeared on Louise's pale cheeks, and though she smiled still her eyes were hard and angry. "Iris shall marry in a month's time," she said, "and if anything happens to me, I hope you and she will be able to forgive yourselves."

Louise was as good as her word. A date was fixed, a trousseau of great magnificence was ordered, and invitations were sent out. Iris and the very good lad were radiant. On the wedding day, at ten o'clock in the morning, Louise, that devilish woman, had one of her heart attacks and, gently forgiving Iris for having killed her—died.

1925

Give Her a HOOVER and You Give Her the *Best*

CHRISTMAS finds the world with a common purpose — and a common question, "What shall I give?"

What will you give *her*? Something that is beautiful not only in appearance, but in use, and in the thought that goes to the giving. Something that will add to the joy of her New Year. Something memorable, the years through, by its constant help and service.

Isn't that "something" the Hoover?.... To be her helpmate in the home, to lighten her housecleaning tasks, to give her the greater leisure that is surely her due.

The Hoover—the only carpet cleaner that, beating, sweeping and suction cleaning in one easy, electrical operation, will do her hardest work quicker and better than she had ever imagined possible.

HOOVER LTD., 229-233 REGENT STREET, LONDON, W. 1, and at Birmingham, Manchester, Leicester, Leeds and Glasgow

1925

An Xmas Gift
—Well chosen, well received

From one woman to another, from husband to wife, or from any man to any woman, one sane, sensible gift, sure of a grateful reception, is some "4711" Eau De Cologne. Insomuch as this world-renowned numbered Eau de Cologne has been a delight to multitudes of women for toilet purposes, aiding them in retaining and maintaining a beautiful complexion, the cherished dream or possession of every woman—insomuch is a gift of "4711" Eau De Cologne an ideal Yuletide remembrance. It is more than a token of esteem, a passing gesture of the Season—it is a source of something fine and priceless, not to be forgotten with the passing of the Season.

"4711" Eau De Cologne may be obtained in groups or single bottles as follows: 2/6, 4/9, 8/9, 14/-, 15/-, 30/- and 56/- per bottle.

If you would like to give a complete Set of Toiletries, the following will provoke grateful appreciation, as each is fragranced with "4711" Eau de Cologne. A harmonious setting for Miladi's Toilet Table.

"4711" Bath Salts 1/6 & 2/6 per bottle.   "4711" Vanishing Cream 1/- & 2/- each.
"4711" Soap 2/- box of 3.   "4711" Cold Cream 1/6 & 2/6 per pot.
For Men Folk: "4711" Shaving Stick (in aluminium case) 1/3.

"4711" Eau De Cologne awaits you at all Dealers or High-class Perfumers, where they may be viewed at leisure.

By Rose Macaulay

HOW to

A Delightful this Writer

There is no harm in Christmas, it's the way it's kept

CHRISTMAS is, in one respect only, like pigs, of which animals it is sometimes said: "There's no harm in pigs themselves, it's the way they're kept." This is not true of pigs, who are essentially obnoxious creatures, but it is true of Christmas. There is no harm in Christmas, it's the way it's kept. The way to deal with Christmas is so to keep it that you enjoy it (nearly, anyhow) as much as the other seasons of the year. This is what Christmas is for. You must enjoy it, or you will be looked on as a churl and a curmudgeon, and will even so regard yourself, which is painful. So, somehow or another, you must contrive some way of dealing with this great season which will render it innocuous and yourself happy. The method you adopt will, of course, depend on your individual temperament and inclinations, but here are a few suggestions.

Do not attempt to enter any shops in December; they will not make you happy. It has been well said—or, if it has not, it is well said now—that, if there be a hell, it is probably much like a large shop at Christmas time. And you should not enter hell before you are compelled to do so. Let your children do so: children do not mind. Their hell will not be this, but quite other. Depute any shopping that you may require to have done either to your children or your servants, if any. If you possess neither of these, do not shop. Above all, do not venture into post offices, which from the last day of November on are crammed with people obediently Posting Early, in the hopes that, thus, their communications may arrive on Christmas Day. As a matter of fact, things posted on the 1st of December normally arrive on the 2nd, though, if you post after the fifteenth, your communications, lying near the bottom of a large pile, will probably not be delivered until early in the following year.

But never mind these postal speculations; you will not need them, for the only way to enjoy Christmas is not to post at all. Let others post to one another and to you, but do not attempt to participate in this feverish activity. If you do, you will have to stand in queues in post offices for more hours than you probably care. This is not the way to be happy at Christmas.

Having dismissed shops and post offices from your visiting circle, it is quite obvious that you can give no presents. Receive them if you will, or if others will; the passive part is the more blessed in this business, and you may chance to get something you like. But do not give. For one thing, you probably cannot afford it. If you give one present, you will have to give others, and it comes expensive.

Neither should you write letters or send cards—unless, indeed, someone should go out and purchase the cards for you, put them in envelopes, address

You will also have to suffer the weather, which will be bad at this season

them, and lick the stamps. Even so, it is a mistake to enter the card game. It is full of snags. You will doubtless have forgotten who are the people who are likely to send cards to you; even if you made a list last Christmas and kept it (and this is certainly no way to enjoy Christmas) it is no adequate guide, for how should you guess into whose heart the devil, ever rampant at holy seasons, may not this season place the thought of sending you a card?

However, if you feel you must send cards, there is no need to go to the desperate expedient of buying any; you should send those which, having been posted early, arrive for you throughout December. You should be careful, on the whole, to send each card to another than to him or her who sent them to you; probably he or she will be none the wiser even if you do so, but still, it is something of a solecism. There is, however, one exception to this rule. When the sender of a card has been

Illustrations by Bert Thomas

ENJOY Christmas

Dissertation by amusing at her best

1925

so inconsiderate, lazy and selfish as to write his or her name on the card itself, instead of writing it on a separate piece of paper or leaving it to your imagination, you should immediately return his or her own card, merely altering the "from" to a "to." This is a just retribution, for those who send inscribed cards at Christmas are among the least to be considered of humankind.

Christmas cards are usually poor. There is only one good kind, and that is a snowy landscape with a lighted church in the distance and a robin and a wreath of holly in the foreground. There are not very many of these now, and you are more likely to receive a calendar, or a representation of a bunch of foolish spring flowers, twined round

German music for a time tottered, but never the German Christmas

a silver horseshoe, or a reproduction of an Italian Holy Family, or a stable scene with illuminated verses under it, or something amusing, such as black cats. However, any of these do to send away.

You will get a good many letters and cards from persons of whom you have taken no notice, on the feasts of St. Stephen, St. John, the Holy Innocents, and subsequent days up to Epiphany. After the feast of St. Stephen, you should not try to reciprocate them in time for Christmas Day, as if you had thought of the sender all along, but should wait until New Year's Day.

There is only one thing to be said in favour of the card game—it is better than writing letters. Some people have time, and suppose that others have time, to write letters at Christmas. You should not attempt to deal with these poor people after their own folly; a garland of pansies or a funny cat will meet their case.

All this advice is on the assumption that you are, like most of us, weak, and have succumbed to the Christmas business. If, by some unlikely chance, you are strong-minded, and can sit, like M. Romain Rolland in the one-time war, above the battle, so much the better for you. You will then only have to suffer the minor inconveniences of crowded streets, inaccessible shops, and the general derailment of your life's normal running.

You will also, of course, have to suffer the weather, which will be bad at this season. It will most probably be wet, dull and cold, with a disagreeable wind. It may, however, be what shopkeepers call "seasonable," which is worse, for this means frost and snow

and an even lower temperature. You do not get seasonable weather except at Christmas; you get frost and snow, but it is not called seasonable. Nor is hot weather in summer, nor even wet weather at the same season. It is an adjective reserved for Christmas, and means cold.

Besides the weather, you will find the streets even less agreeable than usual, for there seems to be even more getting about at Christmas than at other times, and this is to say a great deal. People who live in London and are annoyed by the crowds say: "Why can't all these people from the suburbs do their shopping there?" for people like to think that other people come from the suburbs, which are not nice places to come from; in fact, if you are so unfortunate as to reside in a suburb, you should not come from it, but stay in it, for so long as you do that you will only be despised (except from afar) by the other suburbians, and no one minds being despised by suburbians.

We stray from our point, which was, if I remember rightly, that during the Christmas season the streets are crowded. The omnibuses are also crowded, so crowded that you will not succeed in getting into them, so you had better not try. At Christmas every hour is a rush hour, and the rush hours of omnibuses are standing-in-the-street hours for you and me.

In fact, London, like other large British towns, is no fit place in which to spend Christmas. You should, if you can manage it, leave Great Britain, well before what is called the Christmas Rush Abroad. You should rush first, somewhere near the end of November, before the (continued on page 130)

It may, however, be what shopkeepers call "seasonable," which is worse . . .

1925

A Gift Every Woman will Welcome

NO other gift will yield such a measure of helpfulness to the woman of the house as the new Johnson Floor Polishing Outfit—the new easy, liquid way of cleaning and polishing linoleum and floors. It eliminates the old method of getting down on one's hands and knees.

Just pour Johnson's Liquid Wax on the Lamb's-wool Mop and apply a thin, even coat to the floor. A few brisk strokes with the Johnson Weighted Brush will quickly bring it to a beautiful, durable, glass-like lustre that is not slippery or greasy. It's much quicker—only a few minutes required.

31/- *Floor Polishing Outfit for* 22/6

This Offer consists of

A SAVING OF 8/6			A SAVING OF 8/6
	1 Quart Johnson's Liquid Wax	7/6	
	1 Johnson's Lamb's-wool Wax Mop	7/-	
	1 Johnson's Weighted Floor Polishing Brush ..	15/6	
	1 Johnson's Book on Home Beautifying.. ..	1/-	
		31/-	

This Outfit is obtainable at Ironmongers, House Furnishers, Stores and Grocers. *If any difficulty in obtaining, write us direct.*

THIS XMAS GIVE A JOHNSON FLOOR POLISHING OUTFIT. A WELCOME GIFT IN EVERY HOME.

S. C. JOHNSON & SON, LTD. (Dept. G.H.), West Drayton, Middlesex
"The Wood Finishing Authorities."

JOHNSON'S LIQUID WAX

How to Enjoy Christmas

end of any scholastic terms sets others rushing too. Of course others are really rushing all the time; Britons, in their zeal to leave their native land, rush abroad in every train, every boat, and every airship that leaves it. As to where to rush to, you must, of course, please yourself in this, or, alternatively, go as far as such money as you possess will take you. Personally I should always avoid places where there is likely to be seasonable weather, i.e. ice and snow, for two reasons; one, ice and snow are disagreeably cold, two, you will meet too many other Britons playing in them, for Britons like the cold, and what they call *winter sports*. For my part, I would rather seek some warm and secluded spot, in some land where Christmas is not much thought of, such as Italy. The trouble about Italy is to find in it a secluded spot, but still, it can be done. Or there are the smaller and less frequented of the Balearic islands.

But neither Italy nor Balearic islands nor anywhere else in Europe will be really warm at Christmas time. To secure warmth you must go further afield, and this you probably cannot afford. So, on the whole, you may as well save your money and stay in England, keeping a good fire in your home and remaining by it. If you stay by the fire you will avoid the worst of the seasonable weather, the seasonable crowds, and many of the other seasonable annoyances which you would encounter if you were to venture forth into the open. Lay in plenty of good food and drink well beforehand, have such friends assembled about you as please your taste, and such occupations as intrigue your fancy, and when your door bell is rung take no notice, for it may be carol singers. By these means you will be able to ignore Christmas as nearly as may be, and revert to the good old days of our ancestors, when this season passed without much more of a hullaballoo than Easter or any other festival. It was the Germans who first kept Christmas in the modern manner, and our German-loving Victorian forbears introduced it into Great Britain. Somehow it succeeded in weathering the recent anti-German war, which was a heavy blow to other German importations. German music for a time tottered, but never the German Christmas.

Well, it is an amiable custom, this corporate rejoicing, and does credit to humanity. Those who prefer to rejoice less corporately are less Christian of soul. I am almost ashamed to offer them my counsel. But, after all, there they are, and there is no reason why they, too, should not be happy in their own ways. So let this pass for a Christmas greeting to the selfish, the idle, the unsocial, who, though they may dislike brown paper, string, cards, letters, crowds, shops, post offices, and all forms of taking trouble, are, nevertheless, God's creatures too. A happy Christmas, then, to both those and these!

By
Nora
Mullane

If You Have Short Hair

1926

HOW pleasant they are to look at—the proud, smoothly-coiffed, youthful, brave bobbed topknots of to-day, hair brushed and clipped until it outlines charmingly the line of the back of the head! So different they are from the grotesque shapes and sizes we have seen since the twentieth century ushered in the towering pompadour. Here is freedom and simplicity and a lightness of head—physically speaking, of course—that seems to have a strange connection with lightness of heart. Hats are easy to buy, headaches from hairpins and heavy coils disappear, and hairdressing takes less time—though more thought. Naturally these good things must be paid for; all good things must sometime and somehow be paid for; and the price of short hair—once you face it—sounds rather high. It's perfection.

Perfection, nothing less. You can't have bobbed, cropped, shingled, or any style of short hair and be even passably prepossessing, if you have lazy little habits that betray you into tousled, uneven, oily, straggly, stringy, dusty, or lifeless locks. You can't do it, because every defect shows up so fearfully. You must choose your style of hair-cut more carefully than ever you chose a coiffure heretofore. If you have a round, youthful face with nice features, you can do almost anything—be as babyish, or as boyish, or as daringly sophisticated as you like. But if you have large features, a prominent nose, or irregularities that you don't want to emphasise, be careful! Very likely you should keep your hair long. Straight, boyish hair is sweet on the trim, slim girl. Youth and perfect features are enhanced by the severe Eton bob. But if life has dealt harshly with you, stolen your complexion, marked you with anxious wrinkles, or given a defiant look to your lips and eyes, don't wear your hair too short, too straight, too daring in contour. A soft, wavy effect is better for you. The size of your head is another factor. Big, bushy heads and large rolls are now regarded as ugly. Choose a style that makes your head look small and well-shaped.

Whatever style you select, though, it must be flawless.

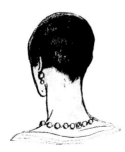

Your hair must have the sheen of satin, of velvet, and be sure you do not confuse the glitter that comes out of bottles with the gleam that comes from constant, intelligent care. Here are a few suggestions that will help you.

Don't get into the habit of wetting your hair when you take a shower. Wash your comb and brush every day, but wash your hair only once in every two weeks. If it needs freshening oftener than that, brush it with a good hair tonic.

Immediately after shampooing, rub a little vaseline into the scalp. Vaseline is preferable to oils, because it does not become rancid.

Don't use hot curling irons if you can avoid it. They make the hair brittle and lifeless. Frizzy hair is never pretty, and is especially unbecoming when the hair is short. Choose the round curl or big, soft waves.

If you want to avoid that unmanageable period just after a shampoo, try this: before it is dry, part and arrange your hair as you like it, and tie over it a light veil firmly knotted. Then fan the hair dry. The result is a perfect arrangement, without any tedious training.

If your hair has been permanently waved, and is straight only where it is growing out near the scalp, put in combs after a shampoo, and let it dry with the combs in.

Don't procrastinate when your hair needs trimming if you want to look perfectly groomed. Wear a strong net at night to keep your hair in its proper position, so that you won't be bothered by a lot of incorrigible strands.

Remember that your neck is infinitely more noticeable now that it is not shadowed by knots and coils of hair above it. Keep the neck firm, round, smooth and white. If there is a roll of fat at the back of it, do not crop your hair. Get rid of the extra flesh first.

Cultivate the habit of watching the back of your head. See that the style of your hair-cut does not spoil its fine curve. Study until you have found just the right hair line across the neck, dipped or curved, but never straight. It is best to follow the natural hair line as nearly as possible, but keep the neck well groomed.

Things You'll

Decorations by Elizabeth Montgomery

1926

A Nest Box

For the Bravest Robin

BE kind to the birds just now, won't you? And do place a nest-box high up in the shrubbery, where you can look at it from the window. You can hang up suet balls at the end of a string, coco-nuts cut in half, and bones to attract the tits.

See that the birds near you have a happy Christmas. Hide behind the window curtain after spreading all the crumbs from a meal on the window ledge and see what a beautiful busy crowd will visit you. If you have Mrs. Gatty's *Parables from Nature,* read that delightful story of the very bravest robin you have ever heard of.

The Only Child

I've got the very thing for Jane's stocking. It is a little green plate. On one side is fixed a white egg-cup and near by stands a darling yellow china chicken. He will be a nice friend for Jane who is an only child.

All mothers should have a few real flowers given to them just now, even if it is only a bunch of Christmas Roses to bloom in a clear vase among the scarlet and silver crackers at tea.

Masked Balls

Why not have a masked Christmas party? It is so little trouble to cut out a mask of black sateen, put tapes to it and hide your eyes. Arrange that your guests shall unmask before supper-time.

It is sometimes easier to have a fancy headdress party than a real fancy dress ball. A chef's cap, a pierrette's peaked hat with black bobbles, a nurse's cap with long scarf streamers, are easy.

Oh! and if you want some good words for Charades, try, *Speck, Tay, Tor* (spectator), or *A Part Meant* (apartment), or *Fur Knit Your* (furniture).

Christmas Eve

Hanging the Stockings

DON'T wrap up the parcels all anyhow, but try some crimson crinkly paper—it only costs 2*d.* a large roll. Then draw and paint pretty little pictures and verses on the back of Mother's old visiting cards. Holly berry and green leaf ribbon is prettier than string to tie with.

All Tens!

Here is a capital card trick. You can do it when the fire is burning low, and all the crackers have been pulled, and it is nearly time for bed. It's a very easy trick, so cheer up! All you have to do is to prepare two packs of cards beforehand. Place the four "tens" on top of one, while the other simply consists of ten odd cards.

Write on a piece of paper, "*You will choose the ten pile,*" and give this to someone in the room. Then tell the audience that you are going to deal out two packs of cards and that you will make them of different sizes. You will then choose any member of the company voted for and pretend to hypnotise him into choosing the particular pack you select.

The whole secret of the trick lies in the fact that you do not mind which pack your friend picks up. If he chooses the little pack, bid him look at its contents—all tens—if he chooses the larger, bid him count them and they will be ten. Then read the paper!

A Christmas Tale

Little Girl Left Out

ELSA was not asked! And she knew that the Macintyres next door were giving a Christmas party. Had they forgotten her, or was it because she was so shy?

She was an only child, you see, and Daddy was an invalid and always lay propped up on a sofa writing a book, and Mother was always busy. So Elsa was left out of a lot of things.

There wasn't going to be a party at Elsa's house of course, there never had been, absolutely never. But oh, just next door, what fun was going on!

A few days before Christmas, Elsa had watched the beautiful green Christmas tree being carried in. Hadn't she heard its fragrant branches stirring; whispering away about the lovely time the children would have, when it stood radiant and robed in splendour, in the very centre of the Macintyres' jolly drawing-room?

"I should go to the party," boldly advised Rose, the housemaid, and Elsa's crony, on the great day, as she came to watch two baker's tray-loads of white and orange cakes go round to the back door; followed by a boy from the florist's bearing a great bunch of red-berried holly. "Go. You know them, miss. They've only forgotten you."

Getting Ready for the Party

"Oh! I couldn't," said little Elsa. "I heard Laura Macintyre say to Barbara just now in the garden, that the fairy doll had just arrived," she added wistfully.

"And I hear there's to be a present for each child," said Rose, nodding wisely. "Oh, Miss Elsa! And they'd be so glad to see you, I know. You ought to talk to the little girls more than you do. If you come into my bedroom now, miss, you can see right into their night nursery, and there are two pairs of pink satin slippers and two party frocks on the bed; one seems all white flounces."

"If I was invited, I'd have nothing much to wear," said Elsa. "Only my old, old green. Still, it wouldn't matter. Oh, how I should love to see that tree and that fairy doll! I believe it's dressed in gold sparkles!"

And she followed Rose up and just next door lay the dainty little slippers that were so soon to be prancing cheerfully to the strains of "Sir Roger."

Like To Know

By
Marjory Royce

Gold Sparkles

In the Study

OH, mercy me, dreary fiddlesticks, imagine being left out of a party! When it's going on under your very nose too! But she wouldn't tell Daddy or Mother. Later on she slipped into her father's room. Daddy had a very bright smile on his face.

"Hurray, Elsa!" he said. "I've got my book finished before Christmas, old lady, after all, and I do feel so relieved. Help me up, darling, I've a good mind to sit up for tea for a change."

"Oh, Daddy, *do*, I'm so glad," said little Elsa.

Even as she helped him to his place, she heard the sound of a taxi. The guests must be arriving next door! Her heart sank and she blinked hard.

"What's that letter there on the ground?" asked Daddy.

Elsa ran and picked it up.

Happy After All

"Why, it's addressed to *me*, Daddy!" she cried, holding the envelope up in bewilderment.

"My darling, I'm so sorry! It came days ago, and must have got all tangled up in my papers," said her father. "I forgot all about it, pet. What is it, Elsa?"

For a sad face had turned into a bright face. It was an invitation to the Macintyres' party! She had not been forgotten after all! She could go! In a trice Elsa had bounded upstairs and was wriggling out of her dress, and in a twinkling Rose had her green frock laid out, and Cook was rummaging in the cupboard to find her best shoes, and Mother was brushing her hair as hard as she could, and there was laughing and tumult and gorgeous excitement.

"I shall see the Christmas tree and the fairy dolly," were Elsa's last words as she skipped through a gate in the hedge.

See it she did, after a glorious tea, and many games. She was handed a large parcel from the tree containing a doll's tea-set, and when they all drew lots for the fairy dolly it was Elsa herself who drew the lucky number!

So she carried home Miss Gold Sparkles in her white tulle skirts carrying her starry-bright, magic wand.

Carols

On Starlight Nights

SINGING carols on frosty, starlight nights is great fun and I advise everyone to buy Curwen's fourpenny book, *Christmas Carols for Children,* at once and begin to practise, "Gently falls the winter snow," and "We three Kings of Orient are."

Marble Bagatelle

You can all make this game and it is splendid fun at Christmas parties. Find a long cardboard box lid and take off one narrow end: this is now your marble board. Now cut a strip of stout cardboard about the depth of your lid. Push it three-quarters of the way up your lid and see that it exactly fits, then cut out into little arches with sharp scissors, and above each arch write a number in bold black ink. Push the arches carefully into position and pick out your twelve prettiest marbles.

The game consists of rolling each marble gently up the board and trying to get it into the arch with the largest number. Take turns with your friends and write down the score. I suggest each person has three tries, three times over. The one who scores the most, of course, wins.

Holidays

Yuletide Wanderings

MANY readers of this page will be coming up to London to go to the pantomime and see the sights. I think they should ask for Methley's delightful *Child's Guide to London* (Methuen, 7s. 6d.) for a present beforehand.

It is sometimes hard to choose the right gift for a boy; Miss Dorothy M. Stuart's charming volume, *The Boy Through the Ages* (Harrap, 7s. 6d.), is just the thing. It has over two hundred pictures and gives stories about boys of all countries.

Noel

Vincent is going to ice his own Christmas cake. You see, the twenty-fifth of December is his sixth birthday. Isn't that exciting? He ought to have been called Noel, perhaps.

It will be quite a simple icing. He will sift a pound of icing sugar into a basin, add to it two whites of eggs and a dessertspoonful of lemon juice. Then when it is stirred till it is well mixed, he will beat it with a wooden spoon for a long time. Probably Cook will help here, don't you think?

Six Chocolate Mice

The icing must not drip from the spoon. If it is too thin, put in more sugar; if too thick, more white of egg. Now for the colouring matter. Vincent has chosen green for this year's cake, so in go several drops of green colouring.

Six noble chocolate mice will be placed round the Christmas cake. Father Christmas clasping his tree will be surrounded by six candles.

1926

W. HEATH ROBINSON.

1926

Why Gardeners

Illustrations by
W. Heath Robinson

IT has frequently been noticed that, although gardens are often very beautiful places, gardeners as a class are depressed. Three young gardeners were once standing talking at Reigate, Surrey, upon a large open space. They saw approaching from the distance, accompanied by his wife and children, the most dismal-looking man they had ever seen. "Look at this faller," said one of the three. "Oi betcher whatcher loike he's a ga-ardiner!" He was right: the most dismal of men was in fact a gardener. He was head-gardener at a large house in that neighbourhood, and his face was seamed with cares. This story is a true one, narrated to me by one of the three; and it has its plain moral.

Gardeners notoriously cry for rain when the rest of men long for sunshine; if one remarks cheerfully to gardeners: "How nice the roses look to-day," they shake their heads, and crush one by saying miserably: "Ain't what they *should* be. Them plaguèd floi; them cuckoo-spit . . . Blessèd mildew. . . ." Too well do gardeners realise the truth. Closer examination by the amateur does indeed reveal both fly and mildew, and a small, sinister patch of white froth. The froth conceals a lethargic yellow insect which presently will jump headlong about the garden like a grasshopper or the Death Watch beetle.

Once started upon wretched thoughts, the gardener can but add to one's dolours. "Carrots won't come to nothin'," says he. "Nor turnips: they've got the fly" or "the beetle." "There's thrip on the peas; woolly aphis on the apples" (but in England he will not say "woolly aphis," but "American bloight," while in America I think he says "Irish blight"). "Me lettuce is boltin'"; "Sha-ant 'ave no anemones—not the 'Cayenne' (Caen); them there woireworms has bin a-after them." "Blessèd slugs. . . ." And so on.

Very quickly does the amateur discover that his or her easy satisfaction with the superficial appearance of a garden rests entirely upon ignorance. It is all very well for Francis Bacon, in his essay "Of Gardens," to lay out thirty acres of what he calls "prince-like" garden, with divisions into three parts, of which no fewer than twelve are to go to the main garden and the rest to "green" and "heath." In his day, if we are to judge by report and by his omission of all reference to pests, a garden could be "the purest of human pleasures," and so without blemish or anguish to the gardener. But nowadays matters are different. A garden is a field of incessant battle—a siege warfare —in which man is always at a disadvantage. As amateurs we may still stroll in the gardens of friends with a sweet unconsciousness of rust, deformity, and the innumerable woes of failure and disease; but if we are in ever so slight a degree professionals—if we have, that is, gardens of our own—we shall find ourselves

gradually—as other gardeners are— weighed down by the strain of incessant struggle with the elements and the ills which affect every kind of crop. Then we shall understand why gardeners are gloomy. They are gloomy because their minds are concerned less with blooms and verdure than with disease, decay, insects, birds, weeds, and even with blank spaces which ought to be smiling with brilliance. They are gloomy because they know what the garden *ought to look like*.

I will not dwell upon the coloured lures of seedsmen's catalogues, or the strange, wicked photographs which one sees of whole fields crammed with perfect flowers. These are but the flares shown to poor mariners by malignant wreckers. We "follow the gleam" year after year, and dash upon disastrous rocks very much as deceived mariners must have done. Nothing will cure us of that trustingness. After all, seeds must come from somewhere, and I take it that one seedsman's packets contain seeds not greatly unlike those in the packets of another seedsman. Moreover, there is an unpromising

gaudiness in some of the drawings. It threatens vulgarity, and blowsiness.

Only the really professional gardener, who longs for all his blooms to be in-

1926

are GLOOMY

By Frank Swinnerton

sufferable giants of disgustingly crude colour, will aim at such results as the packets promise. The rest of us will be content with something smaller. Besides, we have lost some of our faith in the packet picture, and we take what we can get. We *must* buy seeds, or obtain them gratuitously from other gardeners; and seeds are seeds all the world over. It is what happens to the seeds when planted in our own gardens that makes gardeners like ourselves the most despondent of human beings.

For a thousand ills may attend a seed. It may rot where it lies. That is the most likely event. The wet and the cold may destroy it. Or it may swell and burst, and wireworm or the grub of the leather jacket may nestle to the roots and consume them. Or, with good fortune, the plant may show its first green shoots, and they may be eaten by somnolent slugs. An inch or two more, and a caterpillar of voracious type may nip them off close to the surface of the earth. Sometimes they may catch the eye of a dear little bird, and yield themselves as succulent morsels to him.

If they escape these early ills (and wireworm and grub may set to work at any time), frost may destroy; fly may settle and consume; damp and cold may so weaken the plant that it cannot resist

the spreading plagues of the garden. Its leaves may curl and shrivel, may stain, may drop off. Its flower may never come; or, if it comes, may be but half a flower—a wretched caricature, not only of the seedsman's jubilant representation, but even of what one sees actually blooming in other gardens. And when it grows tall and strong, a shelled snail will climb its height, or a shrieking wind may rise suddenly, and blow it flat. Misshapen, discoloured, slain in the darkness by summer frost, or by boisterous wind, the flower is a single item in the daymare of the gardener. Each single flower is but a detail, for in a garden no more than an acre in extent there must be well upwards of a million of such delicate lives. All of them in danger; all at death's door.

There is drought to consider — when the earth cannot be dug; when the flowers and the vegetables parch; when lawns crack, and banks, through the pitiless glare of the sun, indulge in paralysing landslides. Watch the flowers wilting; see the young cabbages turning

yellow, and the young rows of peas drying a dull brown. " Lovely summer weather! " laughs the amateur, stretching easily in bed, and feeling exhilarated by the blue sky. " Makes you feel good to be alive." " If it don't rain *soon,*" mutters the gardener, " all my young cauliflowers will go. The beans ain't settin'. All of them violas—they ain't nothin' but water—will die."

A terribly grim expression appears upon his face. Even though the Water Board may recommend economy with water, he steals out secretly in the evening, snaffles his hose-pipe on to the scullery tap, and sprays the dying garden. And, while he does this in desperation, he knows that water from the tap is only a wetness; it has not the nourishing properties of rain. It may choke the plants, instead of doing them good. " Plaguèd noosance, these beamy days," grumbles the gardener. " All my young pla-ants a-goin'. And I'm doin' more 'arm than good be waterin'." I have a theory that if one waters one's pet plants the mere moisture draws to the spot innumerable underground consumers, so that watering in patches is plant-murder.

And now comes Sir Jagadis Bose, who tells us that we ourselves, if the plants do not like us, may cause them such a trembling of agitation as to induce nervous breakdown. If we go near the plants—though we tread quietly—they are aware of it; they faint from dislike of us.

to make a dish interesting add
Dromedary Dates

The only dates cleaned and packed by machines and not by natives' hands—twice pasteurised!

NO COOKING, no extra trouble; just stone enough Dromedary Dates for everyone to have a generous spoonful over each helping. See how quickly they eat it up. Bread and milk, milk puddings, porridge – the family fairly clamours for wholesome dishes made interesting with Dromedary Dates.

Dromedary Dates make it possible for you to make dates a regular part of your children's diet. You can use them plentifully with the certainty of their entire purity—so essential in the case of food you set before your children. Dromedary Dates are the only dates awarded the Certificate of the Institute of Hygiene, London, for purity and cleanliness. They are packed in the gardens by machines and not by natives' hands. They are even pasteurised before and after packing.

While you eat Dromedary Dates you are enjoying not only one of Nature's choicest delicacies but one of her most valuable foods. Dromedary Dates are packed with health-giving properties—with the lime salts that build bone with tonic iron. Their delicious flavour satisfies the natural craving for sweet things and makes it a source of strength and nourishment.

You will be glad to know that you can enjoy Dromedary Dates all the year round. They are always in perfect condition summer and winter. Each carton carries a guarantee under which your money is returned if you are not absolutely satisfied.

Try Rice Pudding the Dromedary Date Way!

Stone and chop a good handful of Dromedary Dates. When your rice pudding is nearly cooked, sprinkle a layer to cover the top about a quarter of an inch thick. For a delicious change leave to get cold and turn out like a shape.

For dozens of new ways to enjoy Dromedary Dates as a fruit, in sandwiches and salads, write for the Dromedary Recipe Book "New Ideas to help you please the whole family." Simply fill in and post the coupon. A halfpenny stamp only is necessary.

10½d. per packet

Awarded Certificate of Institute of Hygiene, London, for cleanliness and purity

COUPON

Dromedary Ltd., (Dept. A12), Finsbury Court, E.C.2.
Please send me a free copy of the Dromedary Recipe Book which contains many suggestions for serving Dromedary Dates and Dromedary Grapefruit (in cans).

Name ....

Address ....

....

My Grocer's Name and Address is

[Dr.-2-27] ....

1927

"4711" Eau de Cologne
With the Blue and Gold Label.
Sold from 2/6 to 56/- per bottle.

"4711" Face Powder
Perfumed with "4711" Eau de
Cologne. Shaded in Rachel,
Naturelle, Rose and White.
1/3 per box.

CHOOSE XMAS GIFTS NOW

YOUR choice now extends from the world-famous "4711" Eau de Cologne to other beautiful items of dainty feminine "4711" toiletries. And what more delightful and seasonable gifts for remembrance! Such gifts, not dear as to price, however, prove precious to those who appreciate all that is beautiful and, moreover, useful.

"4711" Eau de Cologne is obtainable in all sizes from Chemists, Perfumers and the leading Stores at **2/6, 4/9, 8/9, 14/-, 15/-, 30/- & 56/-** per bottle.

Whatever items you propose giving, be sure they each have the distinctive Blue and Gold label, with the world-famous numerals "4711" — *The Hall-Mark of Quality!*

"4711" Vanishing Cream
Perfumed with "4711" Eau
de Cologne and of unsur-
passed quality. In Pots
at 2/- and Tubes 1/- each.

"4711" Cold Cream
Perfumed with Otto of Rose of
superlative quality. In Pots, 10½d.,
1/6 and 2/6. In Tubes at 1/- each.

№4711 Eau de Cologne

Advertised Goods are Good Goods.

L. HUMMEL

RELA

Weighed in the Balance and Found

By Lady Violet

THE word "relations" is a chilly label, implying obligations and indifference; "distant relatives"—the indifference is increased, the obligations are diminished, and a note of shame creeps in. One sometimes wonders whether relations (saving their feelings and our own, for we, after all, are *somebody's*) are things we should really be happier without?

I have one friend who frankly admits her sincere regret that she was not a foundling, but this is, I think, a rather uncommonly extreme view to take. On the other hand, I know many (mostly, it is true, belonging to the last generation) to whom blood-relationship is an almost holy thing and for whom all relatives, even the most remote and unprepossessing, are sacred.

I think one may reasonably draw a very clear distinction between one's attitude towards one's immediate family, i.e. brothers—sisters—father —mother, etc., and its more distant offshoots, like uncles, aunts and cousins, first, second and third. However critical one may be of brothers and sisters, however uncongenial and incompatible one may find them, one has in relation to them, however involuntarily, the sense of passionate solidarity which might be felt by one wolf towards the rest of the pack. Their credit and discredit are to some extent our own. They are bone of our bone. We have a horrible understanding of their most unpleasant traits. We need not have the same friends, but we must have the same enemies. Taken at its

worst the relationship is bound to be a close one; for that very reason, you may maintain, the more potentially jarring; still, one which it is impossible to deny or dissolve.

Cousins are a different matter altogether. We feel no responsibility for them whatever, nor, if it comes to that, much kinship with them. I remember as a child complaining that cousins were people one was made to pray for, and even supposed to like without ever having made friends with them.

It is this provocative assumption that we all have a fund of ready-made liking at the disposal of relations in general which does more than anything else to queer our pitch with them.

It is difficult to say which are the more annoying, relations who are rather like one, only better, or relations who are rather like one, only worse. Their best chance is to be as different as they possibly can. This rule appears to me to be peculiarly applicable to sisters, and perhaps especially to elder

sisters. There is no doubt in my mind that among the really close relations the least *enjoyable* must be an elder sister. Elder sisters can't help being interfering, curious, managing; it is inherent, not perhaps in their own nature, but in the nature of their position in the family. Even their undoubted kindness and comfortingness in moments of adversity is slightly tinctured with patronage. They know everything about one, and want to know more. " I know where you got *that* from—out of that book you were reading yesterday"—or, " So-and-So said that before you—it's not original, you little copy-cat."

Then they do everything first, and tell one about it, handing on their experience with their old clothes, flaunting their seniority almost vulgarly, as it seems to us juniors. We turn resentfully away from their *nouveau-riche* knowledge-of-the-world, so recently acquired, so ostentatiously displayed.

Elder brothers, on the other hand,

1927

Scissorcut illustrations by L. Hummel

TIONS

— *Sometimes Wanted, Sometimes Not!*

Bonham Carter

are perhaps the most perfect relations it is possible to possess. It is quite impossible to have too many of them. They cannot come amiss in any situation in life. From the moment they leave home for school they have the keys of Heaven in their pockets, mixed up with knives and bulls'-eyes and many other desirable possessions, and all through life they are unlocking doors for us which, but for them, must have remained for ever closed.

Their physical prowess is impressive, but even this does not dazzle us like the brilliance of their wit, which seems to us Talleyrand, Edwin Lear, Rabelais, George Robey rolled into one, and then outshone.

As a child, to be alone with one of them was in itself an adventure, combining the most romantic risks with the most complete security. It might mean being physically hoisted to undreamt-of heights on a tree- or rock-climbing expedition, or being shown (as a deep secret) the Greek alphabet, or taught a card-trick, or told a ghost story, or

being given one's first sip of claret (very nasty, but a privilege), or being allowed to play a small part in a chemical experiment, the skinning of a bat, or a complicated offensive against the grown-ups; always armed with the comforting certainty that however heterodox the proceeding, no evil consequences could attend it, as one was partnered by licensed revolutionaries.

Year by year the keys unlocked new doors and ever better ones. Tastes of Homer, and Sherlock Holmes, a first Shakespeare play (*Julius Cæsar* it was, in my case) *at night*, sitting alone with a brother in red plush seats; foursomes at golf with a brother as partner, who said "Good shot" to one's poorest efforts. One felt yoked to victory as one watched the ball soaring like a lark at the touch of his brassey two hundred and fifty yards straight down the middle of the "pretty." Then, later still, magical days at Oxford. Teas with anchovy toast in rooms for which one is perhaps allowed to choose

the chintzes, to re-arrange the furniture and to dethrone a few of the Landseer dogs which paper the walls with monotonous nobility of expression. For some obscure reason, our brothers no 'longer seem ashamed of our being seen by their friends (as they so naturally and rightly were at school), and there is the amazing discovery, which comes as a greater surprise to them than to ourselves, that their friends appear to take us quite seriously. With the sharing of friends as well as books we have the intoxicating sense of pulling up abreast of them, and assuming almost the dignity of a contemporary. But though we may feel full-fledged grown-ups, they still hold the keys of liberty for us. They count as "chaperons." Throughout our youth an elder brother has it in his power to give us the most coveted of all prizes, freedom and independence, combined with what the grown-ups and the "world" consider to be the necessary make-weight of conventional safety and respectability. If only it were possible to arrange that every family should start with boys, the happiness of women would be assured!

This is a sister's view of brothers. What brothers feel about sisters I cannot say, but of one thing I am sure—that as an insurance in happiness, no less than as an education in living, one cannot have too many of both. Nothing that happens in after-life can begin to compensate that infinitely forlorn object, the "only child," for the brothers and *(continued overleaf)*

1927

Relations

sisters it has never had, and the loss of the gayest and closest, most protecting and developing intimacy in life.

Mothers are, and have always been, so heavily "written-up" that any mention of their merits and demerits as a relation must be omitted from this brief summary, but mothers-in-law, I think, deserve an honourable mention.

The mother-in-law has become a music-hall figure. She has been firmly planted by convention, along with sea-sickness and policemen, in the sphere of almost classical knock-about. Was she placed there by art or nature? One sometimes wonders. I think there is no doubt that nature had something to do with it. It is the (very natural, though possibly ill-judged) refusal of the mother to abdicate completely and immediately in favour of the upstart stranger who has—almost casually—carried off her child, which forms the *leit-motif* of the farce in which the mother-in-law is chronically pilloried. All in-lawship is tainted (tarred would be too strong a word) with this same brush. "My in-laws are coming here to-day." It is almost impossible to say the words without a slightly apprehensive inflection. "I have completely re-arranged this room, which horrifies my in-laws." This is the expression of the eternal conflict between the old tradition and the new broom which sweeps away its patina as though it were a cobweb.

We can enter into the point of view of both combatants with a sympathy and understanding born of the fact that most of us at different moments of our lives have been militant members of both

camps. It is so natural to feel when one has just married somebody that no one has ever understood him before. It is equally natural to resent the sudden annexation of one's favourite brother or son by a (necessarily unworthy) stranger who does not appear to take her good fortune in a sufficiently amazed and humble spirit, nor to realise how little she must know about his tastes, needs and habits.

When there is the additional complication of a country house thrown in, the situation fairly bristles with explosive material. Those who have been brought up among, say, Morris chintzes—or varnished Gothic oak—or the relics of any past or passing school of taste, cannot be expected to see these things with a dispassionate or judicial eye. They are hallowed by a thousand memories and associations. We may learn to condemn them elsewhere, but at home they seem fraught with an indefinable rightness and charm, and to be a part of the "character" of the place.

The new daughter-in-law sees them for the first time in the cold light of the present. For her they are not shrouded in hallowing antecedents. She is not unnaturally appalled at the prospect of living among them, and she has not the slightest intention of doing so. Even the fact that her husband walked his first tottering steps at the age of fourteen months, clutching hold of the Buhl cabinet in the drawing-room, does not reconcile her to this odious piece of furniture. She scraps the old order ruthlessly, banishing tenderly treasured "landmarks" to basements and bathrooms, and subjecting the swept and

garnished rooms to the most daring and (to us) jarring experiments. How can we help regarding her as a sacrilegious Vandal? What can she do but think of us as touchy Philistines?

Grandparents are certainly not what they were. I am just old enough (and only just) to remember seeing them "go out." I just caught sight of the disappearing tails of the last surviving of those silver-haired, pontifical grandparents, with the sunset in their eyes, and a blessing on the tip of each finger, who made one feel that it was a privilege and an achievement to be old, and not a disgrace. They are now quite extinct. In these days "Granny" is a forbidden word in most nurseries. Ingenious pet-names are devised by tactful parents to cloak the unfortunate fact, and children are trained to spare their grandparents' blushes by using them. The children of to-day will remember their grandparents (at least, the female ones) as supremely unwise, short-skirted, shingled gad-abouts, with three times the vitality, enterprise and gregariousness of their own quiet, domesticated mothers, and always busy urging these to spend more on their clothes and waste less of their youth in early bed and country holidays.

Aunts used to have a curious importance, which they appear now completely to have lost. The maiden-aunt was a traditional figure, a symbol of—something or other which has entirely disappeared. In the works of Mrs. Molesworth and other Victorian nursery classics there was always a graceful, beneficent figure called "Auntie," hover-

Relations

ing about the children's lives, and playing a really significant part in them. I believe that there exists to this very day an agency called "Universal Aunts," which undertakes to supply efficient women charged with human sympathy, who will (tactfully) fill any gap, rise to any emergency, discharge any function, however ticklish and responsible, from taking strange children to the dentist downward. . . . What *real* aunt of to-day would we entrust with a task as delicate as this? A frank answer to this question will give us each some inkling of the decline in aunts. We must face the fact that aunts (and uncles, too, for that matter) have lost all sense of duty. They do not even remember birthdays nowadays (unless they happen to live in India) let alone make wills. . . .

What of sons and daughters? They are too big a subject for such an article as this. I will only say this; that being a good mother of sons seems to me to be as easy as fishing with worms. A son presents no problems to a mother. Here is a wholly luxurious relationship, quite without jars or jolts, and yet infinitely passionate, tender, romantic and exciting.

Daughters, on the other hand, offer the possibility of a very sporting, touch-and-go relationship to their mothers. There are great risks of failure and catastrophe, there is a chance of brilliant success, made more rewarding by the fact that it is a success against some odds. What are the dangers? To begin with, mothers can't help expecting daughters to be rather like themselves, whereas in reality they are nearly always absolutely different. Nor can they help falling into the even greater snare of expecting the plot of their own life to be re-spun in their daughters'. It is difficult to realise how entirely irrelevant one's own experience is to nearly everyone else's life, but almost impossible to believe that it is perhaps particularly inapplicable to one's daughter's. Daughters are determined to have brand-new lives of their own.

Again, the relationship between mothers and daughters is one in which there is ample scope for friction over the detail of life—health, clothes, the way daughters hold themselves, their hair, and even the angle at which their new front teeth are coming in, and these tiny preliminary encounters are apt to queer the pitch for the big struggle when it comes, over a love affair or a career. A wide toleration and passivity over trifles is, I am sure, the only chance of preserving intact an influence which may be worth throwing into the balance later on, on an occasion that really counts. I am inclined to think that the sisterly mother who "feels the same age" as her daughter makes for a more irritating relationship than the frankly older one, who recognises the gulf of years and tastes, and flings her imagination consciously across it.

These observations may (with luck) be true to-day and yet utterly inapplicable to yesterday and to to-morrow. There are no doubt vogues and fashions in relationships. Their value fluctuates, ebbing and flowing like that of other commodities in the markets of the world.

To continue the commercial analogy, one may sum up the present position somewhat as follows: mothers booming, sons steady, fathers quiet, daughters appreciating rapidly, cousins neglected, aunts sagging, grandparents still slumping and bottom not yet reached. In-laws: this market continues to be a happy hunting-ground for the bears, but bargains may occasionally be picked up at knock-out prices.

Things You'll

Decorations by
Elizabeth Montgomery

1927

Oranges and Lemons
A Jelly You Can Make Yourself

MIX an eighth of a pint of freshly squeezed orange juice with the same amount of fresh lemon juice. Finely grate a very little outer rind of the orange and the lemon into a quarter of a pint of cold water. Put the water in a saucepan to warm with three ounces of white sugar OR (not AND) three ounces of honey and a quarter of an ounce of isinglass.

Pretty and Golden

As soon as the isinglass is quite dissolved remove from the fire and stir in the orange and lemon juice. Pour your mixture into an old breakfast cup or small mould previously rinsed in cold water. Whip the white and yolk of an egg first separately and then together to a stiff froth. Thoroughly stir this into your tepid jelly mixture before it has set. Leave the jelly to jell before turning it out to eat.

Baby's Present

With his cosy furry cape, a Christmas gift from Mrs. Tape, Baby's little shoulders drape. Right into the hood of fur, Baby goes without demur. I'll tie the soft white ribbon in, underneath his double chin.

If by any chance you meet Baby's pram along the street, your eyes will open very wide, for a white bunny lies inside! Kind Mrs. Tape to give him this. He shall reward her with a kiss!

Hickstone
Daphne's Game

PUT a stick to mark home with a ball near, then choose someone for He. One of the others throws the ball and the rest run and hide. Before chasing them He must fetch the ball and put it in home. Those hiding try to rush home without being seen. Everyone spied by He must stay in home and the others try to rescue them by running in without being seen. No touching is necessary, to be seen is to be caught.

Filling Stockings

Of course Daddy must hang up his stocking, but it's not so easy to fill Daddy's as Mummy's; for Daddy does not like so many things. Here are some suggestions: a little notebook and a pencil; something suitable (if he's a motorist a motorist's diary, a golfing diary if he's a golfer).

Then a pair of warm gloves, that's always right. And a pipe if he smokes one. (Of course the family's all got to join in!)

How about a padlock and a key if you live in the country and have outhouses? A sixpenny store has these. Certainly give him a good pencil; none of your very cheap ones for Daddy! If there is a rich aunt in the house longing to help I don't think Daddy would mind finding in his stocking, rolled up very tightly, a Christmas number of a picture paper. Socks? Yes. Toffee? Why not. He can give it to you if he likes! Oranges and crackers? Of course.

To Oblige a Fairy
On Christmas Eve

SUCH a funny thing happened to Mary Violet on Christmas Eve. She was asked to do a fairy a favour. *Imagine* the honour!

Mary Violet was just stumping up the snowy path to her house after posting some late Christmas cards for Mother, when a fairy came and sat on her shoulder.

"Oh, Mary Violet!" said she. "*The very person!* Will you oblige a fairy?"

Mary Violet was thrilling from tip to toe. A fairy at last! And she was eight; and knew it would be too late soon to catch the slightest glimpse of one.

"I have been *so* rushed with my Christmas shopping," went on the darling voice. "And I hear that Mother Goose is shutting her eiderdown shop in a quarter of an hour; and it is my last chance to slip along to buy the Fairy Princess Lightsome the scarlet silk eiderdown I promised her. But I am due at the Wood of the Singing Pines immediately. It belongs to us; and the Queen always sends one of us up there on Christmas Eve to bring her best Christmas wishes, and to sing them the latest carol. Then they sing one back; and whoever goes dances for them. Oh, I know what you're going to say. But I'll take you there, and fetch you back. And I shouldn't really be more than two jiffkins away at the shop. Meantime, you could just sing them a new carol."

The First Nowell

"What were you going to sing?" said Mary Violet nervously.

"*The First Nowell.* It's always new."

"Oh, I know that one!"

"How lovely! Come on, there's a darling, I see you smiling." And the fairy with a wave of her wand transported Mary Violet up to the wood above the hill. White snow was lying on the beautiful pine branches. The fairy set Mary Violet down, threw a high silver fence all round in a twinkling, gave her a breathless kiss, whispered, "Stay till I come again, sweetheart," and flew off.

Then Mary Violet opened her round rosy mouth and sang *The First Nowell.* The trees heard it in silent delight. Then they sang a wondrous carol in return, rustling and sighing happily.

Like To Know

By
Marjory Royce

Happy Dancing
Among the Pine Trunks

"NOW dance, darling," said the trees. "It is a treat for us," and Mary Violet, who was rather fat, at once began to do the Highland Schottische.

The trees then did a graceful dance of branches for her, waving them here and there.

"The fox will be coming in to-morrow, and he will teach you the foxtrot," said one of the trees presently.

"Oh, but I shall be at home for Christmas Day," cried Mary Violet, suddenly afraid.

"I don't suppose you will. That fairy is very charming; but she has no memory. And you can't get out till she comes back!"

"The robins will sing to you more sweetly than any choir," said another pine.

"Instead of pulling crackers you can crack some of Mr. Squirrel's nuts," said yet another. "Oh, you'll enjoy a Christmas Day in the woods!"

"But I shan't get any presents," said Mary Violet, sadly.

The Best Christmas Present

"We'll tell you lots of splendid wild stories. Stories are much the best presents," remarked a very tall old tree.

"And I shall have obliged a fairy," thought Mary Violet to herself. "That will be something."

But Mother's dear face and the face of Daddy, Brother Phil, Baby Jack, and Nanna would keep rising before her.

"But there will be no games in the evening," she said suddenly.

"Yes, the wind is coming to see us to-morrow night, and he and you can have hide and seek between us in the wood," cried the trees. "It will be glorious. The moonlight makes all our trunks bright for us on Christmas night."

"But I'd *rather*——" said Mary Violet. And then shut her lips tight, because she didn't want to be rude.

Just at that very second she saw the fairy flying back swiftly, against the delicate blue winter sky.

"I'll come another time if I may," cried Mary Violet to the trees.

A Jolly Game
Are You Ugly?

WRITE down lots of awkward questions adding the words, "Step forward if true." Read them out quickly one by one, not giving people time to think. This makes great fun as many step forward when they mean to stand still and *vice versa*.

The Way with Red Ribbon

Emily, who is a dull little podgeration of a stodge (do you understand me?), gives her presents round the Christmas breakfast table tied up anyhow in stupid old brown paper, with thin string in lots of knots. She never tiptoes down early to decorate the table.

But Jacqueline, another little girl I know, takes lots of pains and lays out a few pennies on various useful things. *She* has sheets of pink paper in which she wraps every present and a whole roll of holly-berry ribbon. Each gift is wrapped in pink and tied up smartly with ribbon, and she then ties on it one of those pleasant Christmassy labels you can buy everywhere with a picture on. Round the table Jacqueline is sure to put bits of mistletoe and tawny chrysanthemums (her gift to Mother).

A Christmas Play
The King's Wish

HERE are a few ideas for a tiny play to be acted by three weeny players. It is called *The King's Wish*, and the three people are:

King. He wears a crown which you can make out of cardboard and gold and silver paper, any old cloak, and he must have a little black beard. This you can mark on with boot blacking.

Fairy. Buy a roll of yellow crinkly paper. Just make a hole for the head and have a long bit front and back. A long thin strip will make a sash, of a different colour, if possible. She should carry a wand, with a gold paper star at one end.

King's Daughter can be dressed in pink crinkly paper or in her best party frock. She should wear a crown.

Enter Fairy to give the King a wish, King seated in big chair. Fairy offers a wish. King says, "I wish that everything may turn into gold." Fairy waves wand and says, "It is so."

There must be a little table beside the King on which are various objects. These the Fairy must cover with some little bits of golden crinkly paper she has ready. The Princess is sitting on the ground. Fairy, taking for granted the King means exactly what he says, turns her into gold too. (Covers her all over with a yard or two of yellow crinkly paper.)

The Princess cries out; King very miserable; Fairy has gone. And now you must make up a new wish and a happy end.

By Lady Violet Bonham Carter

The Voice of the Young Women

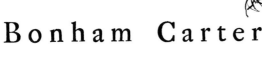

1928

WHAT will be the result of extending the franchise to the young woman of twenty-one and over? This is the question I have been asked to answer, and being neither a prophet, nor a crystal gazer, nor even a particularly young woman, I feel hard put to it to make a reply.

It would be easy to write an orthodox "feminist" article, enumerating the inequalities that still undoubtedly exist in the lot of men and women, and asserting confidently that all these will now be swept away and the balance between the sexes righted with one sharp jerk. And it is very likely that this will in fact happen incidentally, for whatever women themselves do, or do not do, the immediate result of adding some five and a quarter million of them to the register must be to mobilise the minds of the male politician not merely in the direction of their needs, but even of their most unreasonable desires.

By their mere passive existence women have now become a vast new electoral force to be reckoned with, and already every party is concentrating on the auction of "appeals" which must be made to them at the next general election. A vote to be caught is a vote to be catered for. An instinct of self-preservation alone will ensure that in the future the interests of women must bulk large in the programme of every party, for without their support no party could survive. But apart from the tremendous influence which their mere presence in the political field must exercise (if only as bait to the highest bidder) I will fairly confidently commit myself to one forecast, calculated to soothe and reassure the panic-stricken and soon-to-be-outvoted male, who feels the shades of the Matriarchy closing round him.

I think that we shall seldom if ever see a sex-alignment in politics. There are all kinds of men; there are if possible even more kinds of women. They will fall into their natural political categories and sockets, either as fiery progressives, or as stick-in-the-mud reactionaries, or as tepid mug-wumps, just as men do.

How will they use it—this tremendous access of political power to the tune of some five million votes? In view of the vital nature of this question, which opens up infinite vistas of achievement, we have specially asked this brilliant writer to handle it in an article which every woman, irrespective of her politics or her married or single state, will find of the most absorbing interest

Again, I feel confident that the majority of women will not use their new weapon solely for narrow or selfish purposes. There are no doubt certain vital questions which have quite unaccountably escaped men's notice in the past, and these will most certainly be raised and brought into prominence now. But I believe that equality and a sense of justice and fairplay should exorcise sex-consciousness in politics once and for all.

It is said that the newly enfranchised are always reactionary and that long spells of conservative government have usually followed any extension of voting powers. Will this apply again? I think it will depend on how long it is going to take women in the mass to

learn to think in terms of politics; to establish in their own minds the connection that exists between the things we read of in the newspapers and our own everyday experience. Once women have learnt this trick and have realised that the vote is an instrument which can be used to bring about direct and practical results in the sphere of their own daily lives, I think there is no fear (or hope, as some would put it) that they will prove a sluggish or reactionary force, a drag on the wheels of progress. In the discharge of their new duties once undertaken they will be meticulously conscientious. In the service of any creed they do embrace they will be almost fanatically sincere. They will cast on the whole, in my opinion, a very human vote. As politicians they are still realists who have not yet learnt to think in terms of *clichés* and slogans (though in time no doubt they must do so!) At present no axioms, theories, catchwords, or watchwords, will intervene with any effect between them and the things they feel need doing. The sense that they are betraying some time-honoured canon will have no terrors for them. They are not as yet either guided or perplexed by any conscious political philosophy.

I think the first thing to do in trying to imagine the psychology of the young woman voter of to-day is to try to forget our own past. We must realise that the political dramas in which we were cradled, the "old unhappy far-off things and battles long ago" in which we have grown up and won such spurs as we possess, to her mean less than nothing.

I remember very vividly my own disastrous *début* as a really young

Illustration by
Treyer Evans

1928

widow, who is supporting herself by her own efforts in the labour market.

The woman worker, whatever her age may be, will naturally be mainly concerned by problems affecting her industrial and economic status, and that of others; the demand for equal pay for equal work; the refusal by public bodies to employ married teachers, or, on grounds of sex alone, to promote female civil servants to certain high posts which it is well within their power to fill; the closing of hospitals to female medical students; the precarious frontier between protective and restrictive legislation — these will be a few of the battlegrounds on which she needs must take her stand. That a woman struggling to keep afloat by her own efforts in the choppy sea of the labour market, and making no demands on men for support or protection both needs and deserves weapons to fight with, will hardly be denied even by Lord Birkenhead.

But what about the "parasite," the domestic woman, so conveniently relegated by politicians to that cosy *oubliette,* "the home," there to discharge a variety of "sacred functions" (motherhood, wifehood, daughterhood, sisterhood) without "bothering her head" about politics? The changes that she can, and I think will, bring about are not so generally recognised. Politics affect the home as vitally and as intimately as the labour market and it is my belief that it is from the home rather than from *(continued overleaf)*

woman on a great Committee composed of distinguished veterans of my own sex. When the (to them still burning) question of the State Regulation of Vice was mentioned, I electrified everybody with horror by asking innocently, " But isn't *everybody* in favour of it?" Though born of a political stock and reared in a political household I had never heard the phrase, and never heard of the C.D. Acts. To me the State Regulation of Vice meant nothing more than the policeman having the right and duty to arrest a pickpocket. I think this revelation of my black, abysmal ignorance was almost more shocking to the Committee than my original heterodox opinion.

The struggles over Home Rule and the Parliament Act, the People's Budget, even the battle for the Suffrage itself, are probably just as hazy and remote to the present young voter as the C.D. Acts seemed to me fifteen

years ago. The young feel no gratitude for what has been won for them, nor any interest in how it was accomplished. The new voter will not cast more than a hurried and perfunctory glance at a suffragette's old wounds.

Let us then wipe out the past and try to see the present through the eyes of an "under thirty" unclouded by any memories, associations or traditions.

The age of thirty has been used as an arbitrary boundary line separating young women from old ones, but it is not to my mind the political Rubicon it is made out to be. There is no greater gulf fixed between the mental attitude of a 27- and a 32-year-old than between that of a 21- and a 26-year-old. The real cleavage, or so it seems to me, in interests, and perhaps in political outlook, exists between the young married woman whose stake is in domestic life and the independent spinster or

1928

FOR HOME USE

A book of reference on many
subjects relative to the table.
Published by the proprietors of
ANGOSTURA BITTERS

A Book on Christmas and Winter drinks

. . . and a wealth of other timely
information for the Host and
Hostess. The proprietors of
Angostura Bitters offer a 48-page
presentation book compiled to be
of real help in home entertaining.

In the first half of the book are hints
on, and detailed recipes for, beverages
of all kinds—including some good old
Egg Nogs and Winter Punches. From
page 24 onward is the Domestic Section
in which the way is shown to add a new
flavour to sweet and to meat dishes.
This section will surprise even those
who have known Angostura for years!

Plum Pudding

See page 35 of "The
Home Book" before
making your Christmas
Puddings and Mince-
meat. The addition
of "Angostura" will
greatly enhance the
flavour of both.

*Write to the London Address (beneath) for a
post-free copy of "The Home Book," and
see how useful it will be in your home.*

For over 100 years "Angostura" has
been, as your menfolk will tell you,
a participant in Hotel and Club
amenities. "The Home Book" deals
with masculine interests too, making
it worthy of a permanent place in the
Home, for general use.

Angostura Bitters

(Dr. J. G. B. Siegert & Sons) Ltd.

Sole Consignees for Great Britain and Ireland,
British Colonies and Dependencies: Henderson
& Co. (London) Ltd., Finsbury Court, E.C.2.
Solely manufactured by Angostura Bitters (Dr.
J. G. B. Siegert & Sons) Ltd., Port-of-Spain,
Trinidad, British West Indies.

(120)

the industrial centres of women's activity
that the most drastic and far-reaching
reforms will be inspired and carried
through.

There are certain issues on which even
the least politically-minded married
women cannot fail to have a point of
view. There are questions on which, even
though they may differ among themselves,
they must have a more intimate and
specialised fund of experience than any
man.

The service which women render to the
nation in the making of homes and the
bearing and rearing of children has never
received any economic or political recognition or reward. It asks for neither,
for it is a labour of love, but it should
surely carry with it, as all other work
does, certain rights. It is an amazing fact
that it is only within the last few years
that mothers have obtained equal rights
with fathers over their own children, and
equal rights with men in divorce legislation. It is only within the last year that
the public conscience has aroused the
Ministry of Health to the fact that nearly
four thousand mothers still die annually
in childbirth. Steps are at last being taken
to ensure that this, the greatest of all
"productive" occupations, the task of
creating life, should be made a less perilous
adventure and that those who engage in it
should be safeguarded and protected by
all the means that modern Science has at
her disposal. We should have been more
squeamish about an industrial hazard of
equal magnitude.

The question of whether or not birth
control information should be withheld at
Welfare Centres in receipt of a Government grant (a question which has so far
only been seriously considered by the
House of Lords) is one of such importance to women that it cannot much
longer be kept in abeyance. The whole
problem of birth control is an acutely
controversial one, in which religious sus-
ceptibilities, scientific differences and moral
scruples are all involved. But that information of so vital a character should be
at the disposal of those who can afford
to pay for it, and at the same time withheld from those who cannot, but who as a
rule need it infinitely more, is surely an
impossible state of things.

I believe that the women of the future
will refuse to create life blindly and without choice. Nor will they be accused of
making a sordid bargain if they demand
for their unborn children reasonable
chances of health and opportunity.

The question of housing may be attacked
by the woman voter with more energy
and resolution, possibly also with more
imagination and resource than has been
shown in dealing with it up to now. To
a woman a house is not merely, as it may
be to a man, a lodging, nor is it only

"a home," with all that that word im-
plies; it is her workshop as well, the place
in which she plies her trade, often with
most indifferent tools, carrying on single-
handed, day in day out, her fight for the
future, sometimes against odds she is
powerless to overcome.

Look at the aching, bent and twisted
figures of old women toiling between two
heavy buckets from the cottage to the
pump. Surely young women will insist
that before long no house in England shall
be without its tap of running water.

Look at the mother, often compelled
to use the same room as wash-house,
living-room and bedroom, trying to cook
meals for her family with pots and pans
precariously poised on the bars of an
ordinary house grate. Think for one
moment of the appalling degradation of
life implied in the word "overcrowding"
—the suffering, the immorality and the
disease which are its inevitable results.
To thousands of women these are not, as
they are to so many M.P.'s, mere rows of
"disquieting" figures, extracted by their
private secretaries from Blue Books. They
are tragic facts, intimately experienced, to
which they and those dearest to them are
being daily sacrificed. Their forbears
have endured these things with tragic
stoicism. The young women of to-day to
whom patience has never, thank Heaven,
been held up as a virtue, will, I hope, refuse to accept such conditions of life as
inevitable.

There are infinite opportunities for the
intervention of women in the regions of
public health, education, and penal reform.
It is impossible not to hope from their
hands the shaping of a gentler, more
sensitive and humane civilisation.

The real test which awaits the young
women electors to-day lies perhaps in the
international field, and by their ability to
recognise and to respond to that challenge
they will be judged. For the first time
since the Armistice the establishment of
peace on a world-wide basis seems within
range of practical achievement. The
Kellogg proposals herald the re-entry of
America into the international arena and
pledge her no longer to stand aside from
the great task which without her help
could never be more than half-accom-
plished. The barbarous futility of making
force the arbiter in any dispute, whether
between nations or classes, must be recognised by all women.

That they, the trustees of the life of
the future, should be prepared to accept
high explosives as a method of settling
disputes in preference to Justice and
Reason is unthinkable. I believe that they
will make it clear that no party which
does not rule out the brutal and archaic
convention of war, has a chance of their
support. If they do this, their page in
history will have been worth writing.

A Gift 12 Times Over

One of the most welcome Christmas presents that you
can possibly give is a year's subscription to GOOD
HOUSEKEEPING. Women friends abroad, in particular,
will appreciate this monthly link with the most brilliant
writers of fiction and articles, the most up-to-date
methods of equipping and running a home, and the
newest trend of women's thought and pursuits. Post
free 17/6 to any address in the United Kingdom or abroad

1928

Le parfum à la mode

THE choice of perfume can make or mar the toilette. From Paris—dictator of fashion in perfumes, as in gowns—comes Pavots d'Argent. Indefinable, yet alluring, its elusive fragrance gives a note of subtle distinction.

Perfume (Half Size) 5/6
And in Lalique Bottles . 10/6 & 21/-
Sachet 1/3
Soap (per box of 3 tablets) . . 7/6
Face Powder 3/6
Lipstick 1/-
Compact Face Powder . . 1/6 & 3/-
Talcum Powder . . . 2/6 & 2/9
Presentation Caskets . . 10/6, etc.
Creams, Bath Salts, etc.

Pavots d'Argent
(SILVER POPPIES)

P.10

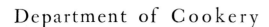
Department of Cookery

*GOOD
HOUSEKEEPING
INSTITUTE*

49 *Wellington Street, Strand, W.C.2*

Conducted
by D. D.
Cottington Taylor

*Certificate Household and Social Science,
King's College for Women, London.
First Class Diplomas in Cookery, High
Class Cookery, Laundrywork, House-
wifery. A.R.S.I.*

1929

MENU I

Chestnut Soup

Poached Plaice

Roast Turkey with Stuffing   Boiled Ham

Bread Sauce

Brussels Sprouts   Roast Potatoes

Christmas Pudding   Foamy Brandy Sauce

Mince Pies   Peter Pan Christmas Pudding

MENU II

Roast Turkey with Stuffing

Bread Sauce

Christmas Pudding   Mince Pies

Foamy Brandy Sauce

*A 7 lb. corner of ham, and
15 lb. turkey, with appropriate stuffing, are suitable
for a family of eight
people*

*Below are the ingredients
needed for the making of
Chestnut soup, an excel-
lent addition to the Christmas menu*

THE lighter side of Christmas catering is suggested by the story of some children who decided that they would be sparse in their diet during the weeks previous to Christmas Day, hoping that Spartan semi-starvation would enable them to enjoy to the full the generous Christmas provender. Anyone who has a little dietetic knowledge will be able to anticipate the sad end to this experiment. The children found that the capacity of their digestive organs, which are controlled greatly by habit, was reduced and the reverse of their expectations was realised. But most people, however, are able to consume, more or less with impunity, a larger quantity of food at Christmas than at ordinary times. This may or may not involve strain on the consumer, but it is very hard on the caterer. The increased quantity of food that will be needed, the probable extra number of persons to be catered for, and the closing of provision shops for two or three days'

holiday, all add to her difficulties, involving financial, nervous and mental strain.

In order that this strain may be minimised, the approximate cost of the simple and more elaborate menu at the top of this page; the quantity of food required for these menus for a family of eight (given under the shopkeepers from whom they can be obtained); suggestions for other Christmas fare; recipes for, and method of cooking the various dishes; and a suggestion for a rechauffé turkey dish for Boxing Day, are all given below.

Although great care has been taken to give the cost of each ingredient as accurately as possible, prices vary so much in different localities that readers will find that a certain amount of adjustment is needed. This is particularly the case with regard to the prices of fresh foods, which are subject to great fluctuation, depending upon climatic and other conditions.

Catering for Christmas

By

G. H. Donald, B.Sc.

King's College for Women, Household and Social Science Department

1929

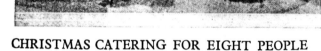

CHRISTMAS CATERING FOR EIGHT PEOPLE

Complete Shopping List for Menu 2

	£	s.	d.
Poulterer and Fishmonger			
14-15 lb. turkey .	1	10	0
Butcher			
2 lb. sausages .		3	0
3 oz. suet . .			2
Grocer			
¼ lb. back rashers bacon . .			6
½ bottle of brandy		6	6
3-4 lb. Christmas pudding . .		8	6
1 lb. mincemeat .		1	0

Additional List to convert Menu 2 into Menu 1

	£	s.	d.
Poulterer and Fishmonger			
2 lb. plaice . .		2	4
Butcher . .			
Grocer			
7 lb. ham (corner of gammon) .		14	0
1 lb. strawberry jam . . .			10
2 oz. glacé cherries			3½
1 piece of angelica			1
4 oz. lard . .			3

When the mistress of the household is solely responsible for cooking the Christmas dinner, it is best to dish up everything together, and keep the food hot in the oven till required

	£	s.	d.
Greengrocer			
1 lemon . .			1
Parsley . .			1
2½ lb. Brussels sprouts . .			7½
2½ lb. potatoes .			2½
Milkman			
4 eggs . .			10
½ pint milk . .			1¾
4 oz. butter. .			6
Baker			
1 small stale loaf			3
In stock			
1 lb. flour . .			2¼
Cloves, peppercorns, herbs .			1
½ lb. margarine .			5
8 oz. icing sugar .			3
1 onion . .			¼
Total cost of Menu 2	£2	13	4¼

	£	s.	d.
Greengrocer			
1 lemon . .			1
2 lb. chestnuts .		1	0
½ lb. mushrooms .		1	6
Milkman			
4 eggs .			10
4 pints milk .		1	2
Baker			
½ doz. sponge cakes			6
1 small stale loaf			3
In stock			
Brown breadcrumbs . .			¼
1 oz. dripping .			½
¾ oz. gelatine .			3
4 oz. spaghetti .			1
2 pints stock .			3
	£1	3	9¼
	2	13	4¼
Total cost of Menu 1	£3	17	1½

(continued overleaf)

A Third Hint on . . . . .

1929

. . . Buying A Wringer

WET floors are a source of annoyance on wash-days, and add considerably to the work involved by washing at home. When buying a wringer therefore, look at the water-board; see that it is wide and deep enough to take the surplus water wrung from the clothes. TAYWIL Mangles have a specially designed, large water-board which prevents the water from running over on to the floors. All real labour-saving devices will be found on TAYWIL Mangles, and each machine carries the makers' printed Guarantee—ask your dealer about them.

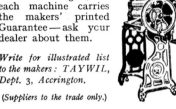

Write for illustrated list to the makers: TAYWIL, Dept. 3, Accrington.

(Suppliers to the trade only.)

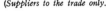

Catering for Christmas

Suggestions for Special Christmas Fare with approximate prices for eight people

		s.	d
1 lb. muscatels		1	6
½ lb. almonds (Valencia) . .		1	3
1 box dates			8
1 lb. box mixed crystallised fruits		4	3
1 drum figs		1	0
1 jar ginger in syrup . .		3	4
1 jar kumquats in syrup . .		4	9
1 lb. mixed chocolates and sweets .		3	0
1 doz. tangerines . . .		1	0
1 doz. oranges . . .		1	6
1 doz. bananas . . .		1	6
1 lb. Brazil nuts . . .			9
2 lb. walnuts		3	0
1 lb. Barcelona nuts . .			9
1 lb. grapes		3	0
1 lb. French plums . . .		1	4
2 lb. apples		1	4
		£1 13	11

Chestnut Soup

2 pints stock	1½ pints chestnuts
1 pint milk	1 oz. fat
Seasoning	1 oz. flour

Cut a slice from the top of each of the chestnuts, and roast them in a moderate oven for about 20 minutes. Remove their outer and inner skins, and cook in well-seasoned stock until tender (about 45 minutes). Rub through a sieve, and return to the saucepan with the stock and the flour which has been blended with the milk and fat. Boil for 5 minutes, stirring all the time.

Poached Plaice

2 lb. plaice	1 tablespoonful parsley
1 pint of milk	
1 lemon	1 oz. flour

Cover plaice with milk in a frying-pan. Bring it to the boil and continue simmering over a gentle heat for 20 to 30 minutes or until cooked. Add milk to flour which has been blended with a tablespoonful of water. Boil for 5 minutes, add chopped parsley, and pour over the fish. Garnish with slices of lemon, and a little parsley.

Roast Turkey

14 to 15 lb. turkey	Chopped parsley
¼ lb. back rashers bacon	1 teaspoonful herbs
2 lb. sausages	3 oz. suet
	½ lb. breadcrumbs
	2 eggs

Prepare the turkey, remove the skins from the sausages, and fill the crop with the sausage meat. Bind the parsley, herbs, suet and breadcrumbs with the slightly beaten eggs, and stuff the resulting mixture into the body of the turkey. Truss the turkey, skewer bacon over the breast, and place in a hot oven at 500° F., lowering the temperature after the first ¼ hour to 350° F. Remove bacon after about 1 hour, and continue cooking for 1¾ to 2¼ hours, basting at intervals. Remove trussing and string.

Bread Sauce

1 gill crumbs	Salt
½ pint milk	4 cloves
1 small onion	4 peppercorns
	½ oz. margarine

Boil the milk with peppercorns and onion in which the cloves have been stuck. Cover and allow to stand for 15 minutes. Strain and add crumbs. Stir in the butter and seasoning. Reheat and serve.

Boiled Ham (7 lb. corner)

Soak for 12 hours, wipe with a clean cloth, and put in sufficient cold water to cover. Bring gradually to the boil, and allow to simmer for 3 hours, removing the scum from time to time. When cooked remove from the water, strip off the skin, and sprinkle with brown breadcrumbs.

Foamy Brandy Sauce

4 oz. butter	8 oz. icing sugar
3 tablespoonfuls of brandy	1 white of egg

Cream butter, add sugar slowly, whipping continually. Add stiffly whisked whites of eggs and brandy. Before serving heat over boiling water for a few minutes, stirring constantly.

Mince Pies

2 teaspoonfuls lemon juice	Mincemeat
8 oz. flour	1 gill iced water
3 oz. margarine	3 oz. lard
	½ teaspoonful salt
White of egg	

Divide the fat into four, rub a quarter of it into the flour and make it into a paste with water and lemon juice. Roll the dough out into an oblong, the length being twice the width. Dot another quarter of the fat over the pastry, fold into three, turn, press the open edges together, and roll out as before. Repeat this until all the fat is incorporated, and then roll out to about ⅛ in. thick.

Cut into rounds with a fluted cutter (a size larger than the patty tin to be used). Put rounds in patty tins, place a little mincemeat in each, wet the edges of the pastry, and cover with a pastry top. Brush with whites of egg, cut a slit in centre and bake in a hot oven at 450° F. for 20 to 30 minutes.

Peter Pan Christmas Pudding

6 sponge cakes	1 pint milk
4 eggs	4 tablespoonfuls of strawberry jam
2 oz. cherries	
1 piece of angelica	¾ oz. gelatine

Scald milk, pour on to beaten yolks of eggs and gelatine, return to saucepan, and heat gently for a few minutes to thicken the custard. Arrange some cherries in the bottom of the mould, cover with a little custard and put in a cold place. Mix broken pieces of sponge cake, cherries, jam, chopped angelica with remaining custard and fold in whipped whites of egg. Pour into the mould to set. Turn out and garnish with a few spikes of angelica.

Turkey Réchauffé

1 oz. margarine	½ lb. chopped mushrooms
1 oz. flour	
1 pint milk	3 oz. breadcrumbs
4 oz. cooked spaghetti	½ lb. cold turkey
	Salt
	Pepper

Cut mushrooms in small pieces, and cook in milk until tender. Melt the margarine, add the flour, and stir in the milk. Add spaghetti, chopped and cooked mushrooms, breadcrumbs and turkey. Place in a baking dish, and bake in hot oven at 450° F. for 20 minutes or until the top is browned. Any bread sauce or stuffing left over could be used up in this dish.

DICKENS
SERIES

1929

FOX'S GLACIER MINTS REG?

for a digestive Xmas

The ideal gift for the Kiddies' Parties.

Obtainable everywhere in 6d., 1/-, and 2/- packages with Christmas Label. Also loose.

The Christmas Party at Dingley Dell.

"WE are all ready, I believe," said Mr. Pickwick, who was stationed with the old lady at the top of the dance, and had already made four false starts in his excessive anxiety to commence.

"Then begin at once," said Wardle. "Now."

Up struck the two fiddles and the harp, and off went Mr. Pickwick in the hands across, when there was a general clapping of hands, and a cry of "Stop, stop!"

"Where's Arabella Allen and Winkle?" cried a dozen voices.

"And where are the Fox's Glacier Mints?" added Mr. Tupman.

"Here we are," exclaimed Winkle, emerging with his pretty companion from the corner, "and here are the Glacier Mints. We did not mean to steal them really, but they're so seductive, so refreshing, so delicious, so cooling; they are a great temptation."

"Well," said Mr. Pickwick, with a very expressive smile, "I think perhaps I should have found them a very great temptation too."

FOX'S GLACIER MINTS, LTD., OXFORD STREET, LEICESTER.

How a Christmas Tree tapping on the
turned a Boarding Establishment
into

A Christmas House

A Story for Children

1929

FROM the outside Miss Ditchling's Boarding Establishment looked very much like all the other houses in the road; each one was neat and quiet-looking, with high windows and a plane tree growing in the front garden. The only difference about Miss Ditchling's house was that the tree in the garden was not a plane at all. It was a large Christmas tree.

Whether this difference had anything to do with what happened inside the house on Christmas Eve it is difficult to know. But the Christmas tree certainly stood close enough to the parlour window to be able to tap with one of its branches on the pane.

On the day this story begins then it was six o'clock on Christmas Eve, and it was snowing. The Christmas tree stood, all its branches white with snow except one; the branch that tapped against the window when the wind blew was dark, for the snow was shaken from it when it tapped. Like a dark finger it looked, pointing at the house.

Inside the house, in the parlour, a small boy crouched over a dull fire, turning the pages of a book. Every now and again he gave a deep sigh.

This was a very different Christmas from the one he had spent with his Mother and Father last year. Then it had been a real Christmas, but this year it didn't seem like Christmas at all. His Mother and Father were away in India and he was staying with his Aunt Matilda (otherwise Miss Ditchling) in her dreary boarding house, where every

penny she spent was grudgingly spent, and the fires were kept low, and the butter scraped on the bread.

That there was a fire in the parlour instead of in the basement breakfast room was due to the fact that Miss Ditchling herself had got a very bad attack of neuralgia and the parlour was less draughty than the breakfast room. Miss Ditchling's neuralgia was very bad all day and got steadily worse and worse until at length she had been obliged to go to bed about four o'clock in the afternoon of Christmas Eve, leaving her little maid-of-all-work, Rosabel, to look after the teas and suppers of the four lodgers in the up-stairs rooms.

Rosabel carried up the four teas on four separate trays and left them in the four different rooms. Then, on her way downstairs, she put her head round the parlour door.

"Master Dick!" she said, a smile on her bright eager little face, and her absurd scrap of a servant's cap on the

window

by

Marion St. John Webb

Illustrations

b y

F r a n k

R o g e r s

The parlour door swung open and Miss Ditchling stood there, a startling figure in her purple dressing gown. Rosabel felt her knees trembling and Dick turned pale

1929

side of her head as usual. "Master Dick! Where are you going to hang up your stocking to-night?"

Dick turned and looked at her gravely. "I'm not going to hang it up at all, Rosabel," he said. "Aunt Matilda said Father Christmas can't afford to come to this house."

"Can't *afford*?" said Rosabel, opening the door wider and edging inside. She stared at Dick for a few moments.

"Anyway, it doesn't matter. It doesn't seem like Christmas," said Dick.

On the window-pane there came a *tap, tap, tap*!

"Only the Christmas tree tapping on the window——" began Rosabel, then she stopped as an idea came to her, and her eyes grew big and her mouth opened in the shape of a small O. All at once she put her hands on the red-plush cloth and leant across the table. "Master Dick, I've thought of something!" she said in an excited whisper. "We'll *make* it like Christmas!"

"How?" asked Dick.

"We'll give a Christmas party!"

"Who?"

"You and me."

"Where?"

"Here."

"When?"

"Now."

Dick looked at Rosabel in puzzled surprise.

"Listen," went on Rosabel quickly. "I've just taken up the tea trays to those four lonely people upstairs—each one shut up alone with a little bit of fire in the grate. Why not make one big fire in this grate and all have supper in the parlour together? It's Christmas Eve!"

"Oo-oo!" gasped Dick. "But what will Aunt Matilda say?"

"She won't know," said Rosabel. "She's fast asleep in bed at the top of the house with a shawl pinned round her head! . . . Now, come on, Master Dick, you and me are going to give this party, so you must lend a hand. You write out the invitations and go and push them under the lodgers' doors upstairs, while I go and see about the supper."

Rosabel's enthusiasm was catching. The next minute Dick found himself with paper and pencil eagerly printing out the invitations. And half-an-hour later Miss Ditchling's four lodgers were

"Bless my heart, shipmate," cried Captain Duff, when Dick gave him the paper-chains, "Of course I'll hang them," and he looped them over the gas bracket while Rosabel made the toast.

astonished to find the following invitation pushed underneath the doors of their rooms:

> PLEASE WILL YOU COME AND HAVE CHRISTMAS EVE SUPPER PARTY PLEASE DOWN IN THE PARLOUR AT 8

Miss Pearce, the thin, fidgety little woman in the second-floor-back room, was thrown into a fluster by her invitation.

"How very nice of Miss Ditchling," she said to herself. "And she's got her little nephew to write out the invitation. How very sweet! Now what shall I wear?" And she turned over her shabby dresses hurriedly, and got out a needle and cotton.

The other lodgers were equally surprised and more or less pleased by the invitation. The old sailorman, Captain Duff, gave a chuckle and filled up his pipe. "What's come over the old girl!" he said to himself, thinking Miss Ditchling had sent the invitation.

The lodger on the first floor, old Mrs. Flouncing, folded up her crocheting, patted her white hair, and pinned on another brooch; she already wore three. Half-a-dozen times she read the invitation to see if there was anything offensive in it. Mrs. Flouncing took offence very quickly. But try as she would she couldn't find anything in the invitation at which to take offence.

The fourth lodger was Mr. Robert, a fair-haired young man with glasses, who worked in a boot stores. He was quite a nice young man, but he never knew what to talk about when he met people. This made him rather nervous in company, and after receiving the invitation he changed his tie five times before he went downstairs to the parlour promptly at eight o'clock.

Meanwhile, Rosabel and Dick had been working *(continued overleaf)*

A Christmas House

hard, and when the four guests arrived a cheerful fire was blazing in the grate and the supper table was spread. Of course, it would have been only the ordinary supper that the lodgers would have had up in their rooms (except that the cheese was in one large piece instead of four small pieces) had not Rosabel been round to Mrs. Tinny's shop and bought a currant cake and some biscuits and oranges and a box of crackers out of her last week's wages. She had also done a daring thing—instead of the usual one cup of tea which Miss Ditchling allowed her lodgers for supper Rosabel had put the teapot on the table and a huge jug of hot water as well; so that there would be two, and perhaps even three cups of tea for each person. If you had ever lodged at Miss Ditchling's you would know what a tremendous thing this was for Rosabel to have done.

Dick and Rosabel had decided exactly what to do when the guests arrived and looked round expectantly for Miss Ditchling. Rosabel said at once, "Oh, please ma'am, and please sir, Miss Ditchling is very sorry but her neuralgia is so bad she has had to go to bed, please. So will you please have supper here just the same, and Master Dick and me'll look after you?"

"To be sure we will," cried Captain Duff heartily, and spread his hands out towards the welcome fire. "This is much more cheery on a Christmas Eve than having supper alone. Eh, ma'am?" He turned to Mrs. Flouncing.

The old lady glanced round suspiciously. "I agree with you, Captain Duff, up to a point," she said. "But I should like to know why Miss Ditchling invited us down here and then went straight to bed, Captain Duff! I should like to know that."

Miss Pearce, all in a flurry, took a seat by the fire, and nervous Mr. Robert stood behind her awkwardly rubbing his hands together and wondering what remark to make to the company in general. Before he could think of anything Rosabel put a plate of sliced bread on the hearthrug, and kneeling down began to make toast before the fire.

Everyone began to thaw under the influence of the cosy fire and the smell of the toast, and soon there was much chattering and laughter around the hearth.

Presently Dick edged up to Captain Duff and whispered to him.

"Why, bless my heart, shipmate, of course I will!" said the Captain, and taking the paper bag that Dick offered he unrolled from it two long paper chains. "Rosabel got 'em round at Mrs. Tinny's shop, did she? They'll look spanking! Soon make the place a bit Christmassy."

Clambering on to a chair he hung the paper chains across the room, looping them over the gas-brackets with the help of Mr. Robert.

Then they all gathered round the table and sat down, except Rosabel who piled the toast on a plate and poured out the tea, and then moved away towards the door.

The Captain saw her. "Hi!" he called. "Sit down, lass, and join us. It's Christmas Eve, and when there's a Christmas party no one must be left out of it."

Mrs. Flouncing half rose, as if offended.

There came a *tap, tap, tap,* on the window-pane.

"Oh, what's that?" exclaimed Miss Pearce in a startled voice.

Mrs. Flouncing sat down again.

"Only the Christmas tree tapping on the window, ma'am," said Rosabel, as she took her seat at the table. Her eyes shone with excitement.

Surely tea and toast and cheese had never tasted so good before! And as for the currant cake—Mrs. Tinny had surpassed herself in making it! It was a wonderful currant cake. At least so thought the six people gathered round Miss Ditchling's supper table that night. Everyone, even shy Mr. Robert, got more and more talkative as the minutes passed, and by the time it came to pulling the crackers and putting on the paper hats everyone was laughing and it was the jolliest Christmas party imaginable.

Then Captain Duff set eyes on the piano. "I shall sing you a song," he said, and he rose and pulled his chair round towards it.

"Oh, Captain Duff, mightn't it waken Miss Ditchling?" cried Miss Pearce, flushed with excitement, her paper jockey-cap set rakishly on the back of her head.

Rosabel looked up with anxious eyes.

"Not it!" said Captain Duff stoutly. "She'll never hear up all them stairs!" And he started to play loudly, and after a while he began to sing:

"*Oh, let us be merry and sing, if you please,
Of Christmas and currant cake, crackers and cheese,
A fire for our feet so our toes cannot freeze,
And toast that is toasted and eaten at ease.
There's tea in the teapot for so many teas—
Well, thanks to Miss Ditchling for giving us these,
But best thing of all, so it seems to my mind,
Is the kindness of heart and of thought that's behind. . . .*"

The parlour door swung open—and Miss Ditchling stood there.

She glared around the room.

A dead silence fell on the Christmas Party. Miss Ditchling looked a startling figure in her purple dressing-gown, with a faded pink shawl wrapped round her head.

An uneasy feeling crept over Miss Ditchling's four lodgers. Was it possible Miss Ditchling didn't know about the party?

Rosabel felt her knees trembling. She turned very pale, and so did Dick.

As for Miss Ditchling—she stood spellbound. The cheerful fire burning away in the grate, supper laid out on her best parlour table, the paper-chains across the room, the crackers, the currant cake, the paper hats, the teapot. . . . She was astounded! The impudence! The barefaced impudence! The waste of coal! And everybody looking jolly and laughing too! Who had done it? Who was responsible? Her eyes flashed round the room and fixed on Rosabel's scared face!

Ah! So that was it, was it? Disgraceful! The girl should be sacked at once. . . .

Miss Ditchling opened her mouth to speak—when there came three distinct taps on the window. *Tap, tap, tap!*

Captain Duff jumped to his feet and seizing his cup held it up on high.

"Here's a toast to Miss Ditchling, and thanks to her for inviting us to Christmas supper!" he cried. "Your very good health, ma'm!" And everybody picked

A Christmas House

up a cup and drank Miss Ditchling's health.
" Very nice of you to come down to see us with your dreadful neuralgia and all. I hope you're feeling better, dear Miss Ditchling?" fussed Miss Pearce.

" Most kind of you, Miss Ditchling," said Mr. Robert, rubbing his hands together nervously.

" I was afraid our hostess was not coming down to see us at all," said Mrs. Flouncing in a slightly reproachful but dignified voice. " I am glad you've come."

" Hip, hip, hooray!" shouted Captain Duff. " Now then, all together!"

And all together they gave a cheer. Then, before Miss Ditchling could get in a word, they had drawn her into the room and were all around her singing, " For she's a jolly good fellow . . ."

Bewildered, Miss Ditchling sank down into a chair and covered her face with her hands. All her indignation and anger had gone, and she was ashamed, bitterly ashamed of herself.

Of course it was all a mistake. She knew she had given these people nothing to earn their gratitude, nothing at all. The mean fires, the mean food—and she had plenty of money in the bank, saving, saving— To-night they had so little, and yet they were thanking her—they thought she had given it and all the time it was Rosabel.

Miss Ditchling looked up, then reached out a hand and laid it on Rosabel's shoulder. Amazed, Rosabel saw Miss Ditchling smiling kindly up at her.

" Thank you, Rosabel," said Miss Ditchling, gently, " for looking after my guests. Thank you—my dear."

" Let's have another song, shipmates!" cried Captain Duff, sitting down at the piano again.

Outside the house the snow-covered Christmas tree stood with one dark branch, like a finger, pointing at the parlour window.

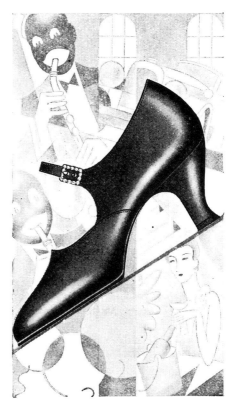

1929

Dog Sense

"as a town dog I need different food"

Speaking as dog to master, I'm all in favour of a comfy' town life, but unless I get my proper Melox, I simply *can't* keep fit. Melox, you see, is specially made for dogs that live my kind of life

There's Melox Concentrated Meal (the all-round diet) and Melox Marvels (the little health biscuits). And, for a change of diet there is nothing to equal Buffalo Bars

There are also bad imitations of Melox and Melox Marvels—be careful to avoid them

Melox and Melox Marvels are on sale everywhere—write to us if you have any difficulty, and we will send you the name and address of your nearest supplier, W. G. Clarke & Sons (1929) Ltd.

MELOX
AND MELOX MARVELS

Give Melox Meal in the morning   and Melox Marvels at night

Stuarts

Every Christmas Hamper

Cheddar or Cheshire, 6, 8, or 12 portions 1/4½

should be completed with a box of 'Diploma'—good English Cheddar and Cheshire worthy companion of the finest Yule-tide fare.

DIPLOMA
The ENGLISH CRUSTLESS CHEESE

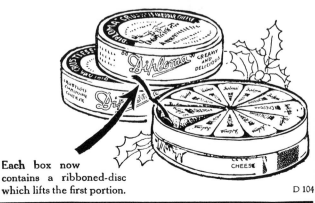

Each box now contains a ribboned-disc which lifts the first portion.

D 104

1929

The new "Ranelagh 20" Limousine is the last word in luxury and convenience. As you glide smoothly through the streets in warmth and comfort with plenty of room for four or five persons and all your parcels, you will realise that had you spent even twice the money, you could have obtained nothing more completely desirable.

AUSTIN

Showrooms:
479-483, Oxford Street, W.1

Service Station and Showrooms:
Holland Park Hall, W.11

A. J. W.

1930

The Moyen Age Lady

This lady of the Moyen Age, who spent her time making tapestry and waiting for her lord to return from the wars, wears a charming costume which can easily be copied to-day. Both the over- and under-dress may be made of sateen. The border may be of a light-weight upholstery fabric in a brocaded design. Her headdress is made of fabric-covered cardboard with a long floating veil of filmy chiffon

LET FANCY DRESS RELEASE YOUR DREAM

HAVEN'T you often longed for an original idea for a fancy dress costume? You're tired of seeing Pierrot and Pierrette dancing with Columbine and Harlequin; pirates and cowboys, Colonial damsels and milkmaids have lost their charm—what you want is a costume which will be sure to have no duplicate.

Perhaps you have always longed to be a grand lady of the Moyen Age, complete with trailing, voluminous gown and floating veil. Or perhaps the license accorded a

The Russians

A suit of cotton gabardine, decorated riding boots, and a plush or fur hat compose the Cossack's costume. The Russian maid wears a headdress of painted cardboard, a blouse of cheese-cloth, and a bodice and skirt of sateen. Designs may be stencilled on these in coloured paints, or floral designs in crêpe paper may be sewed or pasted on

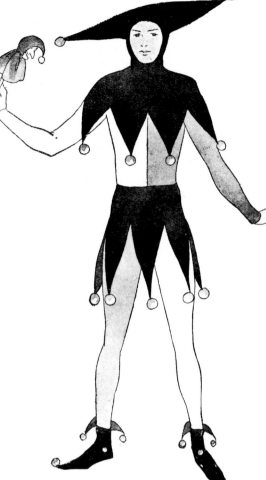

1930

AND BE JUST WHAT YOU'D LIKE TO SEEM

Court Jester will give you an opportunity to tease your friends with impunity. If your taste is more exotic, maybe a dashing Cossack or a colourful Russian girl will appeal to you; while a demure Bretonne, in her spotless coif and sabots, and her sober escort in his remarkable collar have a charm of their own. Both of them wear black.

Whatever costume you choose should suit your type so that you will feel at home in your character.

All the ones shown are authentic in detail and not too difficult to make.

HOW TO ORDER

Patterns for these designs cost 3s. 6d. each post free and can be obtained from Good Housekeeping Pattern Service, 153 Queen Victoria St., E.C.4. Those for the women are in sizes 34, 36 and 38 and for men in sizes to fit small, medium and large figures

The Jester

His vari-coloured costume is founded on a pair of long cotton tights and long-sleeved skirt. The colours are red and yellow, arranged so that the left leg and right arm match and vice versa. The cap, stiffened with buckram or cardboard, like the collar, girdle and shoes, is of red sateen, trimmed with brass bells. The shoes are worn over socks or soft slippers

The Bretons

Loose trousers and a short coat of cotton gabardine trimmed with brass buttons are worn by the Breton. His collar may be made of cardboard. An old hat with a new cardboard brim and a wide, soft girdle complete his costume. A white organdie coif, tied demurely under her chin, and a wide collar to match adorn the Bretonne. Her dress is of sateen and her apron of any figured material. Don't forget the finishing touch of her umbrella

Libelling our GRANDPARENTS

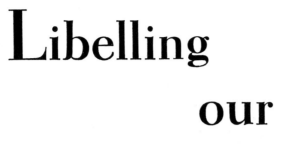

1930

I AM moved to speak up for our grandparents. It is time—more than time—that someone did. Why should these ladies and gentlemen, no worse and no better and no other than ourselves, be perpetually sneered at and maligned in the public press; perpetually have odious characters fastened on to them which, I am sure, they did little to deserve? It is getting beyond a joke, and my sense of granddaughterly fairness revolts.

Every generation, no doubt, has felt impelled by its superiority-complex to invent some mythical character for its forebears, those intriguing beings of whom we know so little, and from whom we have inherited that important quality, our existence. Always ancestors have been fabled, romanticised, mythologised, accused of grotesque qualities, grotesque differences from their posterity. But it seems to me that the twentieth-century posterity goes further in this ancestor-scorn than any posterity before it.

Since a long time now, for instance, we have erected mythical Victorian grandmothers, of contemptible mien, mentality and habits. And just lately these ladies have been referred to more than ever, owing, apparently, to the longer fashion in female skirt-lengths. I do not know why we should mention our grandmothers in this connection, considering that skirts were on the ground as late as 1914, and down to the ankles as late as 1924. (Let anyone who doubts this look up some old photographic groups of six years ago.) Still, we ignore this, and refer back to those unfortunate grandmothers of ours. Well, undoubtedly our grandmothers did wear long skirts; so did our mothers, and so did all of us except the now very young. But we go on from this arbitrary chance whim of fashion, which has no psychological implications whatever, and with which we are now threatened again, to associate with it an array of qualities and a type of female which we have created, I believe, merely to gratify our own sense of superiority. Only the other day I read, in an article by a writer whose comments in general I esteem, something about "our grandmothers, all lavender and prudery." (Shades of George Eliot, Jane Carlyle, and Ellen Terry!) And, during the flight of Miss Johnson to Australia, someone wrote, "What would our grandmothers have said of this girl? They would have swooned six times, and when they were recovered, would exclaim 'How indelicate!'"

Now all this is, as we really know quite well, pure piffle.

Our grandmothers may have used lavender sachets to lay by their clothes in; so, for that matter, do many of us in these days; the use of this scent has no spiritual implications, any more than camphor or verbena have. But as to prudery, and as to swooning, and as to being shocked at a young woman's courageous feat, these accusations are sheer inventions. Swooning is a purely physical weakness, to which some men and women are liable more frequently than others; plenty of people faint to-day, not only from physical causes, but if they see a horrible sight or suffer a bad shock. It depends, one is told, on the strength of the circulation. I see no evidence that our grandmothers fainted more easily than we do. Mine, anyhow, did not. And as to being shocked at

Illustrations by Arthur Watts

By Rose MACAULAY

1930

the daring adventures of young women— well, after all, Victorian young females risked t h e i r necks riding to hounds, dashed about the country on horseback, and later on bicycles, tramped and climbed mountains, rowed, swam, played hockey and tennis, and explored the wilder regions of the globe. The only reason that they did not fly was that no one flew. Mr. R. D. Blumenfeld, arriving from America to Britain in the year 1887 (the very zenith of the Victorian reign), commented on " the athleticism of English young women," on the river

Miss Macaulay, modern of moderns, protests against the attitude of scornful superiority which many people adopt towards their Victorian forebears, and claims that they were much like ourselves

and elsewhere. These young women were, perhaps, not our grandmothers (that is to say, they were certainly not my grandmothers, though they might very easily be the grandmothers of many people now adult). But, whether our grandmothers, our great-grandmothers, our mothers, our aunts, our great-aunts, or ourselves, there they (apparently) were, as active, adventurous, and hoydenish as their descendants of to-day, and active against the heavier odds of long and hampering skirts, even of bustles, so that their actual ability and determination in locomotion must have been immensely greater than ours. An admirable set of Amazons, Atalantas, and Dianas! And, looking back at that lively spectacle, we talk of these dashing young women as if they had been prudes and muffs, who knew not how to use their legs.

And then we go on to say worse than this of them. We call them " leg-conscious." This is the cruellest libel of all. For I am sure that " leg-consciousness" (if we must use this so peculiar expression) only began when skirts went up and the leg became thereby important, a member to be cherished, admired, and elegantly garbed. We are leg-conscious to-day (except at afternoon and evening parties), but we were not so until about five years since, and I imagine

(continued overleaf)

1930

A Xmas Box for Everybody

LADIES'
Initialled Linen Handkerchiefs, No. B60 (illustrated here). Fine quality, size 11". 6 in a box, 3/9. See Catalogue for other designs and prices.

Initialled Linen Handkerchiefs, No. B70 (as illustrated). Size 14". Per doz., 8/-. See Catalogue for other designs and prices.

Fine Hemstitched Linen Handkerchiefs, beautifully embroidered in one corner, size about 11". No. 462 (as illustrated). 6 in a box, 6/3. See Catalogue for other designs and prices.

Fine Sheer Linen Revered Handkerchiefs, size about 11 ins. No. 437 (as illustrated). 6 in a box, 6/6. See Catalogue for other designs and prices.

MEN'S
Initialled Linen Handkerchiefs, No. 120 (as illustrated). Size 19". 6 in a box, 6/3. See Catalogue for other sizes and prices.

REAL IRISH LINEN HANDKERCHIEFS

Huttons offer wonderful Values—See!

Welcome wherever Father Christmas goes, Irish Linen Handkerchiefs make charming just-right Gifts. And, coming from Huttons of Larne, a house known far and wide for the wonderful quality of its Real Irish Linens, these handkerchiefs have the special loveliness that Christmas Remembrances *should* have.

Little lace-trimmed or embroidered affairs for ladies, big snowy squares for men, exquisitely initialled handkerchiefs for intimates—there's a selection to meet every gift-need. ... Make out your list now or send for Complete Catalogue FREE. Remember, you *save* at Huttons.

COMPLETE CHRISTMAS GIFT LIST FREE.

GUARANTEE.—Goods not approved returnable for exchange or refund of money. POSTAGE paid on parcels value 20/- or over—under 20/- add 6d. Send your orders C.O.D.

Huttons

54 Main Street, Larne, Ulster, N. Ireland

Libelling our Grandparents?

that our grandmothers, whose legs were almost completely hidden, never gave them a thought except as means of locomotion. They draped skirts over their legs, because fashion happened to dictate it, then thought no more about them. *They*, we may be sure, did not massage their legs to induce slimness, or enclose them in silken sheaths that they might please the eye. But, in any case, much nonsense is talked about the visibility or otherwise of legs; actually they are, even when skirts are at their shortest, seldom displayed except when their owners are bathing, being at most times closely hidden in stockings. So even about that we have no occasion to brag.

Not only were our grandmothers not leg-conscious, but they were probably far less sex-conscious than we are to-day. Sex has, in these days, become self-important; ceasing to be a simple function and reaction of nature, it has set itself up and become an idol, expecting continual attention, like a petted pug-dog. Our grandparents, from all accounts, took sex in their stride, then went on to think about something else. Our female grandparents did not spend their time and income adorning their faces, painting their lips, cheeks, eyelids, eyebrows, and hair, in order to allure our grandfathers. Coquetry was, surely, less in fashion than among us; the tomboy and the blue-stocking both, I like to think, abounded. We may say, if we wish to accuse our grandmothers, that it was the fashion among them to have less care for appearances than we have ourselves, to be more reckless, less womanly, more epicene. But, after all, why label them or ourselves at all? They were, doubtless, all different, each grandmother from the next. You and I were each, probably, more like our respective grandmothers than these ladies were like one another, for heredity is a much closer link than period.

The same comments, in a lesser degree, apply to our grandfathers. "The Victorians" we call these gentlemen, and proceed to impute to them every kind of humbug, self-righteousness, and cant. "Smug," we call them, "self-complaisant," and "respectable hypocrites." We say that they were "cocksure about the universe, its meaning, and their place in it," whereas we see it all inscribed with a large question mark. But is this true? I believe the Victorians were, on the whole, far more doubt-tossed, questioning, and storm-driven than we are. It was during this reign that the foundations of the religious beliefs that had prevailed through twelve centuries of English life were shaken and rocked by scientific discoveries. The intelligent young men of the eighteen-seventies and eighties were torn by doubts and scepticisms; the words "placid" and "smug" cannot possibly be applied to most of them. I see some excuse for applying some of these adjectives to the beliefs of the eighteenth century, when a firm and pious form of Christian Deism still prevailed, and that anthropocentrism which saw man as the lord of a universe of creatures all existing for his benefit. But to apply such words to the questioning and troubled faiths of our Victorian grandfathers is peculiarly inapt.

I sometimes read novels about Victorian fathers. They are grim beings, like Samuel Butler's terrific papa, or Sir Edmund Gosse's. Often they belong to some form of dissenting Christianity, and carry round the bag in chapel. This is a bad symptom,

I believe; one is never surprised to learn that a Victorian chapel elder, besides being cruel to his children and Jewishly Sabbatical about Sunday, steals the money out of the chapel bag. To be a Victorian father in modern fiction is fatal to charm, and often fatal to virtue. Not, however, in Victorian fiction; and this is, presumably, better informed about its subjects than are the novelists of the twentieth century. Consider the Victorians as presented in their own fiction—Mr. Tulliver, Mr. Micawber, Mr. Rochester, Arthur Pendennis, Dorian Grey, and the rest of the long tale of wild and fantastic gentlemen; consider some of the Victorians of history—Carlyle, Cardinal Newman, Disraeli, Swinburne, William Morris, Rossetti, R. L. Stevenson, Oscar Wilde, Henry Kingsley, Augustine Birrell (happily now a Georgian), and a hundred more. Are they smug, complacent, or narrowly orthodox? Further, were they like one another? Had they any common quality that we can label as "Victorian"? I do not think so. Any more than we have any common quality to-day that we can rightly set down as Georgian. You may meet to-day the twentieth-century counterpart of almost any nineteenth-century type, modern in dress and manners but essentially the same. Humanity changes slowly. We doubtless differ widely, in many ways, from our remoter ancestors. I cannot claim that we have not, probably, changed a little since our first parents gnawed bones in caves, or apples in gardens. We may even have altered a little in outlook since the pilgrims rode to

Canterbury, or since we flocked to see witches and heretics burnt in the market place. Even, perhaps, since the eighteenth century, when stocks and whipping posts were in active public use, and Mr. Fairchild took his infants to see, as a dreadful warning, men hanging on the gallows, and Elizabeth Bennett shocked her friends by walking three miles in the country.

But not, after all, much. How many people still, though no longer allowed to see executions, crowd as near to them as they can get, waiting for hours outside a prison wall, savouring the dreadful moment of some poor wretch's doom? How many people flock to the scene of a murder, enjoying its vicarious thrill? And as to Elizabeth's feat of pedestrianism, we must remember that she was dressed in a long and flowing dress and thin shoes, and any of us returning to-day from such a walk in similar attire (say evening dress) might well be stigmatised, as she was by her contemporaries, as blousy, dirty, and queer.

But, though I suppose even in so short a time as fifty years there must be a little change, if there is to be any in two hundred, it must be so slight as to be barely observable. What a narrow gulf of years divides us from 1870, when, it is reasonable to suppose, the average grandparent of the average modern was in his or her prime. Can the human race have quite transformed itself in so meagre a span of years?

Be Practical in Your Giving!

1930

Big Ben
Plain dial **19/6**
Luminous dial **25/-**

Pocket Ben
Plain dial **8/6**
Luminous dial **12/6**
Packed ready in attractive boxes.

Give Big Ben for the Home Pocket Ben for personal use

Give something that will add beauty and efficiency to the home. Give the new Big Ben—the dependable Empire made clock. Newly designed in charming colours of Old Rose, Blue or Green as well as nickel, it fits in so delightfully with the spirit of Christmas giving.

Big Ben quality facts will convince you of the welcome this gift will receive. Read them and decide for yourself how desirable and acceptable this *unusual* gift will be.

For Sonny or for Dad choose Pocket Ben—the strong, trustworthy watch with all Big Ben's quality points but without Big Ben's alarm—made to stand the strain of strenuous use and guaranteed for 12 months.

Sing
a
Song
of
Sixpence

Annotated
by
A. A. Milne

Illustrated
by
Ernest
H. Shepard

1930

Sing a song of sixpence,
  A pocket full of rye,
Four and twenty blackbirds
  Baked in a pie.
When the pie was opened,
  The birds began to sing.
Wasn't that a dainty dish
  To set before the King?

The King was in his counting-house,
  Counting out his money ;
The Queen was in the parlour,
  Eating bread and honey ;
The maid was in the garden,
  Hanging out the clothes,
When down came a blackbird
  And snapped off her nose.

As my Uncle Kipling (who wrote The Jungle Book) ·said,
when I asked him about Blackbirds:

Nine are the Laws of the Hedge-row
  Which Mavis the Song-thrush wrote.
For blackbirds baked in a pie-crust
  This is the law they quote :
That the blackbird nearest the egg-cup
  Is the one which must give the note.

So that the other blackbirds know whether to start on
B or D, which is very important when singing. I
wanted to tell you why the
cook always puts an egg-cup in
a pie, but when I asked her she
just said that they always did.

Owners do not put their FORD Cars
✤ up for the Winter ✤

1930

NEW DE LUXE FORDOR SALOON, NOW REDUCED TO £225 AT WORKS, MANCHESTER
The Market House, Ledbury, in background.

FEW OWNERS of new Fords put their cars away for the Winter. They find the new Ford too useful to be spared.

Business. Shopping. Parties. Theatres. Week-ends. Touring. These are some of the many things owners use their new Fords for in Winter time.

The new Ford's powerful starter works instantly on frosty mornings.

The welded all-steel bodies with easily raised and lowered windows are always comfortable.

Stainless steel bright parts. Streamline harmony and grace. Sliding Roof may be opened when there is blue sky overhead.

The unsplinterable glass windscreen may be regulated to admit air while at the same time excluding rain.

The low wheels, large tyres, powerful four-wheel brakes, four hydraulic shock absorbers, careful balancing and excellent springing make the new Ford an unusually safe car in any weather.

Luxurious upholstery. Disappearing arm-rest. Roomy pockets in doors. Comfort and convenience far above the price.

Truly, as enquiry among Ford owners shows, the new Ford is an all-year car. Its comfort, convenience and economy last all the year through. Call at your nearest Ford dealer's to-day and let him demonstrate these things to you.

A new Ford Car is now more easily within your reach than ever — since the recent price reductions. Ask your Ford dealer for a trial run.

LINCOLN Fordson

FORD MOTOR COMPANY LIMITED, London and Manchester

Advertised Goods are Good Goods.

CHRISTMAS SHOPPING CHART
FOR BUSY HUSBANDS

1930

IF YOUR WIFE IS A BLITHE YOUNG GIRL

—the kind that never should be chained down to dreary household drudgery ★

IF SHE IS AN EXCELLENT HOUSEKEEPER

—finding the utmost joy in a lovely home exquisitely kept ★

IF YOUR WIFE IS A BUSY YOUNG MOTHER

—with her time and energy taken up by the care of lively youngsters ★

IF YOUR WIFE IS NONE TOO STRONG

—a woman who finds heavy work much too fatiguing for her fragile strength ★

IF YOUR WIFE IS JUST ONE OF THE BEST

—who cares for her home and family wholeheartedly and uncomplainingly, no matter how hard the tasks, but would like to do her housekeeping the quickest, easiest way ★

GIVE HER A HOOVER AND YOU GIVE HER THE BEST

Prices from £10.18.0.   Write to Hoover Limited, Dept. A, 1, Hanover Street, Regent Street, London, W.1

Advertising is the consumer's guarantee of merit.

Illustrations by

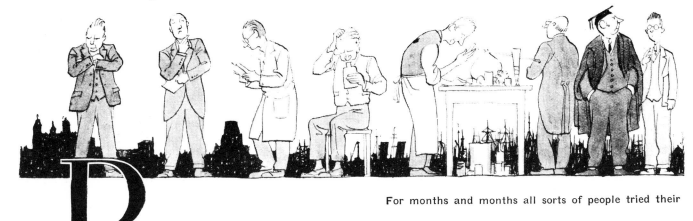

For months and months all sorts of people tried their

Rats—A Story for Children

ONCE upon a time there was a man called Smith. He was a greengrocer and lived in Clapham. He had four sons. The eldest was called George, after the king, and it was arranged that he was to inherit his father's shop. So at school he went to special botany classes, and learned about the hundred and fifty-seven different kinds of cabbage, and the forty-four sorts of lettuce. And he went to zoology classes and learned about the seventy-seven kinds of caterpillar that live in cabbages, and how the green kind come out if you sprinkle the cabbages with soapy water, and the striped ones with tobacco juice, and the big fat brown ones with salt and water. So when he grew up he was the best greengrocer in London, and no one ever found caterpillars in his cabbages.

But Mr. Smith had only one shop, so his other three sons had to seek their own fortunes. The second son was called Jim, but his real name was James, of course. He went to school and he won all the prizes for English essays. He was captain of the school soccer team,

and played half-back. And he was very clever at all sorts of tricks, and used to play them on the masters. One day he stuck a match-head into the chalk. It wasn't a safety match-head either, but one of those blue and white ones that strike on anything. So when the master started writing on the board he struck the match, and nobody did much work for the next five minutes. Another day he put methylated spirits in the ink-pots, and the ink wouldn't stick to the pens. It took twenty-five minutes to change all the ink, so they didn't get much French done that hour, and he

hated French, anyway. But he never did ordinary tricks like putting putty in the keyholes or dead rats in the master's desk.

The third son was called Charles, and he was fairly good at mathematics and history, and got into the cricket eleven as a slow left-handed bowler; but the only thing he was really good at was chemistry. He was the only boy in his school (or in any other for all I know) who had ever made dimethylaminoparabenzaldehyde or even arabitol (which is really quite hard to make, and has nothing to do with rabbits). He could have made the most awful smells if he had wanted to, because he knew how. But he was a good boy, and didn't. Besides if he had they might have stopped him doing chemistry, and he wanted to go on doing chemistry all his life.

The fourth son was called Jack. He wasn't much good at any of his lessons, nor at games either. He never managed to kick a ball straight, and he went to sleep when fielding at cricket. The only thing he was any good at was wireless. He made pretty well everything in the set

To his deep hole specially good Switzerland,

George Morrow

luck—chemists and magicians and bacteriologists and sorcerers and zoologists and spiritualists and lion-hunters . . .

1930

The night watchman
had forgotten to wear
boots without nails.
So the magnet pulled
him along feet first

at home, except the valves, and he was learning to make them when the story begins. He had a great-aunt called Matilda, who was so old that she said she could remember the railway from London to Dover being built. She couldn't walk, and had to stay in bed all the time. He made her ear-phones to listen in with, and she s a i d she hadn't been so happy since Queen Victoria's t i m e. Jack was very clever with other electrical things too. He made a special dodge to get electric light for his father's h o u s e without paying for it, and the meter didn't register anything for a week. Then his father found out what was happening and said, "We mustn't do that, it's stealing from the electric light company." "I don't think it's stealing," said

the rats brought their King food—chocolates from dates from Algiers, and so on

Jack, "A company isn't a person, and besides the electricity goes through our lamps and back again to the main. So we don't keep it, we only borrow it." But his father made him take his gadget down, and even paid the company for the current, for he was an honest man.

Mr. S m i t h had a daughter named Lucille, but everyone called her Pudgy. She doesn't really come into the story, so I shan't say anything more about her, except t h a t when she was little her front teeth stuck out; but in the end they managed to push them in.

Now at this time there was a great plague of rats in the L o n d o n Docks. They were specially fierce rats which had come on steamers from Hong Kong along with tea and ginger and silk and rice. These rats ate all sorts of food w h i c h are brought to London in ships because we cannot grow enough food in England to feed all the people here. They ate wheat from Canada and cheese from Holland, and mutton from New Zealand and beef from Argentina. They bit out

(continued overleaf)

By
J. B. S.
Haldane

The eminent scientist

Rats

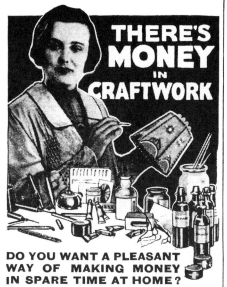

pieces from the middle of Persian carpets to line their nests with, and wiped their feet on silk coats from China.

Now the man who is at the head of all the docks in London is called the Chairman of the Port of London Authority, and he is a very big bug indeed. He has an office near Tower Hill that is about as big as Buckingham Palace. He was awfully angry about the rats, because he has to look after the things that are brought in ships from the time they are unloaded till they are taken away in trains and lorries and carts. So he had to pay for the things the rats ate.

He sent for the best rat-catchers in London. But they only caught a few hundred rats, because they were a very cunning kind of rat. They had a king who lived in a very deep hole, and the other rats brought him specially good food. They brought him chocolates that had come from Switzerland, bits of turkey from France, dates from Algiers, and so on. And he told the other rats what to do. If any rat got caught in a trap, he sent out special messengers to give warning of the danger. He had an army of ten thousand of the bravest young rats, and they used to fight any other animals that were sent against them. A terrier can easily kill one or two rats; but if a hundred rush at him all at once, he may kill three or four of them, but the others will kill him in the end. The rats with the toughest teeth were trained to be engineers, and used to bite through the wire of rat-traps to let the prisoners out.

So in one month these rats killed a hundred and eighty-one cats, forty-five dogs, and ninety-five ferrets. And they wounded a lot of others so badly that they ran away if they even smelt a rat, let alone saw one. And they let out seven hundred and forty-two prisoners from six hundred and eighteen traps. So the rat-catchers lost their best dogs and ferrets and traps, and gave up the job in despair.

The people in the docks sent round to the chemists' shops for all sorts of rat poison and sprinkled it about mixed with different sorts of bait. A few hundred rats were killed that way. But the king rat gave orders that none of his subjects were to eat food unless it came straight out of a box or barrel or bag. So only a few disobedient rats got poisoned, and the others said it served them right. So poison was no more use than the dogs and ferrets and traps.

So the Chairman of the Port of London Authority called a meeting of the Authority in the great boardroom of his office, and said, " Can you suggest what is to be done about these rats? " So the vice-chairman suggested putting an advertisement in the papers. The next week advertisements came out in all the papers. It was on the front page of the ones that have the news inside, and in the middle of the ones that have the news outside. It took up a whole page, and was printed in huge letters, so that almost everyone in England read it. All the Smith family read it except Great-aunt Matilda, who never read the papers, because she listened-in to all the broadcast news.

Now this advertisement made all the competitions in the papers look pretty silly. For the Chairman of the Port of London Authority offered a hundred thousand pounds, and his only daughter in marriage, to the man who would rid the docks of rats. (If the winner was married already, of course he would not be allowed to marry the daughter, but he got a diamond bracelet for his wife as a consolation prize.) There

was a photograph of the hundred thousand pounds, and they were real golden sovereigns, not paper notes. And there was a photograph of the daughter, who was very pretty, with short curly golden hair and blue eyes. Besides this she could play the violin, and had won prizes for cookery, swimming, and figure skating. The only snag was that the competitors had to bring their own things for killing the rats, so really it cost a lot of money to go in for the competition.

Still, thousands and thousands of people went in for it. They had to get three extra postmen to take the letters to the Chairman the next morning. And so many people rang him up on the telephone that the wires melted. For months and months all sorts of people tried their luck. There were chemists and magicians, and bacteriologists and sorcerers, and zoologists and spiritualists and lion-hunters, but none of them were able to kill more than a few rats. What was worse, they interfered with the unloading of the ships, and quite a lot of corn had to be sent round by Liverpool and Cardiff and Hull and Southampton instead of London.

Among the people who tried their luck were Jim and Charles and Jack Smith. Jim thought that if only he could make a trap that looked quite ordinary, he would be able to fool the rats, just as he used to fool the masters at school. Now he knew that there were all sorts of old tins lying about the docks, so he designed a special sort of trap made from an old tin. The rat smelt the bait inside it and jumped onto the top. But the top was a trap-door, and the rat fell through and couldn't get out again. He spent all his spare time making these traps, and he got his friends to help. He borrowed ten pounds from his father, and got Bill Johnson, who was an out-of-work tinsmith, to make more for him. In the end he had one thousand three hundred and ninety-four of these traps, but seventeen of them were pretty bad, so he didn't bring them.

So he went along to Tower Hill with his traps on one of his father's carts, and he saw the vice-chairman, who was a duke, and was looking after all the rat-catching. The vice-chairman said, " Of course these traps aren't enough to go all round all the docks, but we will try them on one." So they tried them on the West India Dock, where the ships come from Jamaica and the other islands round it, with sugar and rum and treacle and bananas. I don't think that was a very good place to choose, because the rats there are quite specially quick and nimble. This is because they are constantly tumbling into barrels and vats and hogsheads and demijohns of treacle. The slow ones get stuck in it, and that is the end of them. Only the quick ones escape. So all the rats round there are very quick, and good climbers.

Half Jim's traps were baited with cheese and half with bacon. The first night they caught nine hundred and eighteen rats. Jim was terribly pleased, and thought he was going to win the prize. But the next night they only caught three rats, and the third only two. The king rat had warned all his subjects to avoid tins, and only stupid or disobedient ones got caught. On the fourth night they moved the traps to the Victoria docks, but they only caught four rats. The warning had been spread. So Jim went home very sad. He had wasted a lot of time and ten pounds, and the other boys at school called him " Tinned Rats."

Charles Smith had quite a different scheme. He invented a special kind of poison with no taste or smell. I am not

Rats

going to tell you what it was, because some murderer might read this story, and use it to kill all sorts of people. He made a lot of this poison, but he also made a lot of the stuff that gives the smell to Roquefort cheese, which is a very cheesy kind of cheese made in France. This is called methyl-heptyl ketone, and I think it has a lovely smell. Some other people don't like it, but rats do. He borrowed twenty pounds from his father, and got a hundred cheap and nasty cheeses. Then he cut each into a hundred bits. He soaked them first in the poison, and then in the stuff with the Roquefort smell, and put them into ten thousand cardboard boxes. He thought that if he did that the rats would not think they were ordinary poisoned bait, which is just scattered about, and not in boxes at all. But the boxes were cardboard, so that the rats could get in quite easily.

All through one day two men with wheelbarrows went round the docks, leaving the ten thousand cheese boxes in different places. And Charles went behind them with a squirt and squirted the cheesy stuff over them. The whole of East London smelt of cheese that afternoon. When the sun set the rats came out, and they said to one another, "This must be marvellous cheese, quite a little box of it smells as much as a whole case of ordinary cheeses." So a great many of them ate it. They even brought some back to the king rat. But luckily for him he had just had a huge meal of walnuts and smoked salmon, and wasn't hungry. The poison took some time to work, and it wasn't until three o'clock in the morning that the rats began to die of it. The king at once suspected the cheese, and sent out messengers to warn his subjects against it.

Also there was a wicked rat which had been sentenced to death for eating its own children, and the king made it eat the bit of cheese that had been brought him. When it died he knew the cheese was poisoned, and sent out another lot of messengers. The next morning they picked up four thousand five hundred and fourteen dead rats, and ever so many more were dead in their holes, besides others that were ill. The Chairman was so pleased that he gave Charles the money to buy another lot of cheeses. But when, two days later, they left them about, only two out of eight thousand boxes had been opened. So they knew the rats had been too clever for them again. Charles was very sad indeed. He had been so sure of success that he had ordered a wedding ring for his marriage with the Chairman's daughter, and written to the Archbishop of Canterbury to marry them. Now he had to write to the jeweller and the Archbishop to say he wasn't going to marry after all. And worst of all, the cheesy smell stuck to him for a month. They wouldn't have him back at school, and he had to sleep in the coal shed at home.

Last of all Jack tried his plan. It needed a lot of money, and though he borrowed thirty pounds from his father, it was not enough. But he borrowed some more from me, and sold some wireless sets he had made, until he gradually got enough. He got some very fine iron filings, much finer than the ordinary kind, and had them baked into biscuits. The biscuits were left about the docks. At first the rats would not touch them, but later they found they did them no harm, and began to eat them. Meanwhile Jack got seven perfectly enormous electro-magnets, which were put in different docks. Each was in the middle of a deep pit with smooth sides. And cables were laid so that current from the district railway and the East London railway could be put through the magnets. Luckily Jack knew the head electrical engineer on the underground railways, because they were both keen on wireless, so he was able to arrange to borrow their current.

When he thought that the rats had eaten enough iron filings, he made arrangements to turn the current through the magnets. All loose iron, steel, or nickel things had to be tied up. And the ships, because they were made of steel and iron, had to be tied up very tight indeed with extra cables. And all the people in the docks that night had to wear special boots or shoes with no nails in them; except the vice-chairman who was a duke, so of course he had gold nails in his boots.

At half-past one in the morning the last underground railway train had stopped, and

1930

Rats

they turned all the current that had been working the trains into the first magnet. A few rusty nails and tins came rushing towards it, and so did the rats, but more slowly. They were full of iron filings, and the magnet just pulled them. Soon the hole round that magnet was full of rats, and they switched the current on to the next magnet. Then they turned on the third magnet, and so on. Of course, only the rats that were above ground were pulled by the magnets. But they turned them on again and again, and as more and more came out of their holes they were caught too.

The king rat knew something was going wrong, and felt himself pulled to one side of his hole. He sent out messengers, but they never came back. At last he went out himself, and a magnet pulled him into a pit. When morning came they turned on water taps and drowned all the rats that had been pulled into the pits. These rats weighed one hundred and fifty tons. No one ever counted them, but they reckoned to have caught three-quarters of a million.

There were some awkward accidents. A night watchman called Alf Timmins had forgotten to wear boots without nails. So the magnet pullet him along feet first. He managed to get his boots off just as he was on the edge of the ratpit, but a rat hung on to each of his toes, and the magnet pulled these rats so hard that all his toes came off. So now he has no toes, like the Pobble, and takes a smaller size in boots than he used to.

But another watchman called Bert Higgs had better luck. Before the war he had been a great billiard player, but he got a bit of a shell into his brain and couldn't play billiards any more. And none of the doctors could get the bit out. So when Jack turned the magnet on the bit of shell came popping out of his head, and the part of his brain that made him so good at

billiards started working again. So now he is billiards champion of Walthamstow.

The next night they turned on the magnets again, and caught a lot more rats, about a hundred tons. Their king was dead, so they did not know what to do. The third night they caught a lot more again. After that, the few rats that were left were so frightened that they all ran away. Some got on to ships and went abroad. Some went into London, and were a great nuisance to the people there, but none stayed at the docks. They caught none the fourth night, and though they hunted with dogs and ferrets the next day, there wasn't a rat in the place.

So Jack Smith got the hundred thousand pounds and married the Chairman's daughter on a ship at sea. He didn't want to be married in church, and he thought registrar's offices were ugly, so he hired a ship, and when they were three miles from shore the captain married them, which he couldn't have done if they had been only two and ·a half miles away, because that is the law. They had two boys and two girls, and Jack got a very good job with the B.B.C.

With all that money he might have lived all his life without doing any work, but he was so fond of wireless that he wanted to go on working at it.

His sister married the duke, so she is a duchess, but of course duchesses aren't so important now as they used to be. She has diamond heels to her shoes to match her husband's gold nails. He gave his brothers Jim and Charles money to start in their professions. So Jim spent it on magic wands and trick hats and tables, and became a conjuror, and a very good one too. And Charles went to the university and became a professor of chemistry. I am a sort of professor of chemistry too, and I know him quite well. So they all lived happily ever after.

Our Shopping Service

1

1. Very smart evening coat in black chiffon velvet, made on the newest lines and lined throughout in coloured tinsel or white artificial satin. Finished with stand-up collar of white coney. In black only. Price 39s. 6d. Post free U.K.

2. A charming two-piece evening ensemble in artificial silk taffeta. The coatee has a slight basqued effect and the graceful skirt has a slim hip line. Available in ivory, pink, pale blue, or pale green. Sizes S.W. and W. Price 30s. Post free U.K.

3. Pretty evening frock in taffeta, with a new back decoration to the skirt, which is arranged with low-set frills. Available in pink, ivory, pale blue, pale green or black. Sizes S.W. and W. Price 49s. 6d. Post free U.K.

4. Evening ensemble in rich quality artificial silk velvet. The sleeveless frock is made on distinguished lines and the coatee has the sleeves edged with white foxaline. In black only. W. size. Price 4 gns. Post free U.K.

6

1931

5. Evening ensemble in good quality artificial satin beauté. Sleeveless frock made on good lines, finished with tucks, and long-sleeved coatee which ties at the waist. Available in nil, grass green, peach, powder blue, turquoise, lemon, ivory or black. W. size. Price 45s. 9d. Post free U.K.

6. Smart evening frock in rich quality artificial satin beauté. Detail is given by lines of tucking. Available in ivory, nil, grass green, peach, rose, lemon, powder, turquoise, red or black. W. size. Price 35s. 9d. Post free U.K.

2

3   **4**   **5**

Order now for Christmas from these new frocks and supplement of gift suggestions

7. Informal party frock in artificial silk with lace trimming at throat, sleeves and forming jabot. Frills at sides of skirt and pleats in centre front. Available in black, navy, wine or dark green. Sizes S.W. and W. Price 52s. 6d. Post free U.K.

8. Afternoon frock in artificial silk made with a cross-over double rever on the bodice and pleats at the side and a plain panel in front of the skirt. Available in black, navy, brown or wine. Sizes S.W. and W. Price 49s. 6d. Post free U.K.

9. Practical frock in a new woollen material with a slight white fleck. The bodice has an inset vest and collar of oyster art satin beauté. Basqued effect on skirt, which is finished with neat details. Available in bottle, chocolate, Lido, red, navy or black. Sizes S.W. 44 in. and W. 47 in. Price 30s. Post free U.K.

10. Effective house or under-coat frock in artificial silk, made with long revers opening over a light vest folded across in front; slim hip line and flared skirt. Available in black, navy, wine, or dark green. Sizes S.W. and W. Price 49s. 6d. Post free U.K.

11. Smart frock in crêpe spiral, a new finely woven wool fabric, trimmed with imitation broadtail on the wide revers and sleeves; the skirt is made on new lines. Available in emerald, chocolate, bottle or wine. Sizes S.W. or W. Price 30s. Post free U.K.

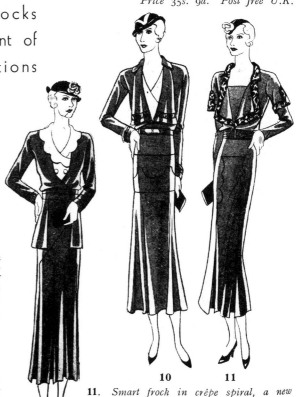

7   **8**   **9**   **10**   **11**

GINGER from Jamaica

The sweet sting of this exotic root mingles with many spices and fruits in this exciting sauce

* * * *

1931

Far away in the Caribbean lie the verdant palm-clad islands of the West Indies. The rich dark loam of their vast plantations yields up luscious fruits and rare spices.

No ginger can equal Jamaican ginger. So from this beautiful island it is brought and blended into that delectable harmony of balanced flavours — Brand's A.1. Sauce.

From oriental gardens come luscious mangoes; from Africa the cooling tamarinds; from Mediterranean shores red-ripe tomatoes and golden apricots. Herbs from the East, spices from the West — all these are mixed together according to a secret recipe devised a century ago by the chef of George IV, Henderson William Brand.

Preferred by connoisseurs of good food everywhere

Today, as then, the same ingredients, the same process of slow blending, make this Royal sauce.

The subtle tang, the inimitable piquancy of Brand's A.1. Sauce adds an exciting flavour to cold meats, grills, or roasts. It is delicious in savouries and made-up dishes.

Grocers everywhere stock Brand's A.1. Sauce in bottles of two sizes. Buy a bottle today and let this Royal sauce add aristocratic distinction to your meals! Brand & Co. Ltd., Mayfair Works, South Lambeth Road, London, s.w.8.

BRAND'S
A.1.
SAUCE

MADE BY THE MAKERS
OF BRAND'S ESSENCES

STUFFED EGGS —
Mix the yolks of 3 hard-boiled eggs with two tablespoonfuls of Brand's fish paste and moisten with 1 teaspoonful of Brand's A.1. Sauce — replace mixture into the white of egg and serve with lettuce and Brand's Mayonnaise Salad Dressing.

The Housekeeper's Dictionary of Facts

When Baking Rich Cakes

TO prevent cakes which require long baking from becoming scorched and over-cooked, they should be protected by lining the tin with well-greased paper, and by tying several thicknesses of strong brown paper round the outside of the tin. When only small ovens are in use additional precaution is afforded by placing the cake on an asbestos board or tray of silver sand.

Preparing Currants and Sultanas

When possible the fruit for cakes and puddings should be washed several days before it is required in order that it may dry. In an emergency, however, it can be dry cleaned by sprinkling generously with flour and rubbing over a sieve, when the stalks and any particles of dust fall through. Fruit—currants in particular—which are small and shrivelled, may be improved considerably by steaming. Place in a colander and put over a saucepan of boiling water. A few minutes are sufficient to cause the fruit to swell.

A Jelly Tip

Quite a novel Lemon Jelly can be made if ginger beer is used instead of water for dissolving the jelly. Exactly the same method should be followed, except that instead of water one pint of ginger beer should be boiled and added to the jelly.

Cream from Butter

The following is a new tested recipe for making cream from butter:

4 oz. salt-free butter	4 whites of eggs
	Little vanilla
3 oz. sieved icing sugar	essence
	Small pinch of salt

Melt the butter slowly and skim if necessary. Allow to get nearly cold, but not setting. Whisk the whites of eggs to a stiff froth so that they stand up in sharp points, and gently fold in the icing sugar, vanilla essence and a small pinch of salt. Then add the butter drop by drop, whisking hard all the time.

This cream may be used in all cases where real cream is used, but is not so liquid in consistency.

Baked Ham

Ham that is partly boiled and partly baked makes a change from one that is cooked entirely in boiling water. Weigh the ham, and allow 20 minutes to each pound and 20 minutes over. Soak it overnight and boil for half the required cooking time. Then take it out from the water and allow it partly to cool. Make a paste with flour and water, and cover the ham entirely with this. It should be about half an inch thick, and should be kept in position by tying with string or by tying the whole ham in muslin. Then place in a moderate oven and bake for the remainder of the time. Remove the paste when the ham is cooked and return it to the oven for a few minutes to crisp it very slightly. Sprinkle with breadcrumbs and send to the table.

Unsweetened Evaporated Milk

The usefulness of sweetened condensed milk is recognised by most housewives, but there are many that do not appreciate the possibilities of unsweetened evaporated milk. This can be used to enrich innumerable dishes, both savoury and sweet, and is excellent for the making of soups and sauces, giving the dishes the flavour of fresh cream. It can be bought in tins from 3½d.

The Christmas Menu

Cream of Corn Soup
Roast Turkey.   Chestnut Stuffing.   Cranberry Sauce
Boiled Ham.
Stewed Celery   Roast Potatoes
Mince Pies   Christmas Pudding
Brandy Sauce
(See recipes for soup, stuffing and sauces on right)

Preparations to be made on Christmas Eve

Check the tradesmen's orders, all of which should have been given not later than the previous day.

Soak the ham in cold water; clean and stuff the turkey and leave ready for roasting.

Stew the giblets for gravy; make and bake the mince pies; make the cranberry sauce.

Preparations on Christmas Day

Cover the ham with cold water and simmer gently for the time required, allowing about 20 minutes to every pound and 20 minutes over.

Put the turkey into a slow oven of 400° F., lowering after 15 minutes to a temperature of about 340° F., which should be maintained throughout the whole of the cooking process. Baste the bird frequently.

For a turkey weighing from 10 to 13 lb. three hours should be allowed for cooking, or from 13 to 16 lb. three and a half hours, from 16 to 20 lb. four hours.

Prepare the vegetables, and put the pudding on to boil; make soup; make brandy sauce.

Put the water on for cooking vegetables; heat up cranberry sauce and cook the sausages. Warm plates and dishes, dish ham, skin it, sprinkle with breadcrumbs and decorate with a frill.

Dish turkey, remove string and place sausages round, then make the gravy, using stock from the giblets.

Dish up vegetables and sauces, heat up mince pies. Turn out Christmas Pudding, and if liked pour over brandy and light it.

Cream of Corn Soup

1 large tin of corn
1½ pints water
1½ pints milk
2 oz. margarine
1 oz. flour
½ a small onion
1 teaspoonful salt
Pepper and chopped parsley

Cook the corn and onion in the milk and water, rub through a wire sieve, melt the margarine, cook the flour in it, but do not allow it to brown, and gradually add the sieved corn. Boil for about 10 minutes, season and serve in tureen with a little chopped parsley on top.

1931

Chestnut Stuffing

1½ lb. chestnuts
¾ lb. sausage meat
3 oz. butter
4 oz. breadcrumbs
Seasoning and stock

Wash the chestnuts, cut a slice from the top of each, using the point of the knife. Place in a saucepan and cover with water, and boil for a few minutes. A few at a time should be taken from the water and the shell removed, using a pointed knife. Cover the shelled nuts either with stock or milk and simmer till they are cooked, and all the liquid has been absorbed. Rub through a sieve, add the rest of the ingredients to the purée and season to taste.

Cranberry Sauce

1 lb. cranberries
1–2 gills water
4 ounces sugar

Wash the cranberries and add the water. Stew until cooked, stirring and pressing the fruit from time to time. Sweeten with the sugar, to be added when the fruit is cooked.

Hard Brandy Sauce

2 oz. castor sugar	4 oz. fresh butter
2 dessertspoonfuls brandy	1 tablespoonful ground almonds

Cream the butter and sugar until light-coloured and frothy, then beat in the almonds. Keep cool until required and just before serving add the brandy.

The quantities given in the recipes would be suitable for eight or nine people.

NOTE TO READERS

The Institute is not only ready to answer readers' household or cookery questions, but their own solutions of domestic difficulties are gladly received. A small fee will be paid for any published.

YOUR DAY IN TOWN

1932

CHRISTMAS IS HERE AGAIN! Doesn't the very sound of it warm your heart with anticipation and set you thinking of the gay weeks of preparation that follow each other through December to the crowning festival of the year? Can't you see the holly and mistletoe and paper chains transforming the dullness of every-day into a happy world of let's-pretend? Can't you see the lights winking in every shop window and the array of presents set out so temptingly that those precious coins are conjured out of your purse almost before you've had time to know they were there? Can't you *see* Christmas coming? Of course you can—and you'll be taking the first opportunity you have of paying a visit to town (maybe London, maybe Liverpool, Edinburgh or Birmingham, maybe one of a hundred other places) to take your part once again in the magic Christmastide pageant of the shops.

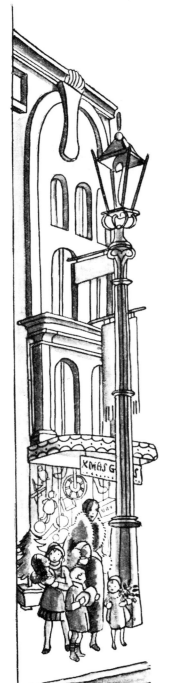

COME ONE, COME ALL

There's no one who need begrudge a visit on the plea : " I've no money for Christmas this year." Most of us are in a state of having to make a little go a long way, and there's a vast amount of enjoyment in expending shillings which might have been pounds and in planning gifts that, for their forethought, will be of more value to the recipient than mere coins can estimate.

THE SHOPS OF LONDON TOWN

So you'll come a-shopping, will you not? And if it's London you're to visit, here's GOOD HOUSEKEEPING to be your guide. In Oxford Street, Regent Street, Piccadilly, Bond Street, Knights-bridge, Kensington—all the great shopping thoroughfares—Father Christmas has paid an advance visit. Every shop has laid in a store of the loveliest merchandise and decked itself in its bravest wear to welcome you. Somewhere here you will find exactly the gifts you want at exactly the price you wish to pay : and when Christmas Day comes and all the presents lie opened on the table, you'll be proud of the results of your expedition to Town.

LET US BRING LONDON TO YOU

There may be some of you who at this point will say with a sigh, " I'd love to come to London for my Christmas shopping, but it is impossible for me to get there." With all such people, GOOD HOUSEKEEPING keenly sympathises—but not in vain. We are pre-pared to show our sympathy in the practical form of help. You readers miles from shops and civilisation—let us bring Christmas to you. The plays and pantomimes and lights and laughter of London, alas! cannot be removed through the agency of the post : but the glittering promise of London shop windows is yours for the asking. Tell us what you want, send us the money and we will buy it for you and despatch it direct to your door. We charge you nothing and our service is guaranteed.

CHRISTMAS GIFTS FOR EVERYBODY

In this special Shopping Guide is a wide selection of attractive presents, specially chosen by the Director of the Shopping Service, on the principle of value for money and in the belief that anything which one would like for oneself is always acceptable to another person. These gifts are not cheap, but they represent the best of their kind. Any of these we will buy for you, or any other thing that pleases you in the advertisement pages throughout the magazine. You will find details of the arrangements for purchase on page 83.

Are you ready, then, for your day in town?

*MAP
OF
LONDON'S
SHOPPING
CENTRE*

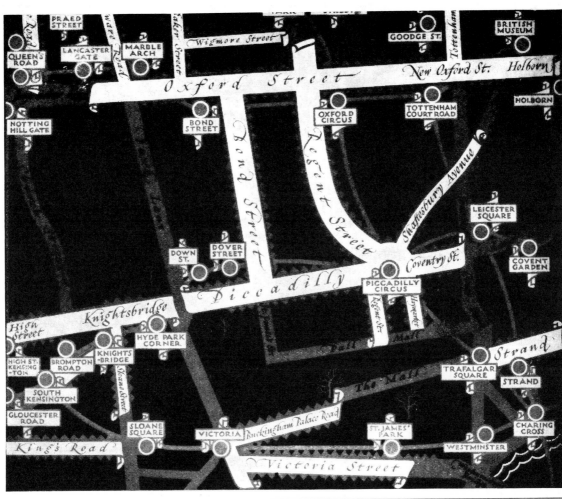

*By kind permission
of Underground Rlys.*

1932

I THINK WE ARE

In our

Working Hours

says FRANCIS BRETT YOUNG

Molly Forgan

1932

"Some men are born with a capacity for elegant idling. I was not : and when I am idle or elegant, I am, frankly, miserable. . . . My happiness is my work"

"GIVE me," says Hazlitt, in that great essay *On Going a Journey*, through which the wind of his enormous zest blows like a dry south-wester—"Give me the clear blue sky over my head, and the green turf beneath my feet, a winding road before me, and a three hours' march to dinner—and then to thinking!" "Give me," I reply, "a crisp September morning with dew or rime of early frost on the lawns, elm-branches touched with gold, briars wreathed in beaded gossamer—give me my desk, my study, a brisk fire burning; no company but the familiar books on my shelves and my dog at my feet; outside, the perfume of the autumnal world; within, the provocative reek of Boer tobacco—and then to writing!"

For work, with me, means writing. It has meant nothing else for the last twenty years of my life. And writing—for better, for worse—is my enforced vocation: not only a "strange necessity" of my (possibly) misguided nature, but my only means of expressing—I use the word in the literal sense of its derivation—the perilous stuff with which my mind is crowded, the sole justification of my existence in this astonishing world. I take no credit for the fact. It is as much a part of my physical nature as blue, astigmatic eyes and dark, rapidly-thinning hair. I find no merit in this. Some men are born with a capacity for elegant idling; and I am prepared to believe that the idle thoughts of these idle fellows express their selves with a satisfaction as great as any that I can find. It so happens that I was born neither for elegance nor for idleness, and that when I am idle or elegant I am, frankly, miserable.

The devil's advocate may say that I am making a virtue of necessity. Perhaps that is true. I am one of those fortunate people whose infant lispings were not impeded by a silver spoon. I have always had to earn my living and to work so hard for it that my mind has had no room for divine (or human) discontents. My first school was medicine, and the life of a general practitioner in a working-class practice has few moments of leisure; yet even when one part of my mind was distracted by the anxious emergencies of that exigent calling the other was forced—I feel there was no choice in the matter—to "work" on another plane, and found, in writing, its greatest happiness. In the midst of the influenza epidemic of 1914, at a time when I was seeing as many as eighty patients in a day, I found time (heaven only knows how!) to write a book called *The Dark Tower*, and wrote it in less than six weeks. During the War, indeed, there came *(continued on page 86)*

HAPPIEST—

In our

Leisure Hours

says
KATE
O'BRIEN

Sasha

MR. BRETT YOUNG lines up with the sheep over this question, and I with the goats. And he is not only on what the moralists would call the right side of this debate, but he has, over and above that, a most unfair advantage in getting at your sympathy, dear readers. For since all of us, or all of us who count, are born to toil and moil in one way or another, since a vast proportion of our precious waking hours are necessarily damped by the sweat of our brows, what could be more reassuring than to have a first-rate intelligence set out to prove to us that that inescapable state of affairs is in fact idyllic, and that we are at our best and brightest when at our wits' end?

Make no mistake. However skilfully and irreproachably Mr. Brett Young may reason you into resignation, however he may wheedle or admonish you, even if, with Dr. Watts, he tells you of the appalling things which Satan finds for idle hands to do—he will be wrong, on the wrong tack. And permit me now to take a rather long-winded way of proving this to you.

Happiness, according to Webster's Dictionary—with which I venture to agree—means primarily good luck, good fortune, prosperity. Its second meaning is so important and so well defined by the same authority that I am going to quote that definition in full—viz. "a state of well-being characterised by relative permanence, by dominantly agreeable emotion ranging in value from mere content to positive felicity, and *by a natural desire for its continuation.* Mental and moral health and *a freedom from irksome cares* are its normal conditions." (In both cases the italics are mine.) And Webster's third meaning is "felicitous elegance; graceful aptitude; felicity."

So much for the moment about what happiness is. Now let us look for a while at work, to see what it means to us. In order to be quite quixotically fair to Mr. Brett Young we will limit ourselves here to discussing only that kind of work which is done because the doers like to do it, because they have a natural inclination towards it, even, if you like to be solemn, a vocation for it. That cuts out all those manifold labours which we must call drudgery—the labours of the famous politician who has yearned all his life to run a hotel and of the bishop who would have preferred to be a farmer, as well as of the kitchen-maid who inevitably desires to be La Garbo. These unlucky people, in the measure in which their dreams control them, are drudges. Their jobs bore them, and assuredly they are *(continued overleaf)*

"Most good kinds of happiness come to us through our relations with our fellows, and are therefore mainly the outcome of our leisure hours"

Illustrations   by

Frederick   Thompson

(continued overleaf)

I think we are Happiest in our Working Hours

1932

to me moments of leisure; but even in the field, where writing was by no means comfortable, the writing of two novels, a war book, and a volume of poetry, gave that leisure its highest moments of happiness. Perhaps I was not a good doctor nor yet a good soldier. Perhaps I am not, after all, a very good writer. But good or bad or indifferent, my happiness is my work.

This article is becoming excessively personal, but that, I fear, is inevitable. So many men, so many opinions—and a man who is swayed, as I am, by one ruling passion, is not, perhaps, qualified to pontificate on a thesis as general as this. But it seems to me that the case of an artist, and particuarly that of a writer, is somewhat exceptional. The "jolly humours" of Stevenson, which Hazlitt has anticipated so zestfully in the passage I have quoted, are all part and parcel of the process of literary creation. I might equally fairly have written: " Give me a mild May morning with just enough cloud in the sky and a light breeze ruffling the water and a good hatch of fly and big trout on the feed— and then to writing ! " For the work of a writer is not limited by the hours in which he sits at his desk. It is always, at the best, sub-conscious. It takes eager cognisance of every sensual impression that enters his brain by his eyes, his ears, his nostrils; there is not one of these that may not " link up " and find itself incorporated in the imaginative tissue on which that mind is engaged, dropping into its allotted place with the neat finality of a complicated shape in a jig-saw puzzle. Why, even when he sleeps, the " little men " are at work, presenting him, when he wakes, with the astonishing results of their nocturnal craftsmanship. In a crowd no less than in the solitude of his study, the in-

ward eye is selecting, seizing, transforming. As he sits in an easy chair, absorbed, and reads, the page blurs and he realises, with a start, that the subconscious mind is still working beneath the surface of thought— he can hear the subterranean tinkle of Nibelung hammers, for ever fashioning and re-fashioning imagination's crude ore.

It is partly because of this—because, willy-nilly, their minds are always consciously or subconsciously concentrated on their work, that writers in general may be considered a happy race. When I practised as a doctor I learnt that the most devastating and incurable unhappiness is usually associated with idle hands and a bored mind—that it depends far less on the pressure of outward circumstances than on an inward emptiness; that the graver diseases of the spirit are those of disoccupation. Now authors write books for a variety of reasons: to supply the necessities of their large families; to provide themselves (or their wives) with the luxuries which they crave, or to achieve the no less material rewards of celebrity; and, above all, to attain that full expression of the inmost nature which life has given them which is—or should be—the principal object and justification of human existence and the only unfailing source of happiness known to mankind. And no writer of considerable stature, as far as I know, has ever attained that full expression without enormous labour. The effects that astonish a reader by their air of easy, careless spontaneity are, more often than not, the result of years of unceasing, assiduous toil. " The last word," as Conrad told us, " is not said—probably shall never be said. Are not our lives too short for that full utterance which, through all our stammering, is our only abiding intention ? "

It is the very stubbornness of this struggle, the fact that it never relaxes and that utterance can never be fully achieved, which gives the writer, man or woman, a happiness that I, for one, would not exchange for all the gold of Ophir. Fame, money, personal popularity are merely by-products, not the main achievement of an author's activity. His richest joy—and I make the admission without shame—lies not in the pleasure his work gives to others, but in the pleasure he derives from it himself. The printed book with his name on the title-page, the applause of a growing public, the praise of reviewers, the cheques he receives from publishers are pleasant, no doubt, and flattering; but the public is fickle, reviewers follow the fashions, and money dwindles most disconcertingly. Yet, even though these forsake him, one thing stands firm: the joy of those hours when, caring for none of them, his whole being, conscious and unconscious, was at grips with the task of creation; the days when he struggled dourly with ideas that would not take shape; the moments—too rare, but all the richer for their rarity—when imagination took wings and swept him aloft on them; the crowning mercy of the last page of manuscript when, shattered but triumphant, he found himself writing *The End*, and staggered to bed with an odd light-headedness and the blessed consciousness of a job more or less well done! For six months of a year, maybe, he has been railing bitterly against his task and telling his friends how he loathed the business of writing. But next morning, though he pretends to be idle and says he enjoys nothing better, he will secretly set about planning another book; and never, until he writes the words *Chapter One* will he be really happy again.

I think we are Happiest in our Leisure Hours

only happy in their leisure hours, which are their hours of fantasy. But it would be unfair to Mr. Brett Young were we to dwell on their sad case. Let us talk instead of our less tragic selves, who are under the happy delusion that the work we do suits us, and that we do it at least as well as we are likely to do anything.

When we are working, doing that work which we have chosen to do, are we happier than at any other time of the day? Are we, as Webster says, in "a state of well-being characterised by relative permanence, by dominantly agreeable emotion ranging in value from mere content to positive felicity, and by a natural desire for its continuation"? Of course we aren't. If we are doing the job at pressure, that is to say, as it should be done, with all our faculties stretched to it, we are in a state of stress and alertness and exasperation, a state of inspiration if you like, which is very superb and valuable and exhilarating, but which is not, cannot be, happiness. Its relation to happiness is that it contains the bud which, presently, when we pause from working, will unfold into the flower, happiness. It is a state necessary to happiness which will arise from it, but it is not happiness. It is far too full of cross-currents, too full of impatience and strain, much, much too full of that maddening awareness of the gap that stretches between what one then, in the enlightenment of labour, sees to be done and what one is in fact doing. To be working hard is to be in a splendid, health-giving state, it is to be invigorated and roused, and sometimes to be intoxicated—

but it is also domination, a state of slavery —it is to be, for the good of one's soul, under the lash. And no one outside a madhouse could contemplate cheerfully the continuation without respite of such a state —but we all, and how vainly, are for ever dreaming of a happiness which shall never pause, never leave us.

No, work is a great bestower of happiness—perhaps the greatest—but the happiness it brings comes after it, not with it —comes, in fact, to reward us in our leisure hours. For the sensation to which, if we are human, we surrender at the end of a good day's work is, I think, real happiness. To stand up from one's desk at sunset, if possible to have the courage to stand up without looking back at what has just been accomplished, to find by a fire or by an open window the armchair that knows one's lounging habits best, to light a cigarette and, preferably alone and in silence, to savour a blessed hour of private ecstasy, an hour of smugness and relief and glorious, virtuous fatigue—that is assuredly one exquisite kind of happiness. To appraise, as one sits, one's own light-headedness, to apprehend that one's hand and eyes and brain are really and honestly tired, not play-acting, to gather from all these signs about which one has learnt not to deceive oneself that there probably is, for once, something fairly good in the bit of work that caused them—that is happiness, happiness with the genuine flavour of precariousness. Because you know, even then, that to-morrow, or even maybe to-night after dinner, you will go back to your

desk and look over what you did, and return at once, as you always do, to despair and to bad-temper; but even that knowledge cannot spoil this blessed hour. Just because you have used yourself up to the best of your powers, and now are relaxed from doing so, you are happy. It is happiness and it is leisure.

But it is not the only kind of happiness. Most of the other good kinds come to us from our relations with our fellows, and are therefore mainly the outcome of our leisure hours. After all, whatever we may find, I think it is mainly happiness that we go seeking in social intercourse or in the relaxations of home life.

The happiness of friendship—who is so brave as to be willing to forgo it? And to be found, to be kept, it must be given something of our leisure. The happiness of love—that elusive and dangerous thing which still persists in revealing itself to us—how are we to taste and treasure that, how coax it to stay with us even a little while, if we give it no playtime, no hours of sheer idle appreciation? Surely for love, for the full understanding of it, we must dawdle and linger and be lazy? If love is happiness—and I think that it is that nearly as often as it is tears and sorrow—then surely we have proved that a great part, the best part of happiness, is to be found in leisure, for who is so clever that he can love and work simultaneously? And is it not arguable that love might become a surer happiness, and a more permanent, if we were so lucky as to have more time to waste on it?

Give PYREX this Christmas

(Regd. Trade Mark)

Your women friends will love to own it!

*Pyrex Entrée Dish —
Oval; No. A283. For
entrées, vegetables and fish.
Price 5/6.*

*Pyrex Pie Dish—Oblong;
No. 146. Excellent for
meat pies and fruit tarts.
Price 3/9.*

*Pyrex Pie Plate No. 204
and Custard Cup No.
410. These charming little
dishes cost only 6d. each.*

1932

For Christmas dinner: Roast goose cooked and served in Pyrex Well and Tree Platter No. 372

THIS year make up your mind not to worry about ideas for Christmas presents . . . solve the problem by giving your friends some of the lovely Pyrex oven glassware!

Mothers who have to cater for families, young brides with modern views on housekeeping, bachelor girls who like to cook a quick meal in the evening — all will be delighted to find Pyrex amongst their gifts on Christmas morning.

There are so many attractive Pyrex shapes to choose from. Fascinating little individual dishes, larger family-sized dishes, or groups of dishes sold in sets *at the new, low prices* . . . whichever you decide to buy will make a really handsome present.

Why Pyrex is such a favourite with women

Clean, economical in use, as easily washed as china, Pyrex casseroles and dishes are at work in thousands of kitchens today! Gently, thoroughly, Pyrex cooks — giving out the heat it absorbs from the oven evenly to the food, so that no part is underdone or overdone.

Carry your Christmas dinner — and all your meals throughout the year — straight from the oven to the table in this sparkling oven glassware — its beauty adds lustre to the simplest meal!

All leading departmental stores, glass and china and hardware shops stock Pyrex. With every piece goes a guarantee against breakage from oven heat for 12 months. Write for illustrated Cookery Book free, to: James A Jobling & Company Limited, (Dept. A.12), Wear Glass Works, Sunderland.

PYREX BLUE RIBBON GIFT SET *makes a delightful Christmas present. It costs only 16/6, and each piece can be bought separately. Round Casserole No. A268, 6/6; Utility Dish No. 231, 3/9; Bread or Cake Pan No. 212, 3/6; Oval Pie Dish No. 404, 2/9.*

PYREX Ovenware

(Regd. Trade Mark)

MADE IN ENGLAND BY AN ENTIRELY BRITISH FIRM

FRIVOLITIES FOR THE GAY

1933

RUSSELL & ALLEN　　　　　　　　PEGGY MORRIS　　　DEBENHAM & FREEBODY

The exquisite Russell & Allen gown, in crisp faille in a tone like powdered chocolate, has an interesting décollétage. The wings of faille give the wide-shouldered look and are held by a strap that continues round the neck, and leaves the shoulders bare. The skirt is full and rustling

The dress in the centre is made entirely of stiff, reversible black and white ribbon, used both sides so that one panel is blacker than the next. The wrap is turquoise velvet fastened with cut-steel buttons. The raglan sleeves are made of rouleaux of the velvet, giving an effect something like quilting

The three-quarter black marocain coat has surprise sleeves of chéné taffeta, where large rosy pink flowers meander over a black ground. The sleeves are definitely " period " and most effective. The dress is straight and clinging with a high neckline in front, low at the back

THE winter mode has settled into its stride and the great question of new coats decided and done with for the majority of people. Christmas parties and holidays, however, bring with them entrancing prospects of new frocks and accessories, and the shops are bursting with delightful ideas for the gay times ahead. Evening frocks have resolved themselves into the stately, trained affairs in velvet and lamé, or the rustling, bouffant, period frock, sometimes in taffeta, sometimes in stiffened tulle, sometimes in stiffened or lacquered lace. This lace has a delicate all-over tracery, so fine as to look like an Edwardian veiling. The accessories that go with

1933

MOLYNEUX

MOLYNEUX

HARTNELL

Black moiré taffeta is cut with a pointed flounce on both skirt and cape. A huge bunch of white violets is pinned to the V of the décollétage, the cape is lined with white which shows as the points float out. The pointed skirt sweeps the floor

The black ring velvet gown has godets set at knee level that give a delightful movement to the skirt. A twist of the velvet marks the waistline. The enchanting black velvet cape, unlined, has full-blown red and pink roses set over both arms

Hartnell's black crêpe roselba, a supple matt silk, has narrow frills of black ring velvet arranged in rows on the skirt, and to make sleeves. The tops of both shoulders are bare. The cape is ermine, with velvet facings to the stand-up collar

either type of dress are feminine in the extreme, fluffy feather collars and boas, floating sashes. flower and lamé capes, huge bunches of white violets or trails of flowers pinned to the waist or the décollétage. Flowers, indeed, are very much to the fore this winter; are pinned to the corsage, nestle under frills on the shoulder, scatter themselves on the hemline or form bracelets.

Another feature of the winter mode is the feeling for something in the hair. Gertrude Lawrence wears a tortoise-shell Alice-in-Wonderland comb over her very curly coiffure in *Nymph Errant*. At the smart First Night many of the audience appeared with snoods of ribbon, tortoiseshell, or black

and silver enamel adorning their sleek heads. Diamanté slides, diadems and little coronets of tiny flowers are set high, like the wreath of white may-flowers worn by Anne of Bohemia in *Richard of Bordeaux*. All are attractive fashions, and as all tend to draw the hair back from the face, foreheads and ears are showing themselves to the light of day and night once more.

Hemlines are stressed in many ways. Look at the sketches on this page and you will see how Molyneux and Hartnell do it. In the lovely Liberty collection, two dresses stood out especially on this account, a dull black crêpe with a flared band at the hem about three feet deep having a Greek key design

appliquéd on in black velvet, and a real Edwardian dress in stiffened, striped black marquisette over taffeta, with a fluffy ruche on the hem. A limp crêpe, in another house, had its pillarlike silhouette broken by organ pleats set all round at about knee level. Trains, both very long and of the fishtail variety, are another way in which the designers take the eye from the shoulder where it has rested so long. Trains, indeed, are seen everywhere: in ballrooms they are looped up over the arm for dancing.

Long evening wraps adhere to simple tailored lines, are always velvet and very often furless, relying for effect on their sweeping lines and a dashing cape or scarf. *(continued overleaf)*

1933

1. *Smart jumper suit for house or under coat wear, made in lightweight wool with waistcoat effect and pockets. Available in good shades of red, green, Lido, brown and black, small fitting. Price 21s. 9d. Post free U.K.*

4. *Dinner or afternoon frock in satin and lace : the lace sleeves are worked with bands of satin. Available in black/black ; black/beige ; brown/beige ; brown/brown. Sizes, hips, 40 and 42 in. Price 2 gns. Post free U.K.*

2. *Becoming house frock in light-weight woollen material : designed on straight, youthful lines with a cross-over fichu and tiny cape sleeve-tops, edged with box pleating. Finished with a belt and side fastening buttons. Available in bottle, red, navy and brown. Size, hips, 42 in. Price 45s. 6d. Post free U.K.*

3. *Charming afternoon frock in embossed velvet made with a flared skirt. The satin vest is visible to the waist-front and a gauging half-way down the vest is finished with a satin-lined bow. There is a soft fullness at the top of the sleeve and the belt fastens with a buckle in front. Available in brown, dark green, black, wine and dark blue. Sizes W. and F.W. Price 49s. 6d. Post free U.K.*

7. *Attractive afternoon or dinner frock in georgette and lace. It is cut on long graceful lines and has a fully flared skirt. Available in black, wine, cherry, beige, Lido and grey. Sizes, hips, 38 and 42 in. Price 35s. 6d. Post free U.K.*

OUR
SHOPPING
SERVICE

A selection of dresses to wear at the Christmas Festivities

5. *Handsome lace and georgette semi-evening two-piece with panels of georgette in the skirt ; a georgette belt from the side panels ties at the back. The coatee has long sleeves and cape shoulders and ties in front with georgette inlets. The dress is lined throughout with georgette. Available in black, Lido, bottle green, brown and deep wine. Sizes S.W. and W. Price 3 gns : O.S. Price 3½ gns. Post free U.K.*

6. *Pretty dance frock in matalassé crêpe ; the small sleeve is flat on top and has inset of fullness from under the arm to the shoulder line. The back is high and the slit is fastened on top with a clasp. Available in turquoise, pink and ivory. Sizes S.W. and W. Price 35s. 9d. Post free U.K.*

8. *Youthful frock for the small figure in a fine artificial silk lace. The spiral flounce in the skirt is stiffened to give a new effect. Silk crêpe de Chine lines the frock. Available in black, wine, Lido and brown. S.W. size. Price 79s. 6d. Post free U.K.*

Little girls' party frocks and other Christmas gift suggestions

9. *Sports lingerie in all light and dark colours, designed for wearing with sports clothes ; made in suède locknit. Vest, price 4s. 6d. : panties with flat yoke, price 5s. W. size. Post free U.K.*

10. *Tiny tot's pretty smock in pink figured crêpe de Chine made with little puff sleeves and smocked across front in blue and green. Size 16 in. length : Price 21s. 6d. Size 18 in. length : Price 24s. 6d. Post free U.K.*

10

12. *Girls' party frock in silk taffeta with little puff sleeves ; made with a high waist and two bows in front. The flared skirt is finished with a band and picot-edged frill. Available in blue and rose. Size 24 in. length : Price 19s. 11d. Size 26 in. length : Price 21s. Post free U.K.*

1933

13

11. *Charming frock for little girl in chiffon velvet trimmed with beige lace collar and edgings to sleeve. Coloured pearl buttons down front to tone. Hand finished. Available in blue and cherry. Size, 20 in. length : Price 52s. 6d. Size, 22 in. length : Price 55s. 6d. Post free U.K.*

11

13. *Cosy dressing-gown in all-wool material ; collar, cuffs and pocket trimmed with contrasting colour and with cord girdle at waist. A useful present for winter use. Available in camel/self ; camel/green ; green/camel ; dark saxe/light saxe ; rose/self. W. size. Price 19s. 11d. Post free U.K.*

12

15. *A lingerie gift that would be appreciated in this pretty set of lace-trimmed princess slip in suède locknit with French knickers to match. These fit neatly to the figure and are beautifully made. Available in ivory, pink, champagne, rose, apricot, sky blue, sunrise and spray green. W. size. Price, princess slip 10s. 6d. French knickers 7s. 6d. Post free U.K.*

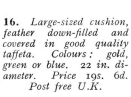

14

14. *Party suit for small boy. Blouse in fine cream spun silk made with picot-edged frills. To fit boys 3 to 6 years. All sizes one price, 14s. 9d. Black velveteen knickers to fit boys 3 to 8 years, all sizes one price, 12s. 6d. Post free U.K.*

17. *Handsome fruit set in semi-opaque apple green British moulded glass—centre dish 11 by 8 in. Price 6s., postage 9d. U.K. Fruit plates 2s. 3d. each, postage 4d. U.K. Finger bowls 1s. each, postage 4d. U.K. Set of centre dish, 6 plates and 6 finger bowls, price 27s. 6d. Post free U.K.*

18. *Charming nightdress set available in all pastel colours. New design in suède locknit with lace trimming and insertions ; coatee, which has lace-trimmed revers and sleeves with wide ends, can be used as a dressing jacket or as an accessory to the nightdress. W. size. Price, nightdress 22s. 6d. ; jacket 16s. 6d. Post free U.K. Either of these garments can be had separately.*

16. *Large-sized cushion, feather down-filled and covered in good quality taffeta. Colours : gold, green or blue. 22 in. diameter. Price 19s. 6d. Post free U.K.*

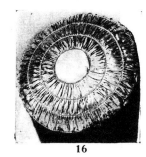

16

15

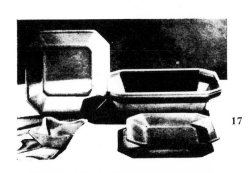

17

18

1933

THE GOODNESS OF 4 QUARTS OF MILK IN EVERY POUND

Wives and mothers are *thinking* more nowadays about the food they give their folk. That's why Kraft Cheese is so popular — there's the goodness of 4 quarts of milk in every pound. It's a *wonderful* food — and digestible, too. Doctors recommend it for growing children.

But its flavour is what will captivate you most. Rich, full and creamy, and the best part is that this wonderful flavour *never varies*. A special method ensures that each piece of Kraft Cheese you buy is exactly the same — stays fresh too. The Kraft process sees to that also for you. Very economical — no waste, no rind, no crumbs. Put Kraft Cheese on your shopping list *now!* Kraft Cheese Co. Ltd., Hayes, Middx.

BRITISH MADE

KRAFT VELVEETA
KRAFT WELSH RAREBIT

KRAFT ◀K▶ CHEESE

"BETTER REST" XMAS GIFTS

The Vi-Spring-Vibase COMBINATION

What better gift this Christmas than one that, year in and year out, will give the recipient nights of sound, refreshing sleep.

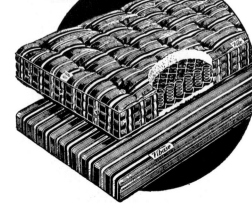

makes a gift that will be appreciated for its sleep-inducing comfort. The "Vi-Spring" is acknowledged as the World's highest standard of bed comfort. Used in conjunction with the efficient Vibase Mattress Support, its hundreds of small, resilient springs impart a sense of luxurious ease that quickly induces sound, refreshing sleep.

The "Vi-Spring" is built by hand throughout and the "Vibase" made with a sturdiness that will ensure years of service. Ask to see this great combination—the finest bed equipment ever made to ensure perfect sleep.

SOLD BY ALL RELIABLE HOUSE FURNISHERS.

Beautifully Illustrated Catalogue sent post free on request to Sole Manufacturers :—

Vi-Spring Products Ltd.
20, Vi-Spring Works, Victoria Road, Willesden Junction, London, N.W.10.

The Vito-Vibase COMBINATION

The great durability of the "Vito" and its low cost make it the cheapest overlay mattress made. The unique shape and assemblage of the small "Vito" Springs prevent them ever becoming displaced. Used with the Vibase Support it makes an extremely comfortable bed, one that will give enduring service.

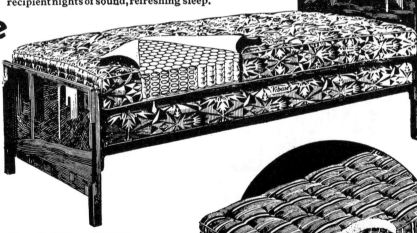

CHRISTMAS FOR AGNES

1933

AT four o'clock on that December afternoon, after a splendid run from London he came into the outskirts of Manchester: Withington first, then Rusholme, the streets rather mean and blowsy after the long humming stretch of open road behind. Though he hadn't been in the wretched place for ten years he remembered it all right, he did . . . same old smoke, same old dirt . . . what a spot! And what traffic! Clanging trams, horse drays, slow, exasperating, dragging across the very nose of his car.

It was a new car, really quite a beautiful car. Twelve hundred pounds it had cost him; yes, every penny of a cool twelve hundred, even after he'd beat the dealer down and cut the agent's commission to the bone. Dear—confoundedly dear! But why not? What good was money if it couldn't give a man the things he wanted? And he'd earned it—that was half the satisfaction—knowing that he himself had *made* the car, made it in the best sense of the word, just as he had made his business, his beautiful house in Hampstead—freehold of course and a bargain at the money—his week-end place in Sussex, his . . . oh, hang it all! Why go on? Say everything and be finished with it.

He wasn't a conceited chap—Heaven forbid!—but the honest fact remained, not many fellows could have done what he had done. Ten years ago, wearing out his boot soles on these same Manchester pavements, a catchpenny insurance agent, slogging round, peddling Safeguard policies to seedy little newlyweds in the suburbs. And now! He smiled richly. It was always honey to remember how he'd lifted himself out of the rut . . . how he'd climbed the ladder—especially that first formidable rung. No good saying his start had been lucky. He'd taken his chance, that was all—a really marvellous chance, of course, but he'd seized it, he hadn't let it slip.

He'd never forget that day, a frosty winter day like this, a sulky red sun hanging above the chimney pots, filling the office with a cold glow, and himself standing waiting to go into the manager's room. Then the word overheard. Amalgamation! The Safeguard amalgamating with the Lease and Life, the oldest, soundest, richest Society in the North. A secret! He'd had the sense to control himself, to go into the office, smoothly, as if he'd heard nothing. He hadn't thought, like a niggling little clerk, is my job safe . . . will they sack me from the new concern? No, no! Even in those days he'd known a thing or two. Like a flash he'd seen that Safeguard shares would double, treble themselves on the market the moment the amalgamation was declared. Buy! Buy . . . he must buy Safeguards on margin, get cover . . . somehow . . . anyhow.

Ah, well! Five thousand pounds he'd made; and clever, clever the way he'd gone about it. Five thousand! Not much, to be sure, in the light of what came after, but enough to let him shake the dust of Manchester from his feet sharp and sudden, enough to start him on the upward grade.

Catching sight of himself in the driving mirror he smiled again—his ready, irresistible smile—and as the traffic held him up he studied himself, not without a modest satisfaction: nice teeth, blue eyes, dark hair neatly parted in the middle. And only thirty-seven! Well, admit it! It was decent, pretty decent to be going back this way.

A fortnight ago when the invitation had come he'd tossed the letter to Sylvia across the breakfast table. The Exchange Club Dinner . . . her well-bred brows had risen, friendly, quizzical, and she'd said: "Two days before Christmas? I can't spare you for Christmas, darling."

"I won't go," he'd answered, laughing, "it's a bore!"

But somehow the idea had tickled him. Rather jolly to take the new car, avoid the crowded trains, make a quick dash over the hard, frosted roads. Do him good it would! Be back home for Christmas Day. The Exchange Club, too. After all, the Manchester Exchange Club was something . . . and to be the guest of honour! Yes, it was definitely a feather in his cap.

He pressed his neat shoe gently on the accelerator, out round the side of a lorry—a smart bit of driving which he subconsciously approved—and swung into the centre of the city.

Then, quite suddenly, quite incredibly he saw her.

She was getting out of a red omnibus at the corner of Deansgate and Peter Street. Wearing a black coat with a rabbit collar. Carrying a brown-paper parcel. On her face was that look of preoccupation, of mild detachment, so familiar, so startlingly familiar that he shoved on his brakes and drew up the car with a jerk.

"Agnes!" He regretted it instantly, but before he could stop himself he had called out her name.

She turned, surprised, her rather short-sighted eyes mildly questioning, her unimportant face singularly alone amongst the crowd of unknown faces. Then she recognised him. She stood

The poignant history of a mother's overwhelming love

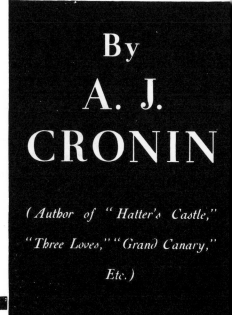

By A. J. CRONIN

(*Author of* "*Hatter's Castle,*" "*Three Loves,*" "*Grand Canary,*" *Etc.*)

Illustrations by Elizabeth Earnshaw

Concealed behind the curtain, Agnes saw Georgie on the pavement, saw the car swing round the corner and George jump out, extending his hands to the little boy. Her face was perfectly wooden as she watched them talk

1933

George drew a sharp, delighted breath. What a great little chap! He smiled warmly, tenderly. "What's your name, old chap?" "Georgie." His own name! "You and I are going to be friends, Georgie"

1933

stock still. For one sickly minute he thought she was going to faint. But all that happened was that the parcel slipped out of her hands and burst open in the gutter—groceries, he could see—and some evergreen stuff, an odd shoot of fir tree, tied up with string.

Instinctively she took a step forward, very flustered, gathering up her parcel; when she rose she was quite close to the car.

"Hello, Agnes!" His smile, though forced and almost sheepish, was not badly done.

"Hello, George!"

A pause.

"Fancy meeting you again!"

"Yes."

Another pause. Seeing her so nervous, confidence came back to him quickly, as it always did. He said, easily:

"Well! We can't stop here, my dear. Not in this jam. Get in and I'll drive you where you're going."

He threw open the door. She hesitated, then she got in, knocking her hat against the roof—it was plain she wasn't used to cars—seating herself awkwardly beside him with the dishevelled parcel in her lap. He drove off.

For a minute neither of them spoke, then in a tone of considered lightness he said:

"Bit of a shock for you, eh, Agnes?"

She did not look at him.

"Yes, George."

"Don't you worry, my dear. I'm really terribly glad. I've wanted us to meet again. Often when I've been in Manchester—hang it all, I'd have given anything to know your address."

Watching her sideways he saw that she took it in. That always was her quality . . . a childlike, a perfectly laughable softness. Soft! He could always do anything with Agnes. His lips twitched, he simply couldn't help it. She was so . . . so unutterably simple. Yet it gratified him strangely to find her beside him again, so intimately, so unexpectedly, here in his richly upholstered car. Naturally she had changed a bit in these ten years; older, a wrinkle here and there, a vague droop at her mouth, yet in many ways the same—plump, rather small, a little soft dumpling of a woman, still pleasant and fresh, with the most remarkable dark eyes—quiet, unresistant. Her dress, of course, was appalling; she had never dressed stylishly. Her stockings were poor, her figure emphasised the cheapness of her corset, and one of her gloves was slightly burst; but for all that she was, yes, she really was a nice little creature.

Making his voice more friendly, he asked:

"And where am I to take you, Agnes?"

Very quickly, rather confusedly, she replied:

"It doesn't matter. I live out by the Eccles Road. But I'd rather not drive up——"

"Certainly, Agnes. Certainly," he soothed her graciously; then, feeling his way, "I quite understand. Your husband mightn't like it if I brought you home."

"My husband!" Wide-eyed, she stared at him, the oddest embarrassment in her gaze.

"Well; well! Sorry, Agnes. My mistake! So you haven't married?"

She shook her head.

He was pleased, tremendously gratified, though he took care not to show it. So she'd never married, she hadn't forgotten him through all these years. He simply glowed inside. Yes, she was a nice little thing; quite common, of course—she couldn't help that —yet placid, restful, kind . . . yes, jolly kind she'd been to him once . . . when they were engaged. Lord! Wasn't it funny to think that Agnes and he had once been engaged! No, no! He recoiled slightly from the thought. He'd never given her a ring, couldn't afford it in those days. Only a stupid silver locket, heart shaped, the obvious sort of thing for Agnes ten years ago. When all was said and done, he couldn't reproach himself for . . . well, for tactfully giving her the slip. Heavens! Agnes would have been miserable as the wife of a successful man . . . miserable!

Turning the glittering bonnet of the car down Chapel Street, past the Museum, he began to drive slowly along by Peel Park. It gave him a feeling of voluptuous opulence to drift round the park with Agnes—the same park where they had sat together after dark, on one of the ridiculous hard seats, his arm round her waist, feeling her youth, her freshness.

He drove once round, then gently drew up opposite the fountain, that fountain they had often heard splashing unseen, threading the harsh mutter of the surrounding city with a strange, reflective beauty. He half turned to her.

"Then, if you're not married, what . . . what are you doing, little Agnes?"

"I'm still at Manton's, George."

Somehow that shocked him.

"It's not a bad place," she added mildly, "in a manner of speaking. We have it fairly easy at the glove counter."

Again the calm reasonableness of her tone horrified him: for the last ten years she had been selling gloves in Manton's Stores at thirty shillings a week. He seemed to see as in a flash those years of drudgery stretching out behind her: it made him feel uncomfortable, ridiculous, angry. And in a voice coloured suddenly by resentment he protested:

"But, Agnes, why in the name of

1933

Heaven didn't you let me know? It was so stupid. I've got on a bit, I'd have helped you! You know I would!"

She smiled faintly.

"I didn't know where you were, George, I hadn't an idea. You went away so sudden. The one night, Sunday, we were courting, and on the Wednesday, when I came to meet you . . you were gone. And I'm not much good at finding people. I'm not that sort, I suppose."

An indignant flush rose to his brow.

"I see," he exclaimed. "You're blaming me. Well, go ahead. I half expected it. No doubt you've every right to think the worst of me."

She seemed a little alarmed at his vehemence.

"I haven't said anything against you, George. I—I wouldn't for the world."

"But you think it, Agnes. You've been thinking it for years . . . thinking that I played you a dirty trick, a caddish trick . . . leaving you without

a word. Come on, now. Speak the truth, out with it."

She looked away, began to twist the loose string of her parcel nervously, guiltily. Then in a low voice:

"I will say I was upset, George, upset something terrible. I loved you . . . I thought we were going to be married. Don't you remember when you gave me that locket, you said: 'I can't afford a ring, Agnes, but this'll stand for one' . . . oh!" She drew a quick, difficult breath. "I don't blame you, George. You always were above me in every way. I suppose it was good of you to notice me at all. But at the shop one of the girls heard you'd come into money—a heap of money. And I . . . I couldn't help knowing you'd chucked me because I wasn't good enough for you. What with that . . . and one thing and another . . . oh, I don't know." She broke off, gazing at him, distressed and helpless.

He shook his head slowly from side to side.

"Well, well, Agnes," he said slowly. "So that's the way you've thought of me. I'm glad you've told me . . . perhaps it's all I deserve." He sighed. "I suppose you hate the sight of me now."

"Oh, no, George," she cried, "not really—not really" Now there were tears brimming her troubled eyes.

"Then haven't you misjudged me, Agnes?" he murmured. "Don't you understand that sometimes the most painful way is the best? If I'd decided we couldn't be happy together . . . that circumstances were altered . . . that we weren't suited to each other . . . a quick sudden cut . . . wasn't that the kindest way?"

She sat tongue-tied; he could see the rapid rise and fall of her breast, and he had, suddenly, the conviction that she still cared for him. Why, it was incredible, but true—he could see it on her neck—she still wore the stupid locket he had given her all those years ago, the (continued overleaf)

CHRISTMAS FOR AGNES

locket in which she had pasted a tiny snapshot of himself. He whispered:

"At any rate, you still carry my photograph about with you." Before she could prevent him, he had the locket in his hand, had flicked it triumphantly open with his thumb.

Then the smile died right out of his face.

It was not his photograph that was in the locket, it was the photograph of a little boy.

He stared and stared at the photograph. Then quite stupidly he raised his eyes to hers. She had gone very white; she was breathing quicker than ever.

"What!" he said, "Who's this?"

There was a long, long pause. Her wounded eyes were fastened upon his like the eyes of a stricken creature.

"That's my boy."

His jaw dropped.

"Your boy," he repeated senselessly. "You mean . . . you mean your son?" His gaze riveted itself upon the photograph again with a sudden, a terrific fascination. He stammered with sudden excitement:

"And mine . . . my son . . . my son, too."

Silence.

"Yes," he declared, his face quite livid with emotion. "That's right. That's right. I can see it . . . see it . . . the likeness!"

Her son! What a discovery! He was really overcome, overwhelmed. His whole body tingled, vibrated, a paroxysm of tremendous feeling of pride possessed him, shook him to the very core. His son . . . his boy . . . his own flesh and blood . . . whom he'd never known, never seen, never touched. Oh, it was too thrilling, too tormenting to endure. A quick revulsion seized him. With a powerful effort he turned to her again. His air of gallantry was gone, all that vague resurrection of his desire for her dissolved, supplanted by this new, this irrepressible emotion. He said intensely:

"Why didn't you tell me, Agnes?"

She was painfully agitated, trembling all over, her very lips trembled as she answered:

"How could I, George? How could I? You left me so unexpectedly, without even a word. I didn't know then. And when I did I was all broken up——"

"It wasn't fair to me, Agnes."

"But you didn't want me, George. You went away. I couldn't find you."

"You could have tried," he persisted. "Advertised, done something or other."

"I'd have been glad to have you, George," she wept. "I loved you . . . I wanted you. I went through a lot . . . in the poor ward of the Infirmary . . . nearly losing my job at Manton's . . . and after, too, it hasn't been easy, I can tell you. I've had my ups and downs."

His silence silenced her. The very thought that the child, his son, had been born in the common infirmary froze him. But he maintained his calmness, his forbearance.

"I've got to see him now, Agnes."

"Yes, George." She fumbled in her bag, dried her eyes with a not too clean handkerchief.

"I'll come out to-morrow."

"Yes, George."

"You'll give me your address."

"Yes, George."

He took it down carefully in the little morocco note-book he always carried in his top left-hand vest pocket. He smiled at her.

"Then we'll see what's to be done."

"Yes, George."

And she smiled back at him, wanly, confidingly.

When he had dropped her at her omnibus station—having made precise arrangements for the following day—he drove to the Midland Hotel. An overpowering elation thrilled through him, mounted in his blood like wine. His son! He had a son! It was miraculous almost, turning out this way, after those years of dis-

---

1933

POSTMAN'S KNOCK

By Fred W. Bayliss

Rat-a-tat-tat !
Who's that ? Who's that ?
Stretching his arm from Mandalay,
Knocking our door on Christmas day,
Knocking our door in London here,
Breathing a word of Christmas cheer,
Rat-a-tat-tat !
It's Uncle Matt.
Rat-a-tat ! Rat-a-tat ! Rat-a-tat-tat !

Rat-a-tat-tat !
Who's that ? Who's that ?
Stretching her arm across the foam,
Knocking our door in home, sweet home,
Breathing a word at Christmas time,
Echoed and heard from clime to clime,
Rat-a-tat-tat !
It's Aunty Pat !
Rat-a-tat ! Rat-a-tat ! Rat-a-tat-tat !

Rat-a-tat-tat !
Who's that ? Who's that ?
Stretching a hand on Christmas Day,
Whispering softly, far away,
Words from the world's remotest ends ?
List to the call of Absent Friends !
Rat-a-tat-tat !
From Medicine Hat,
And Ballarat,
And farther than that !
Rat-a-tat ! Rat-a-tat ! Rat-a-tat-tat !

---

appointment. His son . . . the one thing money couldn't buy.

He entered the hotel where, naturally, they were expecting him. Pleasant, very pleasant it was, the quiet deference; "Your reservation, sir . . . third floor suite facing the inner courtyard." He liked the rich carpets, cool marble, the luxury. He liked his power to command this luxury In the old days it would have been, "Have you a room?" and not at the Midland by a long chip! As he soared in the lift, that feeling of exhilaration, of extraordinary well-being surged over him again.

A big bowl of lovely Christmas roses in his sitting-room and a couple of telegrams. One from Jackson, his manager at the Works: *Houghton deal went through*

O.K. Good! The other from Sylvia: *Don't let the native air overcome you darling.* He laughed delightedly. Decent of Sylvia to have sent that—and like her, too!—he'd bet it was she who had wired them to stick the flowers in his room. He'd never regretted marrying Sylvia, she suited him in every way, breeding and understanding, a cool and never failing good nature, a perfect social flair, not to mention the very tidy fortune she had brought along with her. Thank God he'd had the sense to wait until Sylvia came along. Not necessarily Sylvia, perhaps . . . but a woman of Sylvia's kind. Only one fault he'd had to find: only one fault in that rich vein of gold. But now . . .!

With a start he looked at his watch: half-past six. By Jove, it was getting on; time for him to dress if he was to be at the Exchange Club by seven. His hand hovered over the bell: two rings for the valet. No! he decided not. These fellows expected you to tip them the earth if they so much as pulled out your shoe-trees. Instead he 'phoned down for a cocktail—Martini, dry—turned on his bath and, humming a little tune, put out his things.

He lay in the bath, soaking voluptuously, thinking, thinking again about his son; then, with a laughing exclamation, he jumped up and took a brisk cold shower. Nothing like keeping fit—a man couldn't get the best out of life unless he kept thoroughly fit—not that he would ever be anything else, his health was grand. And to-night he felt marvellous.

He dressed leisurely, carefully, his skin in a glow, sipping his Martini delicately between times. They'd sent up an olive, too—the small French olives he rather fancied. As he knotted his white cambric tie he couldn't, from habit, help admiring his beautiful studs. Onyx and rose diamonds from Boucheron's in Bond Street. Eighty guineas, no less, the set had cost him, but the workmanship was matchless, the taste exquisite. A wrench, of course, to part with real money for trifles like these, but he had a motto which he unfailingly applied: "Get yourself the best, my boy, you'll never regret it." And sure enough he had never regretted the Boucheron studs: they were perfect.

As he slipped on his dress coat the 'phone rang. A voice said: "Sir Charles Bogg has called for you, sir. Shall I show him up or ask him to wait?"

He answered off-handedly: "Let Sir Charles wait." That was the way to do it; treat 'em rough and they thought the more of you. Smiling a little, he stood before the mirror, making the final adjustments to his tie, his hair, his platinum dress chain. Yes, he'd do. As a culminating touch he took a small white bloom from the bowl upon the table, sniffed it delicately, and tucked it in his buttonhole. Then from the dressing-table he picked up the locket which, for the sake of the photograph, he had begged from Agnes. He opened it. Yes, there was the boy, his son. What a nice little fellow, what an open, happy face! His son! George's heart expanded, glowed; his eyes watered suspiciously. He drew a long, deep breath. With a manly self-consciousness he brought the tiny photo gently to his lips. Then he snapped the locket shut, slipped it in his vest pocket, and turned to the door. Now he was prepared for the Exchange Club—for anything. He'd have a wonderful dinner, a wonderful evening, make a wonderful speech. Easily, confidently, he strolled towards the lift.

The next day was Christmas Eve. He awoke with a delightful sense of well-being, of expectation. Marvellously, for Manchester, the sky was blue and bright, the sun brilliant, frosty. After his fruit and morning tea—he respected his figure and never made a heavy breakfast—he lay in bed luxuriously, considering his programme for the day, dallying with the idea of a long distance call to Sylvia. But no, he decided not; and reaching for the telephone he dictated a wire: *Detained here to-day darling utmost importance love George.* Then he rose, shaved, bathed, dressed with unusual care and went down to lunch.

After lunch he went shopping. Heavens! what fun it was, he'd never known he could enjoy himself so much! The streets, the stores, were crowded, crowded with happy people like himself, all buying, buying, buying for their children. It was glorious; for once he let himself go. He bought a box of chocolates, an enormous box tied with orange ribbon; he bought a clockwork train, a fire engine with electric lights and a real rubber hose; he bought a clown that turned somersaults, a swimming duck, a humming top guaranteed to spin for whole minutes on end. Only the sheerest effort of his common sense restrained him from further exuberance, for really he was intoxicated, swept away by the most delicious excitement.

At four he went back to his hotel; had tea. His eagerness grew; he became impatient. Every ten minutes he looked at his watch—time seemed to pass so abominably slowly and Agnes had said she would not be home from Manton's until seven. A nuisance, a confounded nuisance! But at last the hour arrived and, taking his parcels and a taxi, he drove out to the Eccles Road.

It was a poorish locality, a dismal street of the semi-genteel, a street come down in the world, with sunken areas, broken railings, chipped plaster porticoes, and chalk marks scrawled along the walls. The houses were huge, converted into flats. No bright shops here with big plate-glass windows crammed with turkeys and fruit and crackers and toys. A row of barrows stood at the corner, flanked by a fried-fish shop and a pub. And on the ground floor of the building where Agnes lived there hung a notice, brazen as an affront: *Timothy Treacle, Flues and chimneys swept.* It made George frown, despite his eagerness: what a place indeed for the upbringing of his son! But he dismissed the vexing thought, bounded up the stone steps, rang the bell.

Agnes let him in immediately. She seemed smaller than ever without her hat and coat; her hair was brushed back from her brow, her face shone from recent cold water and soap. He knew instinctively she had hurried home to tidy herself up, expecting him.

"It's only a tiny place we have here, George," she apologised at once. "Just two rooms. Not very grand."

He had seen that at a glance: the cheap deal table, plain chairs, cracked linoleum, the common sink. Not very grand indeed, it was certainly not grand. But it wasn't the place he'd come to see. His heart thumping, he asked quickly:

"Where's the boy?"

"In the other room."

As she hesitated, watching him, he said urgently:

"Quick, Agnes! Can't you understand? Can't you see I'm dying to see him?"

She went out, rather crushed. In a moment the boy came in . . . alone.

George drew a sharp delighted breath. His eyes glistened suddenly with a cul-minating pride. What a great little chap! A frank freckled face, blue eyes, *his* eyes, and fine dark brown hair. He'd been right, by Jove! The boy was his living image. Not very big for nine, to be sure, but straight in the back as an arrow. A credit, yes, a credit to him. He smiled, warmly, tenderly.

"What's your name, old chap?"

"Georgie!"

His own name. It thrilled him to the heart. He could hardly speak. He held out his hand.

"You and I are going to be friends, Georgie."

"All right."

A tiny pause; then Georgie asked:

"What's in them parcels?"

George smiled eagerly.

"Something for you, my boy. Something you'll like." And quickly, like a magician, he whipped off the string, the lovely stiff brown paper. . . .

"By gum!" gasped Georgie. And then: "Crikey!" He had never seen such toys, his eyes turned enormous, his little face grew quite red.

"That's nothing," George said swiftly. "Nothing at all, old chap. I like you, Georgie. I'm fond of you. I'm . . . I'm an old friend of your mother's. I'm going to do a lot for you . . . everything."

Georgie touched the train, timidly, as though he doubted its substance, then he took it up, wound the engine, gingerly set it down. It tore along the scrubby linoleum like a tornado.

"By gum!" cried little Georgie, dashing after it in an ecstasy. Ten minutes later when Agnes came into the room again she found George and Georgie down on their knees playing with the train.

Rather self-consciously, George got up. He'd forgotten about Agnes for the moment, quite forgotten.

He dusted his knees carefully, then he stood meditatively rubbing his fingers with his brown silk handkerchief. At last he said judicially:

"Could I speak to you now, Agnes?"

Agnes said to Georgie:

"Go in the next room a minute, Georgie."

Georgie went off with his toys.

A pause. George moved forward, settled himself as comfortably as he could by the small bright fire. He seemed to ponder, then lifting his head he addressed her very seriously.

"Listen, Agnes. I want to say something to you. I want to humble myself before you. You've been right, perfectly right. I'm the one who was wrong. I see it now. I admit it. Yes, I admit it frankly. I shouldn't have cleared out the way I did. Perhaps it was rather a mean trick. Perhaps the money did go to my head a bit. We're only human after all. But I'm sorry, sorrier than I can say." His tone became more grave. "And I want to make amends."

Seated upright in her hard square chair, her pale round face lit up by the firelight, she listened.

"It's been hard, Agnes, considering your circumstances, that you should have been saddled with the upbringing of the boy."

"Oh, no, George," she said quickly. "I'm not complaining. Sometimes it's been a struggle, I will admit," she gave an awkward little laugh. "Once or twice we got down to our last sixpence. The day before pay day, that's always the worst and I'm horribly extravagant Saturdays, when I do get my money. I always bring home a cake for Georgie. He's so fond of that sponge with the sugar icing. But I wouldn't for the world complain. We've been so happy, him and me, oh, honestly you wouldn't believe it . . ." She broke off, flushing at her own fervour.

He said evenly:

"All the same, my dear, he has been a heavy responsibility to you. A responsibility and a burden."

"No, no, George, he hasn't a bit, not really. He's useful, real useful, why you'd hardly credit the things he does for me. Do you know he can make me the loveliest cup of tea, warming the teapot first, infusing it just right, putting the milk in my cup before he pours out, far, far better than I can do it myself. And he'll dry for me often when I do the dishes and never break a thing. Oh, he's such a little man. He goes to school himself and comes back so careful. Gets his lunch at Mrs. Treacle's downstairs. And he's here, George, when I come in at night. Here, at home! You don't know what that means . . . with the table laid often as not. He's a treat, he is. And the cosiest little chap to sleep with in the winter. I'm so fond of him. Oh, really, really you'd never believe the comfort he is to me."

He could have shuddered at these revelations of sad hygiene and sadder upbringing but he restrained himself and said very pleasantly:

"No doubt all that's true enough, my dear. That's your side of the case. But what about his?"

"His?" she echoed, rather blankly.

"Yes, his! Do you honestly think that —living this way—you're giving little Georgie his chance?"

She looked completely dashed.

"It's the best I can do," she said humbly.

"Exactly!"

George paused, compressed his lips; then he said with great frankness:

"You've guessed, perhaps, Agnes, that I'm married."

A slight silence. Her gaze fell.

"Yes, George, I thought . . . I thought you'd be married."

"And happily married, too, I'm glad to say. My wife is . . . well, she's a lady, Agnes. She has helped me in my career, helped me socially, every way. She's a fine character is Sylvia, understanding, generous. We get on well together, Sylvia and I." Then he sighed. "We have only one sorrow in our lives, we have no children."

Dimly, without really understanding, Agnes looked frightened.

"When I get back I am going to tell Sylvia everything . . . everything about this . . . this early indiscretion of mine. She won't be upset. She knows what life is. She's tolerant. As a matter of fact I know she'll be glad."

She stammered:

"But why . . . why tell her?"

Gazing at her, he said gently:

"Because I want you to let me take the boy away with me."

Stupefied, she remained absolutely motionless, her eyes wide, terrified in her colourless face. Then her hand flew to her breast.

"No," she gasped. "No! You can't do that."

He smiled soothingly, compassionately:

"Don't take it that way, Agnes dear. I expect it's a hard thing to face all of a sudden. But don't get upset without considering——"

"No! No! I won't do it. I won't give him up." Her voice was hoarse, unreal, it seemed to make no sound.

"Now, now, we won't be in a hurry, Agnes. We'll be logical, and we must think of the boy. What kind of life has

1933

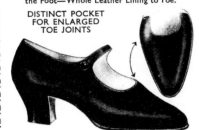

1933

CHRISTMAS FOR AGNES

he got here," he made a gesture which dismissed the room, the district, the neighbourly attention of Mrs. Treacle, "just what kind of life? You've done marvellously, of course. But you really can't give him the kind of upbringing he deserves. Now I've been successful. I admit it. Very successful. I can give the boy advantages that you don't even dream of—a good home, a governess, every attention. Later he'll go to public school and university. As for Sylvia, she'll love him. She wants a child so badly, she's even spoken of adopting one. Think of it! She'll love little George; she'll be a mother to him."

"No, no!" panted Agnes. "It's me . . . I'm his mother."

George shook his head gently:

"Think of the boy, Agnes dear, I implore you. You mustn't—oh, you mustn't be selfish."

Dumbly, in a sort of daze she repeated: "Selfish?"

"Exactly! After all, you've had him all those years. While I, his father, haven't even known of him. For his own sake you'll let him go."

"I won't let him go." Her voice rose, she was quite hysterical now. "You did me out of yourself. You won't do me out of my son."

"Come, come, now, Agnes. Hard words do no good. I beg of you to be fair. You won't have to give him up altogether. You'll see him occasionally, once in a while. . . ."

"I don't believe you," she screamed. "You're taking me in again. I see what you're up to. If I let him go I'll never see him again, never, never."

Her voice rose suddenly, agonised.

The boy, disturbed by the noise, came running into the room, holding the little clown which was still somersaulting over its metal bar.

"What's up? I say, what's up?" His face was unperturbed, curiously wondering.

She answered swiftly, the words stifling her:

"Nothing! Nothing! There's nothing up. Go back and play."

He hesitated, then jerked his head wisely towards George.

"He ain't done nothing, has he, Mother?"

George smiled quickly, engagingly.

"Of course I haven't. Good gracious me! I was only telling your mother that you and I might take . . . well . . . a kind of holiday together."

"A holiday," little George said. "My word, I'd like a holiday. I ain't never had a holiday as I can remember."

"You did," wept his mother. "You had a holiday in the park and a picnic, too, often as often."

"Oh, that," said little George contemptuously, "That wasn't no proper holiday . . . only lemonade and biscuits." And his eyes sought out the man who had given him these wonderful toys, who now miraculously proposed a proper holiday.

"You think you'd like to come one of these days?" George suggested artlessly. "I've got a nice car we would drive in."

"Like to!" said little George with a wide grin. "I say, mister, can a fish swim?"

In a paroxysm of dread Agnes clenched her hands.

"Don't talk that way," she cried. "You're a bad wicked boy. You don't do as you're told. You don't love your mother. You . . . you——" she faltered, trembling, and broke down.

"I didn't mean nothing, Mother. Honest I didn't."

She pointed.

"Then go in the other room at once."

He went in, closing the door quietly behind him.

Silence.

Steadying herself against the table she kept her eyes upon the ground. She felt her breast bursting, her heart lanced by the terrible anguish of mingled love and fear.

With great consideration he did not look at her—at least, only with the corner of his eye. He sighed, as in sympathy, rose and took his hat. Then he stood, all consideration, smoothing the nap with his nicely manicured hand.

"I'm sorry, Agnes," he murmured. "Extremely sorry. I didn't want this to be painful. On my soul I didn't."

Rigid, still supporting herself against the table, she did not answer. She did not look at him. She had not the strength to look at him. She felt weak, helpless, utterly spent.

"Of course it doesn't alter the case. My mind is made up. I'll wait days here, weeks if need be. I'm not going home without the boy. You'll come to see that I'm right. Think of it, Agnes. Do you want your son to be brought up as a slum boy? Or do you want him to be a gentleman?"

Then he went out.

All that night she didn't sleep a wink. She lay quite still, hearing Georgie's breathing, staring into the darkness, passive as a wounded animal. She heard twelve strike outside quite plainly. It's Christmas Day now, she thought wonderingly. Christmas. Such fun she'd had other Christmas times. Stuffing little Georgie's stocking. A penny in the toe, an orange in the heel, some nuts next, a big red apple, polished till it shone, then a bit of a toy—a trumpet, perhaps. And the sport next morning, both of them in bed together, the shrieks of excitement: "Look, mother, look! Watch me blow it hard."

But not now, not this time, they wouldn't do that, the expensive presents had killed it all, killed it stone dead.

A sob, stifled in her breast, seemed to choke her. Oh, it was worse, far worse than that. "Do you want your son to be a slum boy? Or do you want him to be a gentleman." A pendulum inside her head swinging faster and faster: slum boy —gentleman, slum—gent, slum—gent, slum—gent . . . she felt that she was going mad.

"I'll wait days here, weeks if need be, my mind is made up." That's what he'd said, so positive, so inexorable it terrified her. She was in a corner, she wanted to scream, despairingly to beat the darkness with her hands. What could she do, oh, what could she do? Pack up and run away with Georgie? No good, no good at all. No money, no job, and he'd find them in any case. The police: what use were they? A dozen times before she'd been scared the Board would take Georgie from her because she went to work. A lawyer? Impossibly beyond her means. It was all up with her . . . she was absolutely done. Great waves of hopelessness surged out of the blackness and beat themselves upon her.

Then, like a lightning shaft, through the storm raging in her soul came the thought. What right had she to refuse the offer George had made? It was a marvellous, a wonderful offer. No one could deny it, no one in the whole wide world: her son brought up a gentleman. Oh, if only she could have done more, given him more advantages . . . but no, she was no good, helpless, useless, soft.

CHRISTMAS FOR AGNES

That was it—she was soft. She'd never been anything but what she was. She'd only keep Georgie down.

Again she clenched her teeth to keep herself from crying out. Don't be selfish, Agnes. He had said that, George had. And he was right. For Georgie's sake she mustn't be selfish. It was a sickener all right, but she'd have to face up to it. She tried to cast her mind far into the future, to see her son grown up, successful, a gentleman . . . wearing a suit like George's . . . but somehow she couldn't. It was all blurred, her head was hurting her too much, and her eyes.

She lay on her back, quite still, not sleeping yet. The dawn came slowly, filling the small room with a vague grey light.

At eight o'clock she rose without disturbing Georgie, went into the kitchen, began to get the breakfast. Her face was set, singularly expressionless, as she lit the fire and put the kettle to boil. On treat days they had fried bread and bacon. That was what she did now. She cooked the bacon exactly as he liked it with the fat well crisped, then she prepared the little black japanned tray and took it in to him.

He was awake, sitting up in bed, making his top hum on the palm of his hand. The sight of his breakfast delighted him. He hugged her as she set it down.

"Merry Christmas, Mother. I remembered, I said it first. Wasn't that good? Merry, merry Christmas."

Then, propped on his elbow, he started without delay to clear the tray.

She watched him, not seated upon the edge of the bed, as was her usual habit, but standing, quite contracted, withdrawn into herself. It was what she loved, seeing him eat heartily, enjoying every mouthful; really it gave her more pleasure than to eat the meal herself. But this morning, shortly after he had begun she said:

"I've got to go out a minute."

With his mouth too full to talk, he nodded his head agreeably. Often of a morning, when she wasn't working, she went down to have a word with Mrs. Treacle or to buy a paper at Jewsbury's paper shop along the road. She paused as though expecting him to protest, to say "Don't go, mother, stay here with me." But no, he didn't. In the hall she put on her hat and coat, very slowly, as though her arms were heavy and stiff. Then she went out.

On the landing below, Mrs. Treacle, a big-boned Irishwoman with a face like a friendly horse, was taking in the morning milk.

"Compliments of the season to you, Agnes dear. It's early you are for a Christmas Day. But a merry one to you none the less."

"A merry Christmas, Mrs. Treacle."

"Hold on a minute, will you now. I've a present for you in the house. A doty little calendar with a lovely picture on the front, that came from Dublin it did, no less. Wait here now and I'll fetch it."

Obediently Agnes waited, received the cardboard calendar in its tissue paper wrapping. She thanked Mrs. Treacle and descended to the street.

Outside it was very still, a still grey morning fixed in a queer haze of immobility. There was nobody about, the street was quieter than the quietest Sunday. Suddenly, as she walked, church bells rang out coming from a long way off, clear and sweet like sound over water. Unreal. Hurting her deep down inside.

Two streets along she entered a telephone box. It took her a long time to find the number in the book, her eyes didn't seem to be working properly, but at last she found it. She rang up the hotel and asked for George. While she was waiting for him she kept looking at an advertisement on the telephone book. Alfred Nubbin, it said, Funeral Furnishings: Private Chapel: Late of Hope Street.

Alfred Nubbin . . . Funeral Furnishings . . . Alfred Nubbin . . . Private Chapel . . . She found herself going over it, over and over again.

"Hello, hello!" George's voice came across the wire, so loud and near she started confusedly.

"It's me, George . . . Agnes."

"Agnes!"

"Yes, George, I've come to tell you . . ." A pause. She came out with it like a lesson, "to tell you I won't stand in Georgie's way."

She heard him cry out, say something, it all ran through her head like water. He was talking about money now, "I'll see you don't suffer, Agnes, money's no object, I'll look after you." She waited patiently till he had done, then she said:

"Just one thing, George."

A pause.

"Yes, Agnes."

"I can't manage to see you, George. I've got to go out. I've got to go somewhere. But Georgie'll be on the steps. At eleven o'clock."

She left the receiver fall on to its hook, cutting off his gratitude. She didn't see him dash off to send to Sylvia a telegram: "Bringing you the most wonderful Christmas gift in all the world." No! She stepped out of the box and went home again.

"I'll dress you, George."

He made a comical face of disgust.

"Let me dress you this morning, Georgie."

"Oh, Mother! I'm old enough to dress myself."

"Let me, Georgie."

They went into the kitchen beside the fire, where it was warm. She washed him all over with his own flannel and soap, then she dressed him carefully in his Sunday trousers and the new blue jersey she had knitted for his Christmas present. His boots weren't very good, rather kicked out at the toes, but she blacked and brushed them till they shone.

Something unusual in this preparation seemed gradually to strike him; he looked at her, mystified. At last he said:

"Hey, mother! What's all this for?"

She answered very placidly.

"I've been thinking, you might go away for a bit after all."

A slow grin dawned on his freckled face. He broke away and capered about the room.

"I'm going to have a holiday—a proper Christmas holiday! By gum, isn't it great! I like that man, he's a toff, he is. Crikey! what a bit of luck!"

"You'll behave, won't you, Georgie? Remember to say please and thank you and to use your hanky when you blow your nose."

"Course I will, mother! We'll get on a treat, him and me."

She was looking at the clock, her head a little to one side as if trying, trying to make out the time. Three minutes to eleven. Two minutes, one minute to eleven. Still looking at the clock she said calmly:

"Go down in the street, Georgie, and see if he's coming."

Like a shot he took his cap and made a bolt for the door.

"Wait!"

1933

S.17. A smart little patent leather ankle-strap shoe with stout pump sole. From 9/9.

CHRISTMAS FOR AGNES

He turned, surprised, her voice was so cracked and queer. She stood, half turned away, holding her side.

"Give us a kiss, Georgie, before you go down."

"Ah, Mother, you're a bother. I'm not gone yet, am I now?" He gave her a quick, unconsidered kiss and was off, clattering down the stairs as fast as his legs would carry him.

For a moment she stood motionless, then still holding her side she went into the front room and stood concealed behind the curtain. She saw Georgie on the pavement, looking eagerly up and down the street. She saw the car swing round the corner and drive up silently—so silently, it was like a phantom, a vague image in her mind. Then George jumped out, extending both his hands to Georgie. They talked: her face was perfectly wooden as she watched them talk; a short, light-hearted talk with George explaining, demonstrating that everything was all right. They gazed up, once or twice, to the blank window behind which she stood, then, as she had expected, they both got into the car.

Without the slightest fuss the car moved off, turned the corner, vanished.

The street was empty again.

She must have stood at the window a long time, not thinking, for she could not think, not seeing, for there was nothing to see. But at last she moved away, her head hanging, legs dragging as though paralysed. She went into the kitchen, sat down heavily in a chair by the table. Then she saw his blue striped nightshirt lying on the floor. She rose automatically, folded it neatly, sat down again.

On the corner of the dresser the Christmas tree still stood forlornly, half decorated, a little spectre of a Christmas tree. Then the calendar, Mrs. Treacle's gift, caught her eye, and she unwrapped the tissue paper. A lovely picture it was, a Christmas picture, Bethlehem, the Mother and her Child. Agnes stared at it interestedly. Really it was a nice picture, very nice; the baby was just the littlest bit like Georgie had been. Christmas, too . . . nice . . . Sort of different from her Christmas, though.

How quiet it was in the house, how awfully quiet.

Then she remembered she'd had no breakfast, nothing to eat all day. She must make herself a cup of tea, yes, she'd feel the better for a cup of tea—a cup like Georgie used to make, warming the teapot first, infusing it just right, then the milk and sugar in the cup before he poured it . . .

Alfred Nubbin, Funeral Furnishings, Private Chapel, late of Hope Street.

Quietly, rather bewildered, with that mild preoccupation in her eyes, Agnes got up from the table. First she locked the door, pulled the blind down placidly. Then she put her head in the oven and turned on the gas.

FERRANTI

Radiant ELECTRIC FIRES

1934

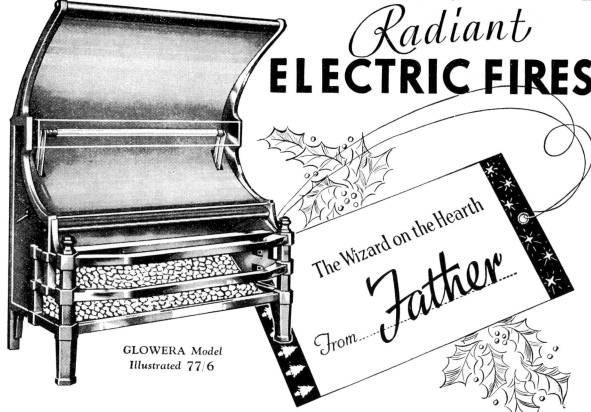

The Wizard on the Hearth

From...... *Father*

GLOWERA Model
Illustrated 77/6

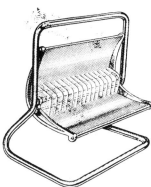

NEWERA Model
Price 75/-

There's a warm welcome awaiting a gift of warmth this chilly Christmas. Such gifts, like charity, should begin at home . . . on the family hearth. There you can place a Ferranti Fire and bask not only in its abundant radiant heat, but in the whole-souled approval of all the family. (A similar reaction is obtained when you give Ferranti Fires to worthy relatives and friends, of course.)

AND why Ferranti?

There are three reasons:

FIRST: The Ferranti was the *original* "high radiation" type of electric fire and cannot be copied in all its essential details.

FOREMOST: Every Ferranti is structurally accurate—built to give maximum electrical efficiency (as its name denotes) and to maintain it indefinitely.

HOTTEST: No other electric fire offers *more* heat comfort—*quicker* comfort and cheaper *comfort*—from each unit of electricity.

GLOWERA INSET Model
Price 110/-

GRANDERA Model
Prices from 12 gns.

FERRANTI FIRES are inexpensive to buy, too. Ask your Electrical Dealer to demonstrate and judge for yourself

See the Red Tag attached to every genuine Ferranti Fire — your protection against imitators.

MINERA Model
Prices from 19/6

There are **35** models from **19/6.** *Let us send you "The Book of the Ferranti Fire FG3."*

FERRANTI LTD., HOLLINWOOD, LANCS. *London Office :* **Bush House, Aldwych, W.C.2**

FF124

Caroline Gray suggests
FROCKS AND TOYS

1934

HERE is a thrill for your daughter's or granddaughter's Christmas—an exciting party frock that she will love wearing as much as you will enjoy making. If she is sixteen or thereabouts, she will create a sensation at her first important dance in the enchanting white taffeta frock with red velvet buttons and belt. She will adore the sophisticated flavour of the slim peplum top and the balloon sleeves. The skirt, on a bodice top, snaps on both, shoulders to the separate outside bodice, and the belt fastens under the bow. A girl of fourteen or even of eight will stand out wherever smart girls of her age meet, in the panelled frock with cape sleeves and neck edged with fine pleating. In pastel shades of silk crêpe, it combines daintiness and tailored simplicity. Even your five- to ten-year-old tomboy will be a credit to you at party or dancing class in the pink or blue silk "best" dress, left below. Last of all, just picture your four-year-old daughter in the white organdie and Irish lace frock with coloured shoulder bows, and you will not begrudge the time it takes to sew every stitch by hand.

P140 *has pleats the length of the back and front to allow freedom of movement and is in two sizes to fit 6–8 and 8–10 year-olds*

The smallest member of the family will greet Christmas as pretty as a fairy in P141, *in two sizes, to fit ages 2–4 and 4–6*

P139

P138

The blouse-and-skirt taffeta party or dance dress, P138, *comes in two sizes to fit girls of* 14–16 *or* 16–18 *years*

Three sizes are available for P139, *the simple crêpe de Chine "best" dress—for* 8–10, 10–12, 12–14 *years*

P140

P141

HOW TO ORDER PATTERNS OF THESE DRESSES

Hand-cut patterns of these party frocks, clearly marked with all working instructions, are obtainable at the following prices, post free, and in the sizes stated: P138, 1s. 6d.; P139 *and* P140, 1s. 2d.; P141, 1s. *Approximate amounts of 36-in. material required:* P138, 5½ yd.; P139, 2¼ yd.; P140, 2½ yd.; P141, 1½ yd., *and* 2 yd. 2-inch insertion. *Send orders to Good Housekeeping Pattern Service,* 153 *Queen Victoria Street, E.C.4*

Mary Baton

as presents these

FOR THE YOUNGER SET

N33

Two sets of dolls' clothes are offered: N32, which includes a complete layette for a baby doll about 10 in. high; N33, which will suit teddy-bears up to 14 in. high, and will make the boy and girl clothes illustrated. Either of these sets costs 1s. 3d. post free

Amusing new soft toys are shown below, which can be easily made from odd pieces of material. Set N34 contains patterns for a clown, clown's dog and cuddly bunny: set D28 includes a comic cat, giraffe, frog and dog. These sets cost 1s. 3d. each post free

1934

N32

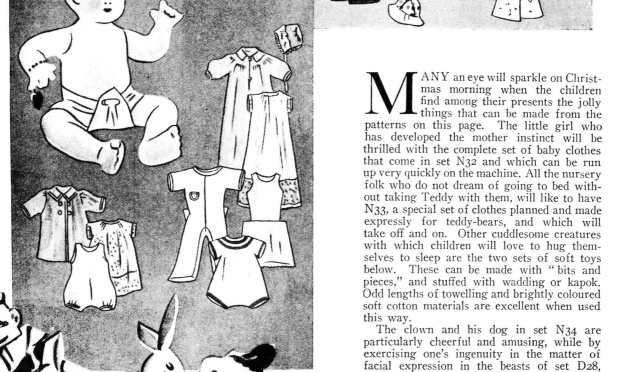

MANY an eye will sparkle on Christmas morning when the children find among their presents the jolly things that can be made from the patterns on this page. The little girl who has developed the mother instinct will be thrilled with the complete set of baby clothes that come in set N32 and which can be run up very quickly on the machine. All the nursery folk who do not dream of going to bed without taking Teddy with them, will like to have N33, a special set of clothes planned and made expressly for teddy-bears, and which will take off and on. Other cuddlesome creatures with which children will love to hug themselves to sleep are the two sets of soft toys below. These can be made with "bits and pieces," and stuffed with wadding or kapok. Odd lengths of towelling and brightly coloured soft cotton materials are excellent when used this way.

The clown and his dog in set N34 are particularly cheerful and amusing, while by exercising one's ingenuity in the matter of facial expression in the beasts of set D28, very comic results can be achieved.

If you have never made a toy before, you needn't be afraid to tackle any one of these designs, which are supplied with full instructions and cutting patterns

Myra G. Sobel   N34   D28

All the four sets shown here are obtainable, at the prices mentioned, from Good Housekeeping Pattern Service, 153 Queen Victoria Street, E.C.4

Christmas and the

1934

" I decided the leaden saucer was for cat's milk, so I filled it with same. But the cat gave the Thing a nasty look and a wide berth . . . "

YOU are either " pro " or " con " Christmas. There can be no half-way measures about it.

Those who are " pro " are those who love children, and the " patter " (though I think it should be called " wollop ") of little feet. If these people cannot surround themselves, on the happy day, with yards and yards of children, theirs or anybody else's, they wilt and take to drink. They also wilt and take to drink when they *have* surrounded themselves, all day, with the little patterers. But that is a cynical reflection unsuited to this fragrant topic.

Those who are " pro " are also those who are so heartily sick of little feet that they palm them off at Christmas on female relations who, for reasons best known to themselves, are footless, I mean, childless. These depraved parents are very " pro " Christmas indeed. They think it is much too short.

I have no feelings one way or another about children. True, I think that babies should never be looked at with the naked eye. Babies should wear veils, and even then, should only be observed, by the sensitive, through smoked glasses. That vacant grin! That awful feeling that it has either just dribbled or is just about to dribble! That sense that it is a sort of human bomb—touch it, and it will explode in all directions. No, you will agree with

me that babies are a grave mistake. They should be abolished at once.

Still, as I say, I have no feelings, one way or another, about children, even at Christmas. Small girls, of course, should be destroyed *en masse.* An agreeable holocaust might also be made of all small boys. But I don't feel strongly about it. As long as they are just all wiped off the face of the earth, I shall not complain.

I have suddenly observed, with astonishment, that the title they have put on this article is " Christmas and the Gardener." May I, as politely as possible, ask why they did that? Can *you* tell me? It is extremely provoking, in the middle of these delicate reflections upon Our Little Ones, to have such a topic thrust upon one. I do not in the least desire to write about Christmas and

" I think babies should wear veils . . . That vacant grin ! That awful feeling that it is a sort of human bomb . . . "

gardeners. I absolutely refuse to do so. No . . . it is no use entreating me. Not even a little line ? About the first snowdrop popping up through the trembling whatnots ? No. Not even a little line.

But stay . . . I *will* write a little line, which does concern Christmas and does concern gardeners, and what happens to them at Christmas.

They are given presents. And they are always given gardening presents.

I speak with particular feeling about this because, a year or two ago, I wrote a book about gardening, which, for some reason or other, has induced everybody who read it to write to me, and not only to write to me, but to send me presents.

Now this was charming when it began, but as the flood of presents grew (and it shows no sign of receding), it became a little worrying.

For one thing, it is wearing out the carpet in the hall. In case this sounds obscure, I should explain that most of the parcels contain earth, and many of them drip, so that as my servant carries them from the front door to my study (registering a hauteur that is worthy of Jeeves), a trail of mud is deposited on the carpet which has to be brushed off every day. Therefore, I should like to drop a gentle hint that instead of sending me any more roots of *hysterica corpulosa* (which don't " do " in my garden, anyway), somebody should send me a new carpet.

At Christmas the flood of gardening presents becomes quite overwhelming. The presents may be divided into three classes :

1. The literary and pictorial.

There will be, for example, thirty-seven copies of the works of Mrs. Marion Cran. There always are.

There will be, roughly, 365 gardening calendars. These are embellished with charming moral mottoes telling me to make my life as beautiful as a herbaceous border. I am not quite sure that I like the thought of 365 people suggesting that my life may *not* be as beautiful as a herbaceous border, but we will let that pass.

There will also be a sheaf of letters containing snapshots of other people's gardens. Nearly all these snapshots appear to have been taken in a deep fog, but this does not deter the

Illustrations by W. Heath Robinson

Gardener

A
not-to-be-taken-seriously
article by

BEVERLEY NICHOLS

1934

" People never send me anything useful. They send things like scarecrows which disclose a cocktail set "

senders from asking me all sorts of gay little questions about them. This sort of thing.

" Don't you think that the clematis over the third arch is marvellous? And is not this a topping picture of my dog? I call him Mr. Wu, and he is a *rogue* among the antirrhinums! That is me, behind the hollyhocks. Of course, you can't tell from a snapshot, can you, but would it be terrible of me to ask you what you thought of me? I shan't tell anyone! I have a few enlargements, and if you'd care, I *could* send you one. But only if you *really* cared. Please forgive this foolish letter, but I've never written to an author before! But I *do* feel that all gardeners ought to be friends, don't you? "

If you think that that is exaggerated, I can assure you that it is tame compared with the average.

Class number 2 of gardening presents is a little more mysterious. I can best explain what I mean by telling you a story.

Last year, a Thing of paralysing ugliness arrived which, for a long time, we stood in the hall. We thought it was some sort of hat-rack - cum - umbrella-stand, and as it was obviously very expensive we decided that we would bear its presence for, at any rate, a week or so, in case the anonymous donor called and asked what we had done with it.

Gradually the Thing, which was made of wickerwork and covered with knobs in the most unexpected places, began to exercise a morbid attraction on us. What *was* it? What the blazes *was* it? If you tried to hang a hat on it, the hat fell off. The holes were too large for umbrellas. There was a sort of leaden saucer at the bottom which, in a bright moment, I decided was for cat's milk, so I filled it with same. But the cat gave the Thing a nasty look and a wide berth, and all the milk oozed through a hole on to the floor.

A few weeks later the problem was solved. Walking down Piccadilly I met a charming creature muffled to the eyebrows in mink. " Oh! " she said, drawing down a slab of mink from her face

" It usually happens that a perpetual simulation of a mysterious complaint makes it tactless of donors to force their presence into my garden "

for a moment, and then hastily replacing it . . . " it's *you*! " Even beneath the mink there was a tone of husky indignation which made me ask what was the matter. It transpired that it was she who had sent the Thing.

" But why didn't you let me know? I can't *tell* you how useful it's been! If *only* I'd known it was from you . . ."

The mink was lowered again. " Has it really been useful? I'm so happy. But I can't understand. I put in a card with the tools."

" The what? "

" The tools, in the other parcel. Didn't you get another parcel? "

" No."

The mink began to rise up again. " Then may I ask *what* you've been using the tool-stand for? "

I blinked. Light began to dawn. So the Thing was meant to hang garden tools on! That was why it had those sinister little wheels at the bottom which made us think it might be a go-cart for a peculiarly depraved sort of baby. And that was why it had those pieces of bass on each knob.

And that was why I had to buy something very expensive, that morning, for a charming creature in mink.

Now, if people really feel impelled to send me presents of this nature, may I make a courteous suggestion that what every gardener wants is an endless supply of clippers of every description? Clippers for hedges, clippers for cutting off stray branches, clippers of all sizes and shapes. Gardeners also need large, sharp and expensive spades. Nor do they despise trowels, watering cans and the like. But people never send me anything useful like that. They always send—well, all I can call them is . . . Things. Things like miniature wheelbarrows fitted with a wireless *(continued overleaf)*

1934

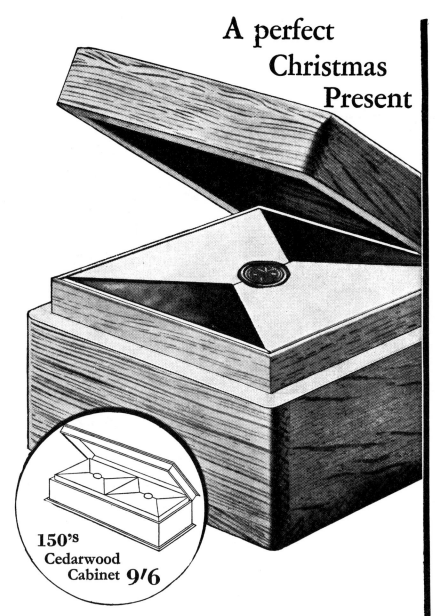
CHRISTMAS AND THE GARDENER

attachment, or hoes that can be used as fountain pens if you turn them upside-down, or scare-crows which may also be used as bird-baths, and, when unfolded, disclose a cocktail set. My tool-shed is littered with such things, and I am growing tired of it.

The third, largest and—strange as it may seem—the most useless class of presents which a gardener receives at Christmas, is . . . seeds.

At the risk of sounding very ungracious, I must admit that gifts of seeds from kindly strangers have become the plague of my life. You can always tell a packet which contains seeds. It is bulky, it is stained, it rattles, and it usually comes from New Zealand. At this moment, I swear, quantities of really charming people in New Zealand are putting seeds into envelopes for me, and sending them off with the most touching little notes, to this effect:

Dear Mr. Nichols,

As you have given me so much pleasure by your works on gardening, I feel I must send you a few seeds of our Hysterica Corpulosa. *It is a blaze of feathery pink flowers, as you will observe from the little snapshot I enclose."* (The snapshot, once again, shows a backyard filled with smoke, with a pair of large feet in the fore-ground.)

I shall be so happy if you will write and tell me how the seeds do in your charming garden. And when I come to England next year may I come up and see for myself . . . just a little peep?
Yours, etc.

I take the seeds up to the cottage and show them to the gardener.

"What *are* we to do with these seeds? There's enough to sow the Sahara Desert here."

"We might feed 'em to the fowls, sir."

"We can't do that. They'll want to know what has happened to them."

"We can tell 'em they were washed away in a flood."

"But it hasn't rained for nearly six months."

"We could say you aren't feeling very well."

That is what usually happens. A perpetual simulation of a mysterious complaint, which would obviously make it tactless of the giver of the seeds to force his or her presence into my garden.

I have no doubt that these remarks will be regarded by many as boorish, heartless and quite inexcusable. I am sorry. But if you received, annually, at least three hundred times as many seeds as any garden would hold (most of them mildewed), together with cartloads of roots, branches and cuttings, and crates of utterly useless tools, your first tender reaction to the donors would turn to a black hatred.

Which brings me to what I really wanted to say. The only thing that anybody should ever send his friend at Christmas, or at any other time, whether his friend is a débutante, a washerwoman or a gardener, is money. It takes moral courage to do this, especially if you can only afford half a crown, but I am sure that your débutante friend would much rather have your half-crown than the bath-salts, which look as if they *might* have cost four-and-six. The washerwoman would much rather have your half a crown than the calendar from which you have rubbed off the price-mark (by the way, a piece of white bread is much better for rubbing off price-marks than india-rubber.)

"Try it with Turkey.."

1936

SAYS HELEN BURKE
Principal of the Symington Cookery Advice Bureau

"WE all of us have failures sometimes (*I know I do*) but there is one meal that simply *must* be a success—Christmas Dinner. This year, mine is going to be a bigger success than ever before, because I'm going to improve something very important but very easy to forget about—the gravy. I shall make it with Vita Gravy, just following the simple directions on the packet and it will be the finishing touch to a perfect meal.

" For Vita Gravy *does* make a very big difference. Quite apart from its extra nourishment, it has a richness, a flavour and a texture which you cannot get any other way. And it pays to be careful about gravy—indifferent gravy can spoil an otherwise perfect meal.

" And when the family have reduced the turkey to scraps, Vita Gravy will come to your rescue once again. There's nothing like it for adding savour and nourishment to rechauffe dishes."

SYMINGTON'S

VITA GRAVY

In 2d. and 6d. packets.

CONTAINING VITAMINS A B D & E.

Made by W. Symington & Co. Ld. Market Harborough—Makers of the famous Soups, Table Creams, etc.

St. John Ervine

gives a

CRAZY CHRISTMAS PARTY

to which he invites the most incongruous set of people he can imagine

1935

LAST year, in the Christmas number of GOOD HOUSEKEEPING, I described a Christmas party I would give if I were able to call to it a number of notable and agreeable people. This time I propose to describe a Crazy Christmas Party to which I shall invite the most incongruous collection of people I can imagine. For the purpose of this party, I shall endow myself with resurrectionary powers so that I may summon people from the past. If I could give a party to which I could invite six historic figures and six living people, whom would I summon? That is the question.

I might, of course, try to put my people of the past at ease with my people of the present by sending invitations only to those who were likely to get on together, but I have a more mischievous intention than that. This is to be a Crazy Christmas Party. I want to embarrass my guests by merely putting them in each other's company, and so that the party shall not become a total failure because each guest has put a gag in his or her mouth and flatly refuses to speak a word to anybody, I shall stipulate that there shall be no reserves, no politenesses, no remembrance of what little ladies and gentlemen all the guests really are. They must be frank and voluble. The party will probably have a sticky conclusion, but that will be part of the fun. It seems to me useless to die and enlarge one's spirit if one cannot speak one's mind freely or is unable to discuss even one's own mistakes with candour. I take it that the object

of dying is to increase one's capacity for listening with patience to the truth about one's self; and I shall expect the dead who are summoned to my Christmas party to be able not only to state the facts about other people, but to listen to those that are disagreeable about their own behaviour when they were earthly.

I should like to ask Queen Victoria and Queen Elizabeth to sit at the same table with the ex-Kaiser; indeed, one of the most entertaining parties I can conceive of myself giving is one at which all the guests are monarchs, past and present. The spectacle of Cleopatra discoursing with the Prince Consort, Albert the Good, while Victoria listened, would, I think, be entertaining. I should like to see Henry VIII taking the present Queen of Holland or Mrs. Franklin Roosevelt —for a President's wife is a sort of a Queen—in to dinner; and one of my dearest dreams is of a party at which all my guests are reigning women or

Illustration by Sherriffs

women who have reigned. A luncheon party at which Lady Jane Grey sat side by side with Bloody Mary, while Elizabeth, Anne and Victoria conferred together on their own behaviour during their reigns would be well worth attending. Imagine Victoria reproving Elizabeth for her relations with the Earl of Essex, and Elizabeth answering back with the statement that Victoria treated Mr. Gladstone very shabbily. Queen Anne might have a few remarks to make on the subject of maternity. She had seventeen children, of whom sixteen died in their infancy. The re-

Here is the party at the close of dinner—six historical figures and six living ones. Can you guess who make up this strangely-assorted gathering? If their identities seem doubtful, turn to page 111 for a table-plan that will give you the solution

maining child, the Duke of Gloucester, died when he was eleven. Anne had not one child left when she became Queen. Elizabeth would probably be impatient with Anne, who was a dull lady, but Victoria would, I feel sure, be solicitous about her. My party of Queens would include Catherine of Russia. No party would be complete without that amazing woman.

There is no limit to the Crazy Christmas Parties one might hold, and I suggest to my readers that they should amuse themselves this Christmas by assembling one. Let everybody say

whom, if they could, they would invite to dinner on Christmas Day. Reasons must be given for the choice. It will not be enough to say, " I should like to ask So-and-so ! " and leave it at that. Each inviter must say why he or she wishes to ask the invitee to the party.

If I were giving a Crazy Christmas Party, I should issue my invitations in a crazy spirit. The first guests I should invite would be Lucretia Borgia and the late Mr. Eddy; *Mister* Eddy, not Mrs. ! I should put Mr. Eddy between Lucretia and Mrs. Naomi Mitchison, who would, I feel sure, tell the little man all about " us Haldanes." I might have trouble with Lucretia, who would, I fear, feel terribly tempted to put something in Mrs. Mitchison's wine. I daresay there would be a general reluctance to taste anything while Lucretia *(continued overleaf)*

CRAZY CHRISTMAS PARTY

1935

was present, and I should put her on my right and have her served first. Then would come Mr. Eddy, to whom it would be immaterial what he ate, and next to him I would very firmly and with malice aforethought put Mrs. Mitchison. She would be encouraged to read extracts from her works, especially from *You Have Been Warned*, to Mr. Eddy. My endeavour would be to provoke Mr. Eddy into saying something. On the other side of Mrs. Mitchison I should seat Signor Mussolini. He would undoubtedly deafen her. On the Duce's right, I would place Anne of Cleves. One side of the table—for twelve persons, including myself, will be present at this party—would then be filled.

Opposite to me, John Calvin would sit, and next to him I would put Joan of Arc, and next to her Servetus, who was burnt at the stake by Calvin's orders. Conversation at that end of the table would, I fancy, be heated, although Joan's sanity would keep Calvin and Servetus cool enough for civility to be maintained. Anne of Cleves might find Calvin a tedious neighbour, and I am sure that Mussolini would frighten her out of her wits; but she was accustomed to finding herself at queer parties and might come very creditably out of her ordeal. Did not her ex-spouse, Henry VIII, invite her to supper with her successor, Katheryn Howard, at Hampton Court the night they were married, and did not Anne go with a thumping heart, entirely delighted at being asked? She even essayed to curtsey to Katheryn, who, to her honour, refused to let her do so. Henry gave his former wife a good resonant kiss, and behaved to her like a gentleman. The fact that Anne kept her head is sufficient in itself to make her an interesting guest at this crazy party. We should all want to know how she did it.

Nine places at the table are now filled, and three remain to be filled. Six of those already named are out of the past, and only three are alive, so the remaining three must also be living people if there is to be a balance of the living and the dead. That stipulation, however, need not be made, though I shall abide by it now.

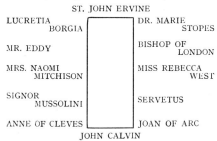

	ST. JOHN ERVINE	
LUCRETIA BORGIA		DR. MARIE STOPES
MR. EDDY		BISHOP OF LONDON
MRS. NAOMI MITCHISON		MISS REBECCA WEST
SIGNOR MUSSOLINI		SERVETUS
ANNE OF CLEVES		JOAN OF ARC
	JOHN CALVIN	

On my left, and facing Lucretia Borgia, I should put Dr. Marie Stopes, who might, however, feel that she ought to sit next to Queen Anne at any party of this kind. As, however, that over-mothered lady will not be at this party, Dr. Marie Stopes will have to sit where I put her—on my left and facing Lucretia. Next to Dr. Marie Stopes, I feel tempted to put the Canadian whose wife gave birth to quintuplets, but instead I shall give her for her left-hand neighbour, Dr. Winnington Ingram, the Bishop of London. If I could give her a neighbour out of the past, I should, and all would applaud my choice, give her the Rev. Thomas Malthus, the author of the *Essay on Population* which made an evolutionist of Charles Darwin. The Bishop would give Dr. Marie Stopes a lot to talk about. On his left, with Servetus on her right, I would put Miss Rebecca West. My first impulse was to put Mrs. Van den Elst in that seat, but her con-

tinual attendance in protest at executions might embarrass both Servetus and Joan of Arc and would certainly cause trouble with Calvin. Miss West, therefore, takes the remaining seat. She will face with courage Mrs. Mitchison and will not blench before Mussolini's frowning eyes. I feel certain that Miss West will do most of the talking at the table, and will compel the men to listen to her by her brilliance. The Bishop of London will, I am afraid, feel uncomfortable between Miss West and Dr. Marie Stopes, but his geniality has pulled him through more awkward company than theirs, and I daresay he will come out of his ordeal with an undiminished head.

Can anyone imagine a crazier Christmas party than that? Probably many people can, and I hope that they will amuse themselves during the holidays by doing so. But not many people will be able to think of more incongruous dinner-table companions than Mr. Eddy, Mrs. Mitchison and Signor Mussolini. Or than Anne of Cleves, John Calvin and Joan of Arc.

It would be fun, I think, to make John Knox, Sir Walter Scott and Robert Burns eat together. Three more dissimilar and, apparently, antipathetic men than these Scots can scarcely be imagined. A gruesome party could be composed of a judge, the counsel for the prosecution and the counsel for the defence, a condemned murderer, and the hangman, but that party might be too gruesome, especially if the condemned man started to complain of the way he was turned off. But perhaps the craziest Christmas party of all would be one at which all the signatories of the Treaty of Vienna were invited to dine with all the signatories of the Treaty of Versailles. It would be a humiliating feast for them all.

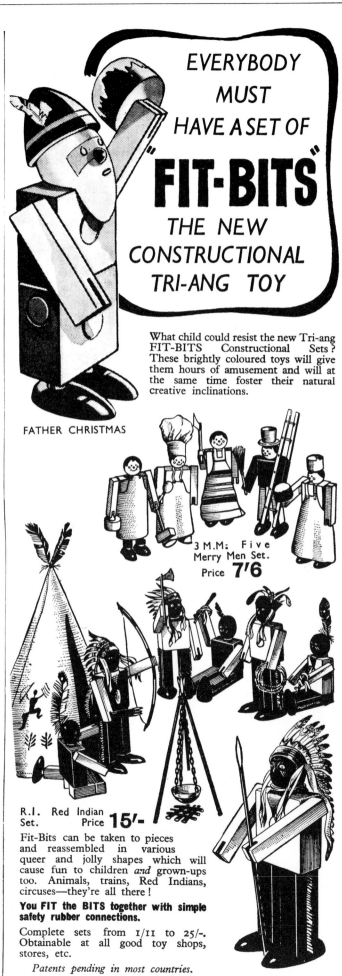

OUTSIDE HELP

With Christmas Catering

1936

Christmas Dinner menus from three famous restaurants

WEST END restaurants, like every home in the country, follow tradition in their Christmas dinner, but each chef has his own way of giving a distinctive turn to the orthodox menu, and it is on this original touch that the pleasure of a meal depends. Surprise is the most delightful of all stimulants. It makes for the verve of the party and the success of a dinner. This maxim holds good for the private hostess and the restaurateur alike, and it is hoped that the menus given on these pages and the suggestions which follow will prove a practical help to those readers who are responsible for the dispensing of hospitality throughout the festive season.

There is, of course, no necessity to include each item on the menu; in fact, in a private house it is far better to serve two or three well-cooked and

M. Jacques Hoerman, chef of the Trocadero Restaurant

Coupe Mireille

Cortillons de Sole aux Mousserons

Dindonneau Farci à la Périgourdine

Boutons de Bruxelles Rissolés

Pommes Rôties

Salade Lorette

Pouding de Nöel aux Flammes Joyeuses

Mince Pie

Dessert

M. Quaglino chooses a brandy sauce to accompany his Christmas pudding, while M. Hoerman lights his and suggests orange sauce or butter with it

Turkey figures in all three menus, but each of these celebrated restaurateurs has his own way of serving it

skilfully flavoured dishes than to attempt a long or elaborate meal without the certain knowledge that it can be carried through with complete success.

M. Jacques Hoerman's Menu

The first choice of a Christmas dinner comes from Mr. Jacques Hoerman, of the Trocadero Restaurant. He believes in using fruit flavourings to counteract the richness of the fare. Here are details of the menu he chooses:

Coupe Mireille. Place the segments of 4 oranges and 3 grapefruit and the juice of both, equally divided, in cocktail glasses. Chill before serving. Add a dash of maraschino at the last moment.

Cortillons de Sole aux Mousserons

2 soles weighing about 1 lb.	1 bunch of herbs or bouquet garni
2 chopped shallots	
¼ pt. dry white wine	1 lb. small, hard white button mushrooms
½ pt. fish stock	
¾ lb. peeled and chopped tomatoes	4 oz. butter
	1 oz. flour
Juice of ¼ lemon	¼ pt. fresh cream
Salt and pepper	

1936

M. Leoni, who has a well-known restaurant in Soho

Canapé Moscovite

Petite Marmite Bouchère

Truite à la Piédmontaise

Noisette d'Agneau Favorite

Filet de Dindonneau Delysia

Zabaglione

Croûte Swaroff

M. Quaglino, of the fashionable restaurant of that name

Royal Natives
or
Caviar

Consommé Madrilène au Xérès

Filet de Sole Maison

Dindonneau Farci aux Marrons

Pommes Bryon

Haricots Frais de Jersey

Salade

Christmas Pudding with Brandy Sauce

Friandises

Wash and fillet the two soles, cut each of the eight fillets into about five thin strips, and tie each one in a knot. Butter a flat saucepan, add the chopped shallots, bunch of herbs (containing a sprig of thyme, a bayleaf and 2 parsley stalks), mushrooms, lemon juice, chopped tomatoes, white wine and fish stock (made from boiling the sole bones in water). Boil for 5 minutes, add the fillets of sole, continue to boil for another 5 minutes. Remove the sole and bouquet garni and take the sauce off the fire. Blend the flour with the butter and stir in slowly into the sauce. When well dissolved, add the cream very slowly, whisking meanwhile. When cooked, return the sole to the sauce, reheat, season with pepper and salt, and serve.

Dindonneau Farci à la Périgourdine

Medium-sized turkey	2 lb. sausage meat
½ lb. fresh truffle	½ lb. foie gras
1½ lb. minced pork	Mixed spice
1 lb. minced veal	Beaten egg
Larding bacon	Salt and pepper

Prepare the turkey the previous night by lifting the skin from the breast, and pushing the hand up very carefully from the neck end, taking care not to break the skin. Slice the truffle very finely and push about 10 to 20 slices between the skin and the breast, leaving overnight so that the truffle seasons the breast. To make the stuffing, mix the pork, veal and sausage meat, with sufficient mixed spice and salt and pepper to season. Add the foie gras in the size of cob nuts, and chop up any truffle left over. Blend with beaten egg. Mix thoroughly, then use it to stuff the turkey. Take great care when trussing to close both ends of the turkey completely. Cover the turkey with slices of larding bacon and cook slowly for about 2 to 2½ hours. Serve with a thickened rich gravy, made in the roasting-pan and thickened with arrowroot.

Boutons de Bruxelles Rissolés. Boil the brussels sprouts in the usual way. Drain well, then fry slowly in butter until golden brown and season with salt and pepper.

Pommes Rôtiés. These can be left whole or shaped, whichever is preferred. They are then baked in the usual way.

Salade Lorette. This is a very excellent winter salad, because lettuce can be dispensed with, being replaced by corn salad. Cut the corn salad leaves, celery, and beetroot into thin strips and blend with French dressing.

Christmas Pudding

1 lb. beef suet	½ chopped apple
¼ lb. flour	1 oz. mixed spices
¼ lb. brown sugar	Zest and juice of 1 lemon and 1 orange
5 eggs	¼ lb. chopped almonds
¾ lb. breadcrumbs	½ pt. old ale or stout
1¼ lb. mixed peels	¼ gill milk
¾ lb. currants	1 gill rum
¾ lb. sultanas	1 gill sherry
½ lb. raisins	

½ teaspoonful salt

Mix well beef suet, flour, sugar, salt, fruits, almonds *(continued overleaf)*

THIS YEAR'S CAKE FASHIONS

The Bluebird Cake

This design has been voted a popular favourite this year, and it is also one of the simplest cakes that we have ever illustrated. I would not advise anyone, unless exceptionally skilled, to attempt to make the birds, but as eight are used on a cake of average size, and they only cost 2d. each, they can be regarded as a very inexpensive decoration. The effectiveness of this particular cake depends very largely on the skilful choice of colouring. The breasts of the birds are in very pale canary yellow, with blue-grey plumage and bright blue wings. The blue is a very beautiful shade, and contrasts extraordinarily well with the pale yellow background of the cake. The only other decoration is an irregular piping, in the same pale blue as the wings of the bird, for which a fine writing pipe was used.

Father Christmas Cake

This design is equally suitable for a family Christmas cake or a Yule-tide birthday cake, and although the decoration looks well on any round cake, it is most effective on a wide, shallow one. The background is white royal icing, the fir trees bright green, the tubs "fern-leaf" brown, and Father Christmas in characteristic scarlet, green and white. Although the Santa Claus candle-holders are by no means essential, they are novel, and make up a very effective scene, while the miniature scarlet candles show up well against the white background. They are made of china, and cost 2½d. each.

The actual design can be carried out either in royal icing or almond paste. If almond paste is used it must be coloured, as described for the cactus cake, then rolled on a sugared board, cut out with a sharp knife, and fixed in position with a little royal icing.

Personally, however, I think that a slightly better result is obtained with this particular design by using royal icing. A No. 01 pipe is again used for the outlines, which are green for the trees, brown for the flower-pots, and scarlet for the Father Christmas. When the outline is dry, the figures are filled in with royal icing, thinned with sufficient white of egg to allow it to flow, and the required colouring added. Those who feel that the creation of a Father Christmas in sugar is beyond them, may like to know that these can be obtained at a cost of about 2s. 3d. each. A finish is given by "seeding" the cake-board with white royal icing, on which the Father Christmas candle-holders are fixed.

The Cherry Blossom Cake

Chinese in conception, this design is carried out in soft shades of palest pink for the blossom, bright green for the leaves, brown for the stalks, and a soft shade of pale green for the background. Each blossom is built up of five individual petals made with a petal forcer, and has a yellow centre. As the whole design only demands nine flowers, the time taken in producing it is not very considerable. The buds, leaves and stalks are piped directly on to the cake.

To copy a design of this kind, the gracefulness of which depends largely on the proportion and arrangement of the spray, a beginner is advised to prick out or pencil in the outline. The character of the cake is such that a heavy finish would spoil the whole effect, but to hide any slight imperfections at the bottom of the cake, a narrow ribbon of icing or a double line of plain piping could be used, but it should be of the same colour as the background and very unobtrusive.

Mickey Mouse Cake

Of certain appeal for children, this cake is also one which is easy to execute, for the outline can be traced or pricked out. The lines are then piped in with a very fine pipe—a No. 0 or No. 00 writing pipe. When the outline is dry, the figures are filled in with royal icing of appropriate colours. The following are particulars of the colour scheme: a background of blush pink, "fern-leaf" brown, obtained by adding a little chocolate colouring to the icing, for the music and the two figures, and bright green for Minnie's skirt and Mickey's breeches. A narrow brown silk ribbon, tied with a small bow, gives a finish to the bottom of the cake.

The Holly Cake

This presents no difficulty to anyone with a steady hand, for its effectiveness depends on the three sets of five parallel lines of narrow piping, which form the main feature. In scarlet and green they look well on an oblong cake. Silver balls, evenly distributed on the top, with greetings and holly leaves, complete the simple design. Three or four scarlet berries—bought ready-made—are used for the holly spray. Similar scarlet berries outline the cake-board, and tiny silver balls mark the bottom of the cake. Red berries can, of course, be made by hand, if time permits, by colouring a little almond paste with scarlet, and then rolling the berries in the hand.

Narcissus Cake

This is not illustrated, owing to lack of space, but it requires little imagination to visualise it, for the flowers are illustrated in the group of decorations. By soaking angelica in warm water, it can be made very pliable and will lend itself to the cutting-out of narcissus leaves and stalks. These elongated leaves were made to grow up the side of the cake, with the single blossoms resting around the top edge. White narcissi with yellow-gold centres and the pale green of angelica make a pleasant picture on a slightly deeper green background or a white one. The advantage of this design is that it can be used by anyone who does not possess a pipe or forcer of any kind.

OUTSIDE HELP WITH CHRISTMAS CATERING

spices, breadcrumbs, and chopped apple. Then add the eggs, ale, sherry, rum and milk. Mix thoroughly, put into buttered basins, and steam or boil for from 6 to 8 hours. When required re-boil and serve.

Do not turn the pudding out until it is ready to send to table. If possible serve it on a previously heated plated or silver dish. Sprinkle the pudding with castor sugar, place on the table and pour rum or brandy over it, allowing some to run round the dish. Light with a match, and baste the pudding with the burning spirit.

M. Hoerman suggests orange sauce or orange butter as alternatives to brandy sauce or brandy butter, both of which are, of course, more traditional.

Orange Sauce.

1½ pts. milk	Zest of 1 small orange
¼ lb. sugar	3 eggs
	1 oz. flour

OUTSIDE HELP WITH CHRISTMAS CATERING

Boil the milk with the zest of the orange. Whisk the sugar and eggs together, then mix in the flour. Pour the boiling milk into this mixture, continue to whisk. Return it to the saucepan and heat slowly, whisking all the time, until it boils. Strain the sauce and serve very hot.

Orange Butter.

Wipe 2 oranges well, and press 6 lumps of sugar on the skins to absorb the essential oil. Then dissolve the lumps of sugar in the juice of the 2 oranges and boil until syrupy. Beat ¼ lb. fresh butter with a spatula till soft, then work in the cooled syrup. If liked, a spoonful of curaçoa can be added.

M. Leoni's Menu

Leoni's little restaurant in Dean Street is famous amongst people who know and appreciate good food and wine. Here are notes on his suggestions for a Christmas dinner:

Canapés Moscovites are neatly cut from brown bread and butter and topped with caviare, smoked salmon, ham, etc.

Petite Marmite Bouchère is best chicken broth, garnished with chicken and diced vegetables.

Truite à la Piémontaise is steamed, skinned, and served with a sauce containing white wine and truffles.

Noisette of Lamb is cooked with *demi-glace* sauce and garnished in any way preferred.

Filet de Dindonneau Delysia. This is the most interesting thing about Leoni's menu—breast of turkey cooked separately from the rest of the bird. It is an ideal method in a household where the children have their Christmas dinner in the middle of the day and there is only a small party to cater for in the evening. Before the turkey is cooked cut the required amount of white meat from the breast and flatten it as you would a veal *escallope*. Make a batter with beaten egg, cream, and a little Parmesan cheese, coat each fillet in this and fry in butter for four or five minutes. When cooked, cover with a thick brown sauce containing plenty of butter and cream, and seasoning to taste. Garnish with asparagus tips and cooked mushrooms.

Zabaglione. Put three yolks of eggs with a little sugar in a strong saucepan, then, using the egg shell as a measure, add three half-shells of brandy, and whisk well together. Place the saucepan in another containing boiling water. Keep the water boiling, and at the same time continue to whisk the yolks of egg and brandy until the mixture thickens. When it is of the right consistency, pour into individual glasses. Those with a long stem look the most attractive.

As *zabaglione* deteriorates if it is not eaten soon after it is prepared, only sufficient ingredients have been given to serve two persons. The quantities can, however, be doubled or quadrupled, as required.

M. Quaglino's Menu

M. Quaglino's menu for the great day rises in a crescendo to his treatment of roast turkey with chestnut stuffing.

Consommé Madrilène au Xérès. This is an ordinary clear soup, with the addition of peeled and diced raw tomatoes and a glass of sherry to every four portions. It can be served hot or cold.

Filet de Sole Maison. Poach the fillets with some chopped shallot, chopped parsley, sliced mushrooms and tomato purée, in a mixture of white wine and good fish stock. When the fillets are cooked reduce the stock, add a little butter, coat the fish with this sauce, and glaze under a red-hot grill or salamander.

Dindonneau Farci aux Marrons. Select a turkey of suitable size. (For a small party one weighing about 8 lb. would be sufficient.) Stuff it at the neck with the following farce. Take 2 lb. chestnuts, make incisions in the skin of each with a knife, and bake for about 10 minutes. Remove the skins. Put them in a saucepan and cook in white stock until tender. Then take them out, leaving them whole, and mix with 2 lb. sausage meat and a little chopped truffle. Stuff the turkey with this mixture and truss and roast the bird in the ordinary way. Two hours should be allowed for a bird weighing about 8 lb.

Pommes Bryon. Bake several large potatoes in their jackets. When cooked, cut them in half, scoop out the potato with a spoon and fry it in butter. Put two teaspoonfuls of olive oil in a round mould about 3 in. deep, put over the gas until it is very hot, then pour off the surplus oil. Place the potato pulp in the mould, add 1 or 2 oz. of butter according to the quantity of potato, and bake in the oven for about half an hour. Remove the mould and press gently to loosen the potato. Turn it out on to a dish and cover with a light creamy sauce. Sprinkle with grated Parmesan and brown lightly under a grill.

Christmas Pudding

¼ lb. breadcrumbs	½ lb. mixed peel
½ lb. flour	1 grated nutmeg
½ lb. moist sugar	½ teaspoonful salt
1 lb. stoned raisins	Milk or beer to mix
1 lb. currants and sultanas	3 eggs
(cleaned)	Rind and juice of 1 lemon
1 lb. suet (chopped)	4 oz. chopped almonds

Prepare all the dry ingredients in the usual way. Put them into a large mixing bowl, mix with the milk or beer and well-beaten eggs. Beat thoroughly to blend all the ingredients. Put into well-buttered basins, which should be filled without pressing the mixture down. Cover with greased paper, then with a floured cloth. Boil for 7 hours. Remove the pudding cloth, and replace with clean ones the next day. Before serving, boil each pudding again for 3 hours.

Brandy Sauce

1 lb. loaf sugar	1 pint water
2 oz. cornflour	2 glasses brandy

Boil the sugar in 3½ gills of water (1 gill equals ¼ pint) for about 10 minutes, removing any scum that rises. Blend the cornflour with the remainder of the cold water. Add it to the sugar and water, stirring meanwhile, and continue to boil for a few minutes. Add the brandy just before the sauce is ready to be served.

Two facts should be remembered when buying brandy: Cognac need not be very old to be good, and all old brandy is not necessarily good. Brandy must be good to start with in order to improve with age. Beware of cobwebby bottles, because brandy ages in the wood and is bottled only when mature. One may judge its age by the symbol on the label. For example, V.O. indicates 15 years' maturity, S.O. ensures that it has been 25 years in the cask, and X.O. means that it has 45 years to its credit.

Orchids on your Budget

1937

by MARJORIE HILLIS

Are You Thrifty or Stingy?

We hope no reader will be offended by being asked to serve as a Case in this chapter, since it is our embarrassed opinion that what really matters is not whether or not your sister-in-law is stingy, but whether or not you occasionally slip into over-economising. If you find that you can give the correct answer of Yes or No, as the case may be, to ten of the questions that follow, you needn't be worried, but if your honest answer is wrong for a larger proportion, our advice is to watch your step

1. Do you take friends whom you don't care about impressing to a cheap restaurant, and smart friends to an expensive one? (Think hard.)

2. At a party, do you talk loudly about ordering a taxi—and then wait to see if any of your friends with cars will offer to take you home?

3. When getting on a train with a friend who has a paper, do you buy a second one?

4. Do you walk instead of taking a taxi when the pavements are wet and you have no galoshes, or when a friend is waiting and you are late for your appointment?

5. Do you keep putting on your old dresses, and saving the new one for a more important occasion?

OF course economising is painful if you persist in applying it in the wrong places. You have to be careful where you pinch, though a lot of people just go ahead regardless. There are economies that nobody can afford unless they're so poor in purse and spirit that they don't care much anyway, and there are forms of thrift that are so expensive that not even a millionaire can pay for them.

First and foremost among these little errors is the extravagance of Letting Yourself Go. The woman who feels that she can't afford to keep herself as young, handsome, and chic as is humanly possible, or that she can do it just as well the week after next when her finances are in better shape (only they may not be) eventually finds that she made a miscalculation that runs into money. The resulting *débâcle* has been known to play havoc with both jobs and husbands, and it is bound to play havoc with her opinion of herself. In fact,

there comes an inevitable day when she just can't stand herself As Is for another moment, and by that time the repairs are pretty expensive.

To make matters even worse for the married ladies, this illuminating hour often comes to them considerably later than it comes to their husbands, with unfortunate results. Lean periods are the times of all times to be as seductive as possible, since it's only normal for a man (or anybody else) to look round for an excuse for his difficulties, and a slovenly wife is as good an excuse as any other, if not a little better than most.

The wives have excuses too, of course, the most threadbare being that they haven't time. Economising keeps them so frightfully busy. But since having plenty of money and all that goes with it also keeps women frightfully busy, and being in circumstances somewhere between the two takes time both ways, this excuse doesn't impress us. All

interesting people are busy anyway, and the intelligent ones are the ones who choose the things that keep them busy most wisely. Keeping yourself up is certainly one of them. And Keeping At It is the cheapest and most satisfactory method.

We have already preached one sermon on the importance of clothes, but we would like to reiterate the moral, with special emphasis on the moments when nobody sees you but the family, or when nobody sees you at all. The kind of woman who gets herself up any-old-how and looks it, when there isn't company, deserves just what she gets, which might be a divorce from her husband or neglect from her friends and relatives. (We can't bring ourselves to talk about the woman who goes to bed, alone or otherwise, but especially otherwise, with her hair in curlers.) And there's no real alibi for not looking at least fresh and trim, whatever your income, what with the crisp little house dresses sold

THINGS YOU CAN'T AFFORD

A heading that includes not only obvious extravagances like sales "bargains" that prove to be white elephants, but also the penny wise, pound foolish type of economy

6. Do you forget to tip the waiter when you haven't got any small change?

7. When you are in a taxi with a lot of women, are you a past-master at the art of fumbling?

8. Do you hang on to old dresses that you don't wear, but think you might have altered some time, instead of sending them to the Salvation Army or some other charity?

9. Do you check your restaurant bill before paying it?

10. Do you wear a nightgown or a slip just once more, even though it's a shade soiled, before putting it into the dirty clothes basket?

11. Do you buy Christmas presents that " will do " for relatives to whom giving is a duty, instead of trying to think of something they would really like?

12. Do you buy second-rate spirits, thinking you can doctor up the taste with the other ingredients in the cocktails?

13. Do you painstakingly untie the string on packages?

14. Do you salve your conscience after the extravagance of buying a hat you didn't need by lunching on tea and a sandwich?

15. Do you forget to pay for telephone calls in other people's houses?

grance, they do not always do the work more efficiently than the less costly varieties—though here you had better check before you choose. (Incidentally, you can get a good makeshift facial by slathering cream on your face after a shampoo and before you get under the dryer, and letting it drip—and this is only one of a dozen tricks the persistent economiser can work out for herself.)

The point is to plan your spending so that you can have the things you really need for good grooming and to plan your time so that you can apply them. A well-groomed woman seldom feels completely licked, and she never looks it. Those low moments come when your hair straggles down in the nape of your neck and your hands look like a washer-woman's.

No salary is so small that the earner can't spend some of it on aids to improve Nature

to-day for a few shillings and all the other bargains.

The beauty problem may present more difficulties, but it is obvious that it can be solved, since the staggering statistics about the sale of cosmetics prove that there is no salary so small that the earner can't spend some of it on these aids to improving on Nature. If you don't do it, too, you are making a sad mistake, unless you are barely out of your teens. The only older women we have ever seen who boasted that they never used any kind of face cream got no contradictions from anybody. Just one look at them proved that they were truthful.

With a little planning and system, such Spartan abstinence is usually unnecessary even when the financial situation is acute. If these periods are prolonged, you can learn to wash your own hair, manicure your own nails, and give yourself a facial, which reduces the time and money spent in beauty shops considerably, but shouldn't eliminate them altogether (unless you're shipwrecked or exploring the African jungle, and even in these emergencies we hope you'd manage a few beauty preparations somehow). Fortunately we all have our good points, which take most of the care of themselves, as well as our bad points, which require constant attention. It is seldom necessary to apply everything from hair-tonic to foot-ease simultaneously, skipping no points between. And such universal needs as tooth-pastes and emollients can be purchased in the less-expensive chemists and in fixed-price stores, as well as in beauty salons. Moreover, while the expensive ones may have a more elegant fra-

1938

WELL IN ADVANCE: Make Christmas puddings and mincemeat and store in a cool, dry place. Favourite Institute recipes for each are given

ONE WEEK BEFORE: Select the turkey and give instructions to the poulterer with regard to trussing and dressing. Provisions, too, should be ordered now, to ensure their delivery well before Christmas Eve

TWO DAYS BEFORE: Check the provisions carefully and make certain that there is enough of everything to last right over the week-end, even with unexpected guests

CHRISTMAS EVE: Make a chestnut stuffing, according to the " Good Housekeeping " recipe, for the crop of the bird, and put any left over into the body. Alternatively, a veal forcemeat may be used

THE TURKEY: Should be got quite ready for the oven on Christmas Eve. Place fat bacon over the breast, and plenty of dripping or butter in the tin for basting the bird

FLAKY OR PUFF PASTRY: Should be prepared and kept in a cold place until required for making sufficient mincepies to last over the entire holiday

SYRUP FOR THE COMPÔTE can also be made before the day of the party. Pour it over the prepared fruit, and serve in one large bowl or dainty individual glasses

BEFORE CHRISTMAS

THE

Beginner's

OUR COOKERY LESSONS

by MARJORIE

AN inexperienced cook might well regard the preparation of her first Christmas dinner with some trepidation, especially if she has to do all the work for it single-handed. In the fourth cookery lesson of our series, therefore, we intend to give detailed instructions, together with a time-table and favourite GOOD HOUSEKEEPING recipes, so that even a beginner may have the triumph of producing a perfectly cooked and served meal, and also sit down with her guests and enjoy the feast to the full.

A golden rule to follow is not to attempt more than the pocket, experience and time will permit. It is therefore most important to plan everything well ahead, and then to work to a definite schedule, using only reliable recipes, and the best ingredients that can be afforded. Choose a menu, such as that we give later, where the dishes are straightforward and there is no need for elaborate accompaniments. It is also a great help to have practised some of the courses beforehand. Finally, the meal should be planned to allow as much preparation as possible to be carried out the day before the party.

For the cocktail or the appetiser we have suggested Iced Tomato Juice, for which a recipe is given, but this could be replaced by any favourite, provided it can be prepared the day before the party and kept in the refrigerator or larder until required.

No fish course need be served if the hostess is without assistance in the kitchen. In any case, it should be a very light dish, and it is inadvisable to attempt to fry fish when so much of the hot plate will have to be used for vegetables and sauces.

Turkey and its accompaniments will in all probability be selected as the main course of the meal, and the bird itself can be stuffed and got quite ready for

Christmas DINNER

BECOME REALLY TOPICAL

BURGOYNE, B.A.

the oven on the eve of the party, so that all the attention it needs on the actual morning is roasting. Bread-crumbs can be made and the cranberry sauce prepared for re-heating the day before they are needed. Brussels sprouts and plain boiled potatoes are probably the simplest vegetables to prepare and cook, and if game chips are needed, the busy cook will be well advised to buy packets of potato crisps, warming them through a few minutes before the meal is served.

The sweet course presents few difficulties; the Christmas pudding requires nothing more than re-heating and dishing up. Whipped cream may be preferred to brandy sauce or butter, and would involve rather less trouble, if time is very precious. Mince pies made the day before can be put into the oven after the heat is turned off and the main course put on to the table, while the alternative sweet for those guests who find Christmas fare somewhat rich could well be a fruit salad, prepared in advance and kept very cold.

The following list of instructions for making each separate item, and the time-table for the main activities in preparing the Christmas feast, should prove a good guide if used in conjunction with the dinner menu given later. The quantities are for a party of six, but a very generous allowance has been made, since we know that the majority of women will like to pack up one complete, hot meal to send out to someone who would otherwise not get a truly Christmas dinner—some lonely or very busy person who might sit down to a fried chop and an orange, for lack of opportunity to provide the traditional good fare of Christmas.

10.0 : Put the turkey in a tin into a hot oven. In case the oven is too small to take the tin, this article gives hints for overcoming the difficulty

10.30 : Place the pudding, covered with a clean, dry cloth, into the upper compartment of a steamer. Water in the bottom must be kept at boiling-point

1938

11.0 : Put all the plates, dishes, and sauce boats to warm in good time, so that the dinner can be served really piping hot

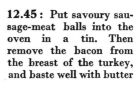

12.0 : Lay the dining-table early. This will avoid a last-minute rush and the risk of forgetting something

12.45 : Put savoury sausage-meat balls into the oven in a tin. Then remove the bacon from the breast of the turkey, and baste well with butter

1.20 : Dish up the turkey, which should be golden-brown. Remove skewers, etc., before sending to table, with savoury sausage balls and potato crisps

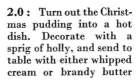

2.0 : Turn out the Christmas pudding into a hot dish. Decorate with a sprig of holly, and send to table with either whipped cream or brandy butter

ON CHRISTMAS DAY

The Beginner's Christmas Dinner

Choosing and Preparing the Turkey

Choose a male bird for roasting (those from Norfolk are deservedly popular) and order it well before Christmas. It should be plump and the breast well covered, with fat on either side by the wings. A turkey weighing from 14 to 16 lbs. should be large enough, as a minimum of half a pound per head dressed weight should be allowed.

If the oven is very small, there are several things you can do. Take exact measurements of the oven and show them to your poulterer, who will truss the bird to fit, if possible. Alternatively, dispense with the roasting-tin, and hang the bird neck downwards from the top grid shelf, or put a shelf in the middle of the oven, cover with several thicknesses of greased paper, and put the bird directly on to this. A tin should be put in the bottom of the oven to catch the drips.

No directions are being given for trussing the bird, as an inexperienced cook will be better advised to let her poulterer do this.

On Christmas Eve wipe the turkey well, stuff the crop with chestnut stuffing, and leave quite ready for baking, i.e. with rashers of fat bacon completely covering the breast.

Cooking the Turkey

Calculate the time required for cooking the bird by allowing 15 minutes for each pound. On Christmas Day put the turkey into a hot oven (400° F.). After 15 minutes baste well with dripping from the roasting-tin, and cut down the heat to 340° F. Butter should be used for basting if this can be afforded. Baste frequently during the cooking period, and half an hour before dishing up, remove the bacon from the breast and baste with butter, dredge with flour and leave in the oven to froth the bird and make it golden brown.

Chestnut Stuffing

2 lb. chestnuts	1 lb. sausage-meat
½ lb. butter	Seasoning
6 oz. breadcrumbs	Stock or milk

Wash the chestnuts, make a slit on the rounded side of each with a knife. Put into a saucepan of cold water and bring to the boil. Boil 3 minutes. Remove a few at a time from the hot water, take off both skins with the point of a knife, and cover the shelled nuts with milk or stock. Simmer slowly until all the liquid has been absorbed, then mash or rub the chestnuts through a sieve. Add the rest of the ingredients and season to taste. Stuff well into the breast of the bird, putting any remaining stuffing into the lower end.

Gravy

Wash giblets and stew in water with an onion and some salt to make stock. Strain. When the turkey is taken out of the roasting-tin, pour off the fat and add a little seasoning to the particles remaining in the tin. Add stock from the giblets and boil up.

Cranberry Sauce

1 lb. cranberries	1 gill water
	4 oz. brown sugar

Stew cranberries in water until tender, rub through hair sieve. Add the sugar. On Christmas Day warm through and serve.

Sausage-meat Balls

½ lb. sausage-meat	2 oz. butter
1 egg	1 teaspoonful chopped onion
3 oz. breadcrumbs	3 mashed cooked potatoes
	Seasoning

Mash together sausage meat, onion and potatoes, the crumbs and butter. Season to taste. Bind with the egg, and shape into small balls. These should be prepared on Christmas Eve, and baked in the oven for 30 minutes in a tin placed under the turkey.

Bread Sauce

3 oz. breadcrumbs	2 cloves
½ pint milk	A few peppercorns
1 medium-sized onion	¾ oz. butter
Salt	

Peel the onion and stick the cloves into it. Place in a saucepan with the milk, salt and peppercorns. Bring almost to boiling point and allow to remain at this temperature for about 20 minutes in order to extract the flavour from the onion. Remove the peppercorns and add the butter and breadcrumbs. Mix well and allow to cook very slowly for about 15 minutes, then remove the onion. It is customary to remove the onion before adding the breadcrumbs, but a better flavour is obtained by allowing the flavour of the onion to penetrate the breadcrumbs by cooking them together.

Brussels Sprouts

2½ lb. sprouts

Choose sprouts with firm, close heads, and the outer leaves as little discoloured as possible. Cut off any discoloured leaves, and wash in plenty of cold salted water. Cook in fast-boiling water with the lid off for 20 minutes. Drain well by shaking in a colander. Put into a hot dish and sprinkle with a little salt and pepper.

Boiled Potatoes

2½ lb. floury potatoes

Peel the potatoes and make as even in size as possible, cutting the big ones when necessary. Put into plenty of cold salted water, bring to the boil with the lid off. Boil about 20 minutes, test with a skewer. Then drain, meanwhile putting the pan to dry over the flame for a few seconds, Replace the potatoes, stand at edge of stove for a few seconds to dry off. Turn into a hot dish.

Brandy Butter

4 oz. fresh butter	4 oz. castor sugar
1 tablespoonful brandy	Nutmeg

Beat the butter to a cream with a wooden spoon, add the sugar gradually and flavour with brandy or rum. The stiffly beaten white of an egg may also be stirred into the mixture if desired. Set the sauce in a cool place until wanted and serve piled up in a fancy dish, sprinkled with nutmeg.

Tomato-juice Cocktail

4 tablespoonfuls of fresh tomato juice	½ tablespoonful of Worcester sauce
Salt to taste	1–1½ tablespoonfuls of sugar
1 tablespoonful of lemon juice	

Press some tomatoes through a fine sieve—one of hair or stainless steel mesh is recommended—to obtain the juice, which must be quite clear of pips. Add the Worcester sauce, lemon juice, sugar and salt. Mix together thoroughly, and chill. Serve in cocktail glasses.

Baked Fillets of Sole

6 fillets of sole	3 oz. picked shrimps or
½ oz. butter	prawns
½ oz. flour	1 gill milk
Seasoning	1 egg yolk
Lemon juice	

Melt the butter in a pan, add the flour and cook for one minute. Add the milk and cook until very thick. Cool, add the egg, seasonings and shrimps or prawns. Spread a little of the mixture on each fillet and roll up. Place on a shallow fire-proof dish, sprinkle with a little lemon juice and bake in a moderate oven for 20 minutes.

A Guide to
CARVING THE TURKEY

1938

1 Are you one of those husbands who are perturbed at the prospect of carving the turkey, because of possible criticisms or unhappy results ? If so, these six sketches and advice will give you courage to tackle the job and leave the family amazed at your authoritative manipulation of the carving knife and fork. First of all, remember that nothing will ruin tempers and turkeys more than a blunt knife, so give your knife a razor-keen edge

2 Before the Day, extract three promises from your wife : to use a dish far bigger than the bird, to go light on garnishes—they only impede progress—to give you plenty of elbow room at the table, or better still, arrange the table so that the carving is done at a buffet. When the turkey comes to table, place its neck to your left and its tail to your right. Commencing on the side facing you, cut the leg from the body—this is best done by pressing the leg outward with a knife, and bending it back gently with the left hand

3 As soon as the leg has been separated from the turkey put it on the side of the dish, or better still on a separate plate or dish. Then, as the drawing shows, hold the end of the leg with the left hand, and with the knife in the right, sever the thigh bone from the drumstick, not at the point of the joint, but over the round bone, then slice portions of the meat from both thigh and drumstick

4 Coming back to the turkey, it is now time to attend to the wing. Insert the fork firmly across the breast bone, as shown above, and with the point of the knife cut down sharply where the wing joins the body. If you have found the right spot, off comes the wing immediately

5 The breast now awaits your attention. With the fork still inserted across the breast bone in such a position that the breast meat is not damaged with fork holes, commence slicing the meat. This can be done in one of two ways—by slicing down from the breast-bone or upwards from the joint where the wing was removed, cutting parallel to the breast bone. Don't forget to slice thinly, otherwise there may not be enough " breast meat " to go round

6 After all the meat has been re-moved from one side of the bird, no difficulty will be experienced in reaching the stuffing. On to each plate put a serving of white and dark meat, a little stuffing, and a sausage. With the serving, the carver's task is completed, unless the guests are of such a number that the dish must be turned, and carving commenced on the other side

Now find a Turkey to practise on !

1939

PRESENTS
at Christmas

Whatever the circumstances of our life may be, nothing can diminish the joy of receiving gifts

PERSONALLY, I am all in favour of Christmas presents. It seems to me that they are very nearly the only remaining signs that we dwellers in the modern nightmare love one another. And when I see the thought, the anxious care, and the charming kindness that take shape in the contents of a parcel, and the delight which those contents so generously give to the recipient, I believe the world is a good place and life is worth living.

These remarks may cause you to imagine me a greedy man, counting his own parcels with a miser's eye. Nothing could be more unjust. We are, as they say, three in family; and if you visited our home on Christmas morning before we were awake (if you wished to find us still asleep you would have to come very early), you would see one colossal pile of packages, one smaller but still respectable and appetising pile, and one little almost nothing lurking under the lee of these mightier assemblies. The last, the almost nothing, is mine.

Long after I have inspected the book, the ties, the box of Carlsbad plums which our cat, Daisy Buchanan, has bought with her pocket money (her gifts are always edible), the electric torch, the slippers, and the beautiful new pipe which is the best of all, I can hear the fevered tearing of brown paper, the impatient cries, the gasps, the ecstatic squeals of the youngest member of the family, and am called upon to admire the dazzling bounty of friends and well-wishers to both my companions.

I admire with rapture. Never have I seen toys and doilies, brooches, dolls, scarves, glass boxes, " knitwear " (horrible term!), china bowls, frocks, bed-jackets, and marrons glacés as beautiful as they are nowadays. Never have friends been kinder or more generous. Never before have I realised as I do in these hate-filled times how the receipt of presents in flowing plenty can lift the heart and make it like a floating balloon of rapture. Indeed, indeed, I am in favour of them all.

Or no, not quite all. There are exceptions, few but vital.

1939

I do not mean only the white elephants—Uncle James's great oil painting of a St. Bernard dog and a mackerel, or Aunt Matilda's monumental sideboard with the knobs and bow-legs—though these, obviously, present a problem. No, I mean smaller misconceptions and maladjustments of taste. Drums and trumpets, for example; concertinas, mouth-organs, and handbells. Anything that makes a noise quellable only by maddened protest. Anything that does not fit the people to whom it is given or the house in which it is expected to find a resting-place. All are exceptions.

There are others. I have a complete detestation of those implements of practical joking, the matches that will not strike, the sugar spoons that gather no sugar, the cigars that explode in the face. Certain ornaments and china dishes send one's spirits hurtling into darkness. There are indestructible monsters in wrought iron and hard wood and imitation brass, and worthless new books which have been sold cheap because at their original price nobody would have them, and mouldy Victorian relics suited only to small museums in country towns far from civilisation. There are bedspreads guaranteed to produce nightmares, and majolica bowls which need large, lofty rooms for their proper oblivion. There are —but I need not continue. What I hate, other men love. Already, in the moment of enumeration, my mood of Christmas benevolence is exasperated, and I cease to feel on behalf of the receivers that gratitude which the

donors, opulently giving, deserve. Nor do I wish to speak ill of any givers whatsoever. Far from it. Taken by and large, they are the salt of the earth.

They are the salt of the earth; and far too many of them suffer from those fixed ideas to which dwellers in our age seem especially prone. They pick up some notion, and ride it to death. Dogmatically, they say: "A present should always (or never) be useful." "A present should always be something the recipient would not dream of buying for himself (or herself)." "A present should be blue, for happiness." Or "A present should last for ever, as a perpetual reminder of my love."

They are quite wrong, of course. Presents are things you give to individuals, to please them. There is much more to be said, in some cases, for the gift of a piece of cheese than for a deplorable footstool that breaks one's shins or a modern painting that destroys one's eyesight. There is a whole encyclopædia to be written in favour of the dress which a diffident young woman would have liked to buy if she had felt sure—as the giver is sure— that it would suit her, or if she had been able to spend two pounds more than her outside limit. The one quality that makes a present perfect is its appropriateness. On a desert island a piece of string might be worth more than a pearl necklace in Mayfair.

Here is a true story of a post-Christmas jumble sale. Once upon a time a white elephant or *objet d'art* which had arrived in a stocking was sent, soon *(continued overleaf)*

by Frank Swinnerton

Illustrations by Clixby Watson

1939

Presents at Christmas

after the holiday, to a sale organised for a very good object. At the pre-view, which was witnessed only by members of the Committee, this *objet* was coveted by one sharp-eyed lady. It aroused the most intense silent longing in the breast of another, who could hardly eat her dinner for thinking of it. Both ladies rose early on the morning of the sale, and hurried to secure their prize. Both found, to their horror, that, early as they were, it had disappeared. Sold. One of them, well able to afford such articles in their pristine state, was disappointed; the other, whose treasures are few and far between, was heartbroken. But within two days the heartbroken lady had a birthday. Among her presents was the *objet d'art*.

You realise what had happened. A third member of the Committee, realising her friend's fierce longing, and well knowing the dreadful resolve of the rival, had risen with the sun, had leapt into the saleroom on her way to work, had snaffled the *objet* before anybody else had a chance to do so, and now gave the purest joy to her friend by offering it as a gift. A lesson for us all. The giver had taken the trouble—either by thought-reading or by subtly-hidden determination at a moment of confidence—to discover what the recipient most wished to have. Her action thereafter was swift and sure. Her reward was a gratitude which I am positive will be lifelong.

The trouble she took is rarely to be endured, and if endured at all it is almost invariably endured by a woman. Men are neither easy to choose for nor ready to take trouble in choosing. In the first place they value their own secrecy, and would prefer to buy their own ugly ties and slippers according to some ridiculous ritual. In the second place they generally leave present-getting until the last minute, dash into a shop, mumble to the saleswoman, a stranger, receive her sophisticated advice, and with preoccupied frowns which are meant to show superiority to this sort of thing, carry off something which, in the event, their wives and female relations probably hate. Thanks, uttered with a sigh, are tepid. The object remains unworn or unused. The giver, who in his bones knows that he is at fault, feels remorsefully sulky; the receiver wishes she had had the money he has wasted; another speck is added to the store of arguments which show that marriage as an institution is a failure.

Not all men, of course, make such mistakes. The wise ones, who have a considerable feminine streak in them, take stealthy stock of possible needs. Months before Christmas they begin to jot down mental notes. They say: "She hasn't got this." "By Jove, that colour suits her better than any other." "Ah, Mrs. Swigg's bracelet made her go all goosey." "I wonder how she'd——" And so on. *When they are alone, they look in shop-windows.* They conquer an aversion from going into these same shops and, in their own eyes, looking idiots. Having entered the shops, they listen to advice but rarely take it. And they stay in the shops as long as they think necessary, and if they do not see just what they want they come out without buying anything and go to another shop. I cannot tell you what moral courage a man needs in order to do that.

He needs courage, and he needs time; but time is always available. Most of the people who say they are "too busy for this sort of thing" are nothing of the kind. They merely prefer to spend their time in some other way, in chatting at the club, in telling somebody else how busy they are, in watching a football match, in playing

billiards. I do not object. I only say that the men who *at Christmas* give their whole attention to the job of choosing presents properly have happy homes.

Shall I tell you why this is? It is not that they love their female relations more deeply than the dashers and darters; it is that they use their imagination to put themselves in the place of each receiver of a present. "If I were Joan or Edith, what —what above everything else—should I like at this moment to be given?" The answer comes like lightning: "Certainly not a tobacco jar, or a card of darning wool, or a pair of blankets." If there is another answer, a more constructive answer, you will hardly expect me to know what it is, seeing that Joan and Edith are strangers to me.

And yet, why should I not make one suggestion? Why should I not say that the art of buying a Christmas present for any woman begins with recognition of the fact that she needs *something of her very own*? It is not enough to replenish the silver canteen, or to hint at marvels with a workbasket, or chance a scarf that would suit every other woman in Chertsey. It is unquestionably an affront to her love to give one's wife only a cookery book or an alarm clock or a new set of aluminium saucepans. By all means give such things during the year, when the mood is upon you: they can be invaluable. Give them, even at Christmas, if they are desired. But never alone. And do not expect that, if they are found resting solitary in the Christmas stocking, they will produce an ecstasy of gratitude. They will not do so.

Yet men give their wives such things as blankets as Christmas presents. I have known it done within my own experience. And if you ask them why they behave so ridiculously they will—to a man—answer that they are at a loss to know what to give, because their wives *seem to have everything they want.* Everything they want! The poor saps! If they could loosen the tact-tied tongues of their wives they would hear of something to their advantage. It would terrify them. It would shrivel them. It might make them better men. It would almost certainly lead to their spending Christmas Day upon all fours in abject shame.

The truth is that no woman has ever or could ever have had everything she wants. It is not to be expected. Though all our lives are to some extent run in grooves— because far too many of us feel safer in grooves—we do not accept those grooves as a final best. Men in the past have been able to escape from them more easily than women, and they are still more fortunate than the majority of women in their opportunities for escape from routine. A woman has to live a great deal in her thoughts. And so, although she may not know what, among possessions, she has not got but must have, and may remain speechless under dreary questioning, her wishes are without limit.

She wants, in particular, a sign that her husband still thinks of her as the girl he married. She wants something that will make Christmas Day different from every other day in the year. She wants something that she has never thought of, or something that she believes her husband has not known she has thought of. If, unpacking her parcels on Christmas morning, she finds it in his gift, memory of that radiant moment of surprised delight will carry her happily onward almost to the following Christmas. Or at any rate until her birthday.

But birthday presents, however agreeable, are not the same as Christmas presents. One is newly born every Christmas morning. I think the postmen themselves know this; for it seems to me that they never show any of the sullen indignation at overwork that most of us feel when we have an unwelcome task to perform. I have a notion that parcels must make themselves light; that they radiate the goodwill of their senders; and that some foretaste of the pleasure they are to give causes the men who bring them to our doors to disregard the labour and relish only the sweetness of the season of giving.

They must need some such kindness at Christmastide. Otherwise the burden of gifts for others would bow them down, and they might throw away a few parcels out of hatred of the lucky ones. It would never do if our heaps were to be mysteriously small, and we were to discover that the postman had decided that we had received quite enough presents for one year. He, after all, has no reindeer to whirl him through the air. He has a van or a motorcycle; but in last year's snow hilly districts were not to be reached by motor, and in our village postmen had to walk miles under abnormal loads through severe drifts.

I wonder what the effect of presents would have been upon Scrooge. I wonder whether I am right in believing that more presents are given nowadays than ever before, because friends are more closely drawn together than they have ever been. I feel sure that gratitude is more keenly felt now; and that is because, with so much that is horrifying and frightening in the over-mechanised world of 1939, we are so thankful to realise that old friendships have lost none of their power. We like our friends the better because of the contrast between their stable affection and the harsh enmity which is expressed abroad towards all that we hold of value. We wish to show our liking. It is shown to us in equal measure. And the showing is done in this gracious offering of pretty and delightful things at Christmas.

How beautiful they are! What ingenuity has gone to their making, and what care to their choice! As we buy, we notice that those who sell them to us are eager for our pleasure. They are not merely polite; they are ready to enter into any difficulty that may suggest itself, and to assist in its solution. And this again is a part of the happiness bred by the season. Would that the spirit of Christmas could by some miracle be prolonged, so that it filled the earth for twelve months in every year! It would then be almost superfluous to give presents, for the millennium would have arrived. So we must be thankful that for those of us who are lucky the millennium does arrive, once a year, on Christmas morning. Then, contemplating our parcels in the darkling dawn, we renew a hope that there is still enough kindness left in the world to go round among those we most love. If, for the younger among us, such pieties are of less interest than the immediate problem of the contents of that whopping great package over in the corner, this is natural. And as the Admirable Crichton says in the play, "whatever is natural is right."

At any rate, I hope you have bought all your presents for this Christmas. And I hope you will have as many as will please you. I expect to have my customary small pile. I expect, without envy, to see two monstrous masses towering, like Mont Blanc and the Matterhorn, above it. And I expect to stagger down the garden, after breakfast on Christmas morning, with the wreckage of all the packing. But I hope nobody has sent a drum or a trumpet or an unstrikable match or a monstrous *objet d'art*; because really any one of these things will spoil my Christmas Day and make me think less well of the institution of Christmas presents than I do at this moment.

1939

1940

by A. G. MACDONELL

I THINK the Christmas which stands out most vividly in my memory is that of 1921. I was in Poland working for the Society of Friends on the reconstruction of the devastated areas. I had been looking forward to a gay Christmas in Warsaw, but at the last moment there was an urgent call for a member of the Mission to visit Rowno, on the frontier between Poland and Russia, to arrange for the purchase of some horses from the Polish Army. I was detailed for the job. On the very same morning my interpreter fell ill and I had to go alone, armed with one single Polish phrase, " *Gdye baraki*," meaning " Where are the barracks ? "

At midnight on December 24th, I arrived in Rowno. It was pitch dark and snowing hard. The station was miles from anywhere. I shouldered my pack and set out vaguely. I met a passer-by and politely put my phrase to him. He gasped and bolted. I met another man. I put my question. He screamed and bolted. Six times I asked and six men vanished, howling, into the darkness. " This is Christmas Day," I reflected bitterly, " the season of peace towards men of goodwill," and then I slipped on a sheet of ice and sat down in a puddle of slush.

The night was blacker than ever. The snow was heavier, the wind colder, and I was soaked to the skin from the puddle. My pack also was saturated and now weighed a ton, and the black forests closed in on either side of the road. Not a light was visible. At last I heard footsteps coming towards me, and I prepared to put my question for a seventh time. But the seventh man must have been one of the six returning, for he bolted with a yell before I opened my mouth. For hours I wandered, until at last the Christmas dawn began to glimmer through the birch-woods and the silver snow turned to pale gold.

In the distance, a huge pile of buildings could only be the barracks, and I reached them at last.

The whole trouble was my Polish accent. Whereas " *Gdye baraki* " means " Where are the barracks ? " " *Gdye buraki* " means " Where is the beetroot ? " I have never touched beetroot since Christmas Day 1921 !

Christmas Days

Appropriately enough, Charles contributes one of these six

by HOWARD SPRING

I REMEMBER few Christmases of my childhood clearly. But one stands out, rounded and complete. It was the Christmas following my father's death ; and I was twelve years old : a long, long time ago, when there were no motor-cars, and winter roads were mud.

Christmas Day that year was on a Sunday, and on the Saturday I was to begin what I fondly hoped would be a permanent job as week-end assistant to a Cardiff baker. I was ordered to present myself at the bakehouse at seven in the morning. I was there before seven, and a very nice place the bakehouse seemed to me, arrived as I was out of the raw, damp street.

Mr. Forest, the baker, arrived at seven, harnessed a smart-looking pony to his van, and we loaded up ; I climbed alongside him on the driver's seat, and off we went through the pale, damp morning.

Mr. Forest was well wrapped up, and I not so well, but it seemed good to be perched up there behind a neat pony, spanking through the morning. We went through street after street, splashing up the mud, calling at house after house. Wherever we called, I had to jump down, run to the door, take the order, and then carry in the stuff from the van. Always, before driving on, Mr. Forest would flourish his whip and

shout : " Compliments of the season ! A Merry Christmas ! "

He didn't speak to me all the morning, except in the way of business. At midday we pulled up at his own door, and I was feeling pretty hungry and very cold. When Mrs. Forest opened the door I could see down the passage into the kitchen, where a bright fire was burning and food was on the table.

Mr. Forest didn't wish his wife the compliments of the season. He looked at her more crustily than one of his loaves. She looked at me and said : " Is the boy coming in to dinner ? "

" The boy is going to look after the horse," *(continued overleaf)*

by DOROTHY WHIPPLE

I WAS rash when I said to the family whose bosom I had but recently left : " You must come to *us* for Christmas Day." They

demurred. They probably thought they would fare better at home. Until my marriage I couldn't even boil a potato, and I hadn't had much chance to learn since. I had been domineered over by an elderly housekeeper, and when she left a week or so before Christmas, it was a matter for relief, not concern, to me ! I blithely engaged a maid even younger and more ignorant than myself.

It was fun buying the turkey, the tree, holly, tinsel, crackers, but on Christmas Eve serious preparations began. I went into the kitchen to make peppermint creams. I found them very difficult to handle, but at last I got them off my fingers and on to the surface of a large, flat dish. Then I began on the strawberry whip. I had seen this made at home. In whipping it rose to treble its size and was piled in a pale pink *(continued overleaf)*

We Remember

Dickens' great-granddaughter sharply contrasted anecdotes

1940

by LORD DUNSANY

MEMORIES of Christmas in Ireland in the early years of this century are for a sportsman, and for many others besides sportsmen, memories of a golden age. In County Meath these memories are dominated by a great personality, John Watson, who was Master of the Meath foxhounds and hunted something like a thousand square miles of country in five days a week. The jovial faces of Perg Maynard, Master of the Ward Stag-hounds, and his huntsman Jim Brindley, shine very clearly, too, through those mists of time. A run for an hour with the Meath was perhaps to see

more country than many a traveller sees in a hundred miles, for you have to see every yard of it if you are to get across it and keep it all in sight of the hindmost hound; and not only see it, but understand it. There is not space here to say what a fox-hunt is, but it is always a vivid thing among the memories of all who have ridden to hounds.

Sometimes frost came about Christmas-time, and that brought other interests. That brought the woodcock into the coverts for certain, and might bring the gray lags into the country too, or the white-fronted geese. Sitting for geese in the twilight is one way of learning of the beauty of the world, which seldom looks lovelier or feels more enchanted than it does at this hour, and when one is near water, the sky's beauty is multiplied.

Christmas Eve was the day on which I always used to give presents to a few men who had always been accustomed to receive them on that day, and their fathers and grandfathers before them. I remember I used to have to be in early then, because they had to get back to their homes, and Ireland is a queer place, and always was, and if you were not home on Christmas Eve before the very first of the darkness should come down on the roads, there was no knowing what spirits might not overtake you.

by ETHEL SMYTH

THE Three-Decker was a hideous deal erection which, in the 'seventies, dominated the centre aisle of Frimley Church. In the lowest box sat the Clerk, Mr. Western. He would never see ninety again, and people used to come from all parts to hear his famous long, quavering "Ä-m-ä-ä-ä-n," A narrow staircase led past the second box, from whence the service was delivered, up to the top floor, which was sacred to the sermon.

Our uncle, Dr. Charles Brodrick Scott, Headmaster of Westminster, invariably spent Christmas with us; it was an institution that he should preach the Christmas sermon, and we were assured that the pronouncements of this terrifically learned divine were considered great intellectual treats by the congregation.

One year a very cheery London

lady, who had taken a house in Frimley for the winter, informed my mother that their dear old friend, the Rev. Lord B., would be spending Christmas *(continued overleaf)*

by MONICA DICKENS

UNTIL last year, all my Christmases had been alike. Vast family reunions; unexciting, but profoundly appreciated, because they were unchanging in a kaleidoscopic world. The War, however, landed me with the prospect of spending Christmas in hospital, more homesick than a first-term schoolboy.

I was nursing on a men's ward, and from the break of Christmas Day, when I staggered on duty, shivering in the bleak six-o'clock air, I realised that these men were going to have a good time, and it gradually dawned on me that I was, too. (I learned afterwards that hospital Christmases are famous.)

Routine and red tape, the pulse and breath of hospital life, went on the wind. Doctors and surgeons, unapproachable gods in everyday life, appeared at lunch-time in a slap-and-tickle mood, wearing chefs' caps and frilly aprons, and carved the turkeys on each ward as skilfully as they were used to carving patients. In the afternoon, relations and friends swarmed in with presents, and everybody sat about on the beds (one of the greatest hospital crimes) and watched the concert. I didn't think it so funny, because I had to sing in it, but several patients threatened to split their stitches. Those that had limbs in plaster casts had decorated them with caricatures and festive or saucy mottoes, and when I settled one old boy to sleep that night, he was still wearing a rakish sprig of holly in the bandage round the skull that he had cracked in a street fight!

We had our own dinner party in the evening, and Boxing Day was marked by a feeling of death on rising, and a spate of out-patients suffering from over-eating, alcoholic poisoning and black eyes. We took down the decorations. Our ward had been dressed up as a battlefield, with the iron lung disguised as a tank, and rifles pointing at you over the sterilisers. Even this, however, did not make it seem credible that outside the self-contained little world of hospital there was a war on. Or was it *because* of the War that everyone last year strove, as they will this year, to forget everything but that it was Christmas, and to celebrate to their utmost the birthday of Him whose cause we are fighting?

1940

Christmas Days We Remember

by HOWARD SPRING

said Mr. Forest briefly. Then he took two halfpenny buns from the van. "Here's your dinner," he said. I ate the buns as I held the horse's bridle.

When Mr. Forest came out again we drove back to the bakery, refilled the van, and went through the afternoon as we had gone through the morning. Fog was coming on; lights appeared in windows; briefly glimpsed interiors were festive: holly, mistletoe, alluring fires. The housewives did not dally. They took their loaves and disappeared each towards her own speck of comfort, and to each Mr. Forest shouted heartily: "Compliments of the season! A merry Christmas!" He sounded the best-hearted man in the world.

The afternoon drew on into a deplorable evening. The fog deepened; the whole world became fantastic. The lamps were lit in front of the van. Once or twice Mr. Forest stopped at some Red Lion or Blue Goose and came out wiping his moustache, and shouting behind him at the swinging door: "Compliments of the season! A merry Christmas!"

At about seven o'clock we were back at the bakehouse. I was by now very cold indeed and very, very hungry. But I had to stay till the pony was unharnessed and put into his warm stall.

Then Mr. Forest counted two sixpences into my hand and said: "Don't be late next Saturday."

Even now he had not addressed a word to me all day, except, as I say, in the way of business. But as I disappeared through the fog his voice came bounding after me: "Compliments of the season!" he shouted. "A merry Christmas!"

by DOROTHY WHIPPLE

mountain on a dish when finished. But somehow my strawberry whip wouldn't behave properly. I whipped and whipped; by ten o'clock I was still whipping. My husband kept coming to see how I was getting on. But he laughed, and I was getting too cold and tired to laugh—to encourage the cream to whip, I had let the fire out. My husband went to bed, and I felt bitter that he should leave me to this endless whipping. Ah, marriage, I thought, I suppose this is what one must expect. At midnight I gave up. Instead of being able to pile the sweet on a dish, I had to pour it into a mould. It fell in as if it too were dead tired.

Next morning, I found the peppermint creams had all run together. They had spread, but the strawberry whip had shrunk still farther into itself and lay in a sullen slab. "Well, everything else must be right," I said desperately to the little maid. But in spite of us, when, tired and hot, we at last served dinner, the turkey oozed pink on carving and the roast potatoes were burnt. "This turkey's not done," said my father, who always speaks his mind. I blushed. "These potatoes are very *over*-done," he said. I drew myself up at the head of my table: "Henry likes them like that." "Yes, I do," said my husband, helping himself with magnificent loyalty to the blackest. Ah, marriage, I thought with a glow.

We sat round the fire in our paper caps. We ate the peppermint creams with forks. For the moment it was nice to rest, with the beloved voices talking and laughing round me. The bread-sauce was wrong somehow, I thought; I must ask Mother. . . . That's all I remember. When I woke, horrified, my guests were on the point of departure, having had a very pleasant, if subdued, evening while I slept. I think I may safely say that the following year I did better; perhaps because I could hardly do worse!

by ETHEL SMYTH

with them, and had most kindly proposed to preach the Christmas sermon. "But you know," said my mother, "Dr. Brodrick Scott of Westminster always spends Christmas with *us*, and it is a sort of institution here that *he* preaches on Christmas morning!"

"Oh, that'll be all right," said the other, who was generous and popular in the parish. "I'll explain everything to the rector . . . you know Lord B. is quite a celebrated performer . . . and he does get so dreadfully bored in the country!"

My mother declared afterwards that she had said "something about it" to her brother-in-law; but given his masterful character, perhaps she thought it better to let the clerical gentlemen settle matters among themselves. Anyhow all went well to start with; my uncle ensconced himself behind the altar rails and read the lessons, while his richly-bearded companion-piece declaimed the rest of the service with infinite dignity from the centre division of the three-decker. He had a fine, sonorous voice and was really a very good-looking old thing; in fact, ill-natured people *did* say . . . but that has nothing to do with my story.

Presently, when the service was drawing to a close, my uncle was seen to open the wicket of the altar rails and, at his usual rushing pace, make for the three-decker, while the peer began opening the door of his box. My uncle dashed up the staircase; breathless we all witnessed the collision and endeavoured to catch the words of what was evidently a heated colloquy; and as each reverend gentleman carried his sermon tightly rolled up like a truncheon, the suggestion of Punch and Judy was irresistible. Suddenly, from the lowest of the three compartments, a loud, agitated, more than ever prolonged "A—mä—än" rent the air. . . .

I forget who won the day, but feel sure it must have been my uncle; our square pew was shaken to its foundation by the suppressed laughter of my mother—a sight which inflamed my father's fury at such a scene occurring in his parish church to an almost ungovernable pitch.

Cross-questioned later on, Mr. Western, still much agitated, said he didn't rightly know nothin' about it, but guessing there was a mistake somewhere, he thought it only right to try and put a stop to it by saying "A—mä—än."

TESTS AS USUAL

1940

GOOD LUCK to your Christmas cookery, housewives. May the sirens be kind to you and let you get on with it ! Be sure of *this*, anyway, that we at McDougall's have done all we can to give you the very best results, just as in peace-time.

Our Self-Raising Flour is still milled from the very finest wheats obtainable, and the raising ingredients added with the same scientific exactness. Another reassuring fact is that we continue to give *actual cooking tests* to every batch of flour that leaves the mills. So, now as always, McDougall's back up your efforts to be truly economical. Every bag or tin of McDougall's that you buy is as thoroughly dependable as the last one. Successes every time with McDougall's !

Recipe for Wartime Christmas Pudding

(SUGARLESS)

½ lb. McDougall's Self-Raising Flour

¼ teaspoonful salt · 1 teaspoonful mixed spice · ½ teaspoonful cinnamon

¼ teaspoonful grated nutmeg · ½ lb. breadcrumbs

½ lb. shredded suet · ½ lb. currants · ½ lb. sultanas

¼ lb. mixed peel (chopped) · 6 oz. chopped dates · 1 large cooking apple

1 large carrot · 6 oz. syrup, treacle or honey · 4 eggs

1½ gills milk (1 gill = ¼ pt.) · ½ gill cooking brandy (optional)

Prepare the fruit and grate the apple and carrot on a suet grater. Sieve the flour, salt and spices into a basin, add the suet, breadcrumbs and fruit, etc., mix well. Make a well in the middle, add the beaten eggs, syrup, milk and brandy. Beat very thoroughly. Put the mixture into greased basins, filling them to the top. Cover with greased greaseproof paper, then with a greased pudding cloth. Steam steadily for 5 hours.

When the puddings are cold, remove the cloths and paper, cover with clean paper and cloths and store in a cool, dry place.

To serve the pudding : Put on fresh greased paper and cloth and steam for 3-4 hours. Turn out on to a hot dish, put a sprig of holly in the centre. Hand Custard or Brandy Sauce.

We also have a recipe for an EGGLESS *Christmas Pudding. Write to Miss Janet Johnston for a* FREE *copy.*

GO TO IT !

McDougall's

the self-raising flour that gives sure results

A McDougall's Wartime Recipe Service has been organized by Miss Janet Johnston—McDougall's Cookery Expert, who will welcome any queries you may have on cookery problems. Don't hesitate to write to her at the address in the coupon.

1941

The Second CHRISTMAS

YESTERDAY I lost the amber bracelet. I could not believe it had gone. Ever since you gave it to me I have worn it every day.

Do you remember when we bought it, Geoff, the first Christmas of the war? You'd been called up about two months before, but you managed to get leave. It was the first time I'd seen you in uniform, and I was proud. But I was frightened, too, as if we both stood on the edge of a dark and unknown sea and didn't know how high or fast the tide would rise.

As soon as you knew about your leave you wrote to me to ask mother to let me spend the two days before Christmas with you in town. "Then we can be on our own," you wrote, "and still be back with the family for the 25th. Tell her you'll stay at Anne's."

We were engaged, but mother wasn't too keen. She'd got that bee in her bonnet about me being young. But in the end she gave way. You came and fetched me, and mother said as she saw us off:

"Take care of her, Geoff. You're both very young, you know, even if you are engaged."

And I remember thinking, I wonder why she calls us young? In war it is the old who are young. They cannot protect us any more: it is we who protect them.

Then, going up in the train, you said practically the same thing. You said: "It's funny how parents still think us young, isn't it? They don't think

we're too young to go and fight and get killed, but they think we're too young to be married."

I said "Yes," and tried to explain that we'd always be young to them when it came to marrying or being in love, because that was the biggest thing in their lives. They've forgotten everything else. They've even forgotten what it means to be in love, the ache and the sweetness. They only remember it like a danger sign on a long road.

Then you said: "Do you think we're too young to get married, Kit?"

I said, "No," and couldn't think what else to say, because I suddenly knew what was behind our trip to town, and why you had planned it so carefully. You put your hand in your pocket and gave me a piece of paper, and when I opened it I saw it was a special licence.

You said: "I didn't get it without thinking, Kit. It's no good upsetting your mother again. You remember the scene we had last time? It spoiled things a bit, didn't it? But why should we wait, Kit? We love each other."

For a second I thought, No, we mustn't. But then you kissed me and we were laughing and everything seemed a madly exciting adventure. We got a taxi and went to Anne's house. You ran up the stairs, shouting:

"Hi! Are there any marriage witnesses about?"

Anne came out to meet us, and behind her was Bill. It was the first time I'd seen Bill, and I thought how nice it was to see my greatest friend with yours. Bill was grinning, but Anne looked a little serious. She said to me when we were alone: "Kit, are you sure about this?"

I knew then I hadn't been sure until that moment, but when I realised that if I faltered now we shouldn't get married, I couldn't bear it. I couldn't bear the thought of your going away, overseas, without our belonging. I said, "Yes, I'm sure. It's only I'm a bit worried about mother. She may feel hurt."

Anne said, "She'll feel hurt anyhow." She looked away from me and added: "I wish I'd done what you are doing, Kit, ten years ago. But I didn't, and he went abroad and we lost touch. Yet I know my mother thought she was doing right."

I could only nod. I felt so sorry. Ten years ago! It was the first time I'd realised she was so much older than me. Geoff! Do you think she and Bill like each other? I do. Perhaps she'll be happy yet. I remember thinking so then, all in a flash, because in another second Anne was laughing and we were back with you and Bill, and in a few hours we were married.

You'd thought of everything, hadn't

1941

By Margaret Pulsford

" I could only say 'Darling, oh! darling' But I'll say more when I see you, I promise. . . . In a way I'm glad I had to wait until Christmas to find you "

Illustration by Andrew Johnson

"Let's keep that faith all through the years, not just remember it at Christmas. Wherever we are, however far apart, let's remember and keep faith, faith in the world and faith in each other." I knew you meant by faith in the world, faith in God.

On Christmas Eve we got up late and went out into the country. Do you remember how high and clear the sky was? We sat down on a bank for a little while and the birds came and looked at us, and you told me how the thrush builds her nest in such dark places that the baby birds are born with a phosphorescent patch in their throats, so that the mother knows she's popping down the food in the right place.

And I said: "I'm glad there'll be electric light in our nursery," and blushed, which made you laugh.

Then the honeymoon was over, just two nights and one day. And we went home. I put the wedding-ring in my handbag. We'd decided we'd keep our marriage secret until your next leave. I don't know quite why, except that love is secret, isn't it? But I wore the bracelet.

It was fun nobody knowing we were married, although I did feel guilty, and I think you did, too. Perhaps not telling anyone proves that mother was right and we are very young, after all. But I did love that secret feeling of belonging to you, specially when you said: "Darling, I've arranged about your allowance. You must have some money put by in case anything happens." And I knew you meant in case I had a baby, and I wanted to tell you that I hoped I would. But I was shy again, and all I could do was to put

you?—even to borrowing Bill's cottage for those two nights and that one lovely day. But you'd forgotten one thing— the ring! You yelled out: "Hold everything! No ring, no bride."

We raced out to choose one. In the shop you said: "You won't be able to wear that, so I must get you something else that you can wear, always." And we decided on a bracelet. At first the man showed us beautiful things. We both knew they were miles too expensive, but we played up. I tried on a jade and diamond bracelet, so wide it would have done for a belt. He said it was a bargain at two hundred pounds, and we both laughed. We'd have furnished a flat on less than that!

Then I tried on the amber bracelet, such a little frail bracelet, but it fitted my wrist. The man said: "That belonged to a Mexican dancer once," and we both laughed again. You said to me silently over his shoulder: "Sales talk," but I laughed because I was thinking, fancy me wearing anything belonging to a Mexican dancer, and I had a glimpse of flying skirts and dark hair and gold ear-rings. But the brace-

let suited me and I liked it at once. There was something warm about it. So we bought it, and you made the man pack it up in a little box. I wondered why.

But in the evening, when we were alone in Bill's cottage and the fire you'd lit with the logs was burning, you took it out of the box and fastened it on my wrist and kissed the clasp. The bracelet was featherlight, yet I could feel it on my arm like a charmed circle, and the warmth of your fingers and your lips stayed so long.

You said: "A happy Christmas, darling, my darling wife."

We had supper in front of the fire— sausages, sardines and champagne. What an awful mixture! Then afterwards we could hear people singing in the little church, "Glad tidings of great joy I bring to you and all mankind."

And you said, suddenly solemn: "Kit, this is the greatest festival of faith on earth." I looked at you, not quite understanding, and you said:

1941

my arms around you and lean against your heart.

Then two days after Christmas your leave was up, and we all went and saw you off. You kissed me last of all. "Good-bye, my sweet," you said. "Don't worry. Everything will be all right. Remember what we said about faith."

I needed the faith, because I didn't hear from you after you got to France. But I got the allowance through, and it's all piled up in the bank, waiting to be spent. Sometimes I nearly burst with wanting to talk about you to mother and to tell her we were married, but every time I stopped. It seemed that if I did I would be turning my back on that faith in you. Silly, wasn't it? Then the report came through that you were missing. I can't tell you what that did to me. I seemed hollowed out inside, as if I didn't belong to myself any more but was off on some journey looking and looking for you.

It was on that day, of course, they found out we were married, because I'm your "next of kin," darling, that had to be informed. Your next of kin, and I don't know where you are.

But the parents were sweet. Mother said: "I'm glad that you got married. We old people are apt to get silly about the young. You've had something that nothing can take away from you whatever happens. I can't think why I thought you'd be better off if I stopped you from knowing it."

Then the weeks rolled on like thick, billowy clouds, and the months piled up on the weeks, and I realised that even your own mother had begun to lose hope. Mother kept saying: "Try and be cheerful, darling, try and hope." And now, when I manage to smile and appear normal, she thinks that the time is healing the wounds since I'm young. How little she knows —how little anybody knows! Hope— of course I hope. Even if I didn't want to in my brain, I could not help it. Hope forces into bloom in my heart, like a flower struggling up out of the earth. I've heard tales of men helped by the French to cross the country and get into Spain, and I've repeated them and repeated them. Someone told me there was a Scot who couldn't speak a word of French and had such a brogue that nobody could understand his English either. But when I tell your mother or mine, I can see nothing but pain in their eyes.

Then yesterday I lost the bracelet. When I realised it had gone I was out in the woods—you know the ones, where the big oak trees are and the woodpecker has his nest. I was taking Jinny for her evening walk, and suddenly I looked down at my wrist and the bracelet was gone. Jinny was hunting rabbits in the bracken. I called her, and together we went back over every inch of the ground. But it was not there. It was getting dark when I reached the road again. I asked people if they had seen it, but they only looked surprised and said "No."

And all the time I was looking for it I felt I was also looking for you. Ever since you were reported missing I have searched for you in my mind, but when I looked for the bracelet I searched for you with my body. It seemed that at any moment I'd come across you and you'd say: "I'm here. We've kept faith."

The funny thing is that although the bracelet had gone I could still feel the weight of it around my wrist, and the warmth of your fingers and your lips when you fastened it there returned.

PROOF of LOVE

" When first we loved you brought me roses,

Crimson each on slender stem ;

Chocolates, books—and then, dear lover,

A circlet set with sparkling gem.

The years have passed, and still you love me,

Though no longer roses red

Are the proof of your affection.

But—my morning tea in bed ! "

W. M. C.

My dear love, where are you? What happened to you at Dunkirk? The war has swamped over us, covering us with one crisis after another, and Dunkirk has grown hazy to many of us. I remember being on Victoria Station one day that summer, and people suddenly began to cheer. A man said: "It's some of the men back from Dunkirk." I ran across the platform, and there they were, coming through the barrier, limping, dirty, tired, and smiling. I thought, perhaps Geoff's among them, and I watched. They went past in twos and some of them saluted and smiled at me. But you were not there.

Then one Sunday I was in the garden, and people began clustering on the tow-path. Some of the little boats from Dunkirk were coming down the river. They looked such little boats, bunched together and led by tugs, dozens of them, scarred and frail, and I thought, perhaps he tried to get into one of those.

It seems so long ago since you went away, yet you, yourself, have never left me. I keep thinking of every moment we ever spent together, from the day I met you because I fell off the bus and you picked me up and before I knew what was happening we were having tea together. Then we discovered our parents knew each other, and that you were the son who had been in Johannesburg for five years.

When I went home, I said to mother, "I want to ask a man to tea." She said: "Who is it, dear?" And I said: "He picked me up when I fell off a bus. He's so nice, mother."

She looked rather severe and said: "Really, darling, are you sure he's all right?" And I said: "Yes, *I* fell off the bus, he didn't," and we both laughed, because she knew I understood what she meant by "all right."

Then you came with your mother and it was a huge joke.

Darling, I began writing this last night, and here's good news for you. As soon as it was light this morning I took Jinny and went back into the woods again. I felt that perhaps I should find the bracelet, and I did! It was caught up on some brambles. I remember now I'd jerked my arm free from them. Dear heart, it was like finding you. I put it on and kissed the clasp.

Now it's Christmas Eve again, the second Christmas since we were married. It's so mild that I've been writing to you with the window open. If I look out I can just see the roof of the house where the evacuee children have been living for months now. They're singing a carol—yes, the same one we heard on the first morning of our married life. . . . "Glad tidings of great joy I bring to you and all mankind."

I can hear you saying again, "Wherever we are, however far apart we are, let's keep faith all the years around." I'm holding on to faith with both hands, darling. But it's hard sometimes, like now, when I've written about us. You always used to say our story would make a book, but, you see, it doesn't. It only makes a very little story, and I cannot even write the ending.

Darling, it's hours since I wrote the last word on this sheet of paper. It's late, and the curtains are drawn. I've been sitting here absolutely still, not wanting to move. The room is like an island of silence, but downstairs I can hear mother moving about, and I can hear *your* mother's voice, too, dear. I've asked them not to come up to me, just to leave me alone. You see, I'm only just beginning to believe that it was your voice I heard this afternoon coming over the telephone.

"I'm back again," you said. "In time for a second Christmas honeymoon. It's been a long trip, and I never want to walk again. I've worn my boots out across France and across Spain, but I'm here and I love you."

I could only say, "Darling, oh! darling." But I'll say more when I see you, I promise. But now I want to thank God for bringing you back, and for the courage and the faith in the French people who saved you. I know now that without faith there's nothing. In a way I'm glad I've had to wait until Christmas to find you again. I have kept faith all the time, haven't I?—and I can add it, unbroken, to the world's greatest festival of hope and believing that is starting to-day.

1942

*O*ur compliments and thanks to you all. For it is thanks very largely to you for so loyally and so helpfully working with us that at this, the fourth Christmas at war, the nation's health is on a sound footing. But though "good living" must now be taken in the sense of healthy living, instead of luxury living, and we all must go carefully with fuel, we can still make Christmas fare hearty, appetising and tempting to look at. Here, with our very best wishes, are some ideas which may help you:

✳ Christmas Day Pudding

Rub 3 oz. cooking fat into 3 tablespoonfuls self-raising flour until like fine crumbs. Mix in 1½ breakfastcupfuls stale breadcrumbs, ½ lb. prunes (soaked 24 hours, stoned,chopped) or any other dried fruit such as sultanas, 3 oz. sugar, 1 teaspoonful mixed spice, ½ teaspoonful grated nutmeg. Then chop 1 large apple finely, grate 1 large raw carrot and 1 large raw potato; add to dry ingredients. Stir in a tablespoonful lemon substitute. Mix 1 teaspoonful bicarbonate of soda in 3 tablespoonfuls warm milk and stir thoroughly into pudding mixture. Put into one large or two small well-greased basins, cover with margarine papers and steam for 2½ hours. This can be prepared overnight and cooked on Christmas Day.

✳ Emergency Cream

Bring ½ pint water to blood heat, melt 1 tablespoonful unsalted margarine in it. Sprinkle 3 heaped tablespoonfuls household milk powder into this, beat well, then whisk thoroughly. Add 1 teaspoonful sugar and ¼ teaspoonful vanilla. Leave to get very cold.

✳ Christmas Fruit Pies

This mixture is a good alternative to mincemeat.

Warm 1 tablespoonful marmalade (or jam, but this is not so spicy) in small saucepan over tiny heat. Add ¼ lb. prunes (soaked 24 hours, stoned, chopped) or other dried fruit, 1 tablespoonful sugar, 1 teacupful stale cake crumbs, or half cake, half breadcrumbs, ½ teaspoonful mixed spice. Stir together until crumbs are quite moist. Remove from heat, add 1 large chopped apple; also some chopped nuts if you have any. Make up into small pies, or large open flans. The mixture keeps several days in a cool place.

✳ Stuffed Mutton *With apple or bread sauce, this is as delicious as any turkey!*

1 leg of mutton, or loin of mutton (half a leg does, but is more difficult to stuff). Bone with a sharp carving knife and small kitchen knife, or get your butcher to do it. Spread the meat flat, stuff one end with your favourite savoury stuffing, one end with sausage meat, the two meeting in the centre. Fold meat over, reforming into shape, sew with sacking-needle and stout thread, place sewn side down in baking dish, spread liberally with dripping. Put halved potatoes, peeled or in jackets, in the baking dish. Allow about 40-50 minutes before joint is done.

ISSUED BY THE MINISTRY OF FOOD (S50)

* Don't waste elsewhere the fuel you save at home.

1942

By Christine Palmer

AND AGAIN— POTATOES

Don't forget—every time you use potatoes in place of bread you're helping to save British lives. "Potato Variety" —fourteen stimulating suggestions for varying the menu—send 1d. stamp to Good Housekeeping Institute, 28–30 Grosvenor Gardens, London, S.W.1.

Potato Cake with Onions

1½ lb. potatoes	1 oz. dripping
2 large onions or leeks	1 oz. grated cheese
Seasoning	

Cut the onions into thin slices and cook them slightly in the dripping until they are a golden-brown. Bake the potatoes in their jackets, then remove their skins and beat them up well with a fork. Mix the onions with the mashed potatoes; season well and put into a greased, flat earthenware dish. Sprinkle with the grated cheese and brown in a hot oven.

Scotch Potato Scones

2 lb. potatoes	½ oz. margarine
2 oz. flour	Salt

Choose large potatoes of the mealy variety. Cook and mash them thoroughly, add the margarine and salt and sprinkle in a little flour, the remainder being used for flouring the board and rolling pin. Roll the potatoes out to about ⅛ in. thickness, cut into circles the size of a dinner plate and cook on a girdle or very thick iron frying-pan until lightly brown. Cut into four and serve hot, buttered and rolled like a pancake.

Hampton Pie

½ lb. cooked sausages	1 dessertspoonful chopped parsley
½ gill stock	
1 tablespoonful made mustard	2 tablespoonfuls tomato ketchup
1 onion, chopped and fried	Mashed potatoes to cover

Slice the cooked sausages and mix with the parsley, ketchup, mustard and stock. Arrange the sausage mixture and fried onion rings in layers in a pie-dish. Cover with mashed potatoes and bake in a hot oven.

Potato and Leek Hot-pot

12 leeks	1½ lb. potatoes
1 oz. margarine	Pepper and salt
Little mace	Water

Well wash the leeks, cut off the stalks and remove the outer skins. Melt the margarine, without allowing it to get very hot, and steam the leeks in it, using a very slow heat: after 5 to 10 minutes add the sliced potatoes and continue to cook for another 5 minutes. Add sufficient water to half cover the vegetables, add pepper, salt and a very little mace, and let it simmer until the vegetables are tender—40–50 minutes. You must cook this over a very slow heat, or the mixture boils dry. When the vegetables are tender, remove the leeks, keep them in a casserole, and mash the potatoes. If there is too much moisture in the pan after removing the leeks, take the lid off the pan and boil until it is reduced. Add to the leeks and serve in a casserole. (6–8 portions.)

Potato and Cheese Galantine

6 medium-boiled potatoes	2 tablespoonfuls white sauce
½ teaspoonful made mustard	
3 oz. grated cheese	1 tablespoonful tomato sauce
Pepper and salt	

Boil the potatoes, mash while still hot, and add the rest of the ingredients. Turn on to a floured board and shape into a roll. Bake slowly, covered with greased paper, for about 30 to 40 minutes. Serve on a hot dish and pour tomato sauce around it.

Winter Salad

1 lb. cooked potatoes	1 tablespoonful shredded raw beetroot
1 teaspoonful chopped parsley	1 tablespoonful shredded carrots
1 tablespoonful chopped onion or leek	2 eating apples
1 tablespoonful chopped celery	2 tablespoonfuls salad dressing
2 tablespoonfuls shredded raw cabbage	1 tablespoonful grated cheese
Pepper and salt	

While the potatoes are still warm add the parsley and onion, then the rest of the vegetables and the apples, and finally mix with the salad dressing. Sprinkle with cheese, pepper and salt.

Good Housekeeping

DECEMBER

Vol. XLII   No. 5

Cover Design by Clixby Watson

1942

Fiction and Verse

Special Articles

Service Features

Miniature Features

" *Good Housekeeping* " *Editorial Offices, Good Housekeeping Institute, Good Housekeeping Centre, and Good Housekeeping School of Cookery : 28–30 Grosvenor Gardens, London, S.W.1.*

MRS. SMITH doesn't mention medals when she writes to her soldier husband. She has no medals to mention. Housewives don't get visible decorations for bravery : their medals are worn very quietly, in their own immediate circle, in a few people's hearts.

But Second Lieutenant Smith, serving somewhere in the desert, wears his wife's colours proudly. He knows the job she is doing. Not all the details of it, of course—he just thinks of it as " carrying on." He doesn't remember that her domestic help has gone long since and that the daily helps who oblige grow less obliging every day. He doesn't know that shopping could take a good half of every week now, if she let it : but that she doesn't, because cooking, cleaning, looking after the children, gardening and tending the chickens all have to share her time, too. He hasn't heard much about her Civil Defence duties, her knitting, her regular salvage hunts and the mathematics war-time housekeeping entails.

Mathematics ? That subaltern in the desert would smile if he could see his wife in the evenings now. Busy with pencil and paper working out the points, figuring out her fuel target, adding up her last winter's coal bills. . . . Brave Mrs. Smith, who " always hated figures." She really does deserve a medal for that.

Fortitude—valour—gallantry. Fine words when they are used to describe fine deeds : but they apply equally well to every British housewife to-day. There's a special fortitude about keeping the home fires burning on a minimum of fuel, and gallantry is extra gallant when it has to be practised from seven to ten every day.

GOOD HOUSEKEEPING humbly offers Mrs. Smith its compliments and would like to give her all the medals there are. Meanwhile, if the Institute can help her in any possible way—with facts or figures or advice or tested recipes—GOOD HOUSEKEEPING will be only too glad.

1942

By C. Henry Warren

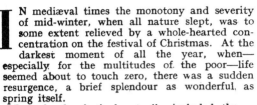

IN mediæval times the monotony and severity of mid-winter, when all nature slept, was to some extent relieved by a whole-hearted concentration on the festival of Christmas. At the darkest moment of all the year, when—especially for the multitudes of the poor—life seemed about to touch zero, there was a sudden resurgence, a brief splendour as wonderful, as spring itself.

Indeed, the festival actually included the idea of a second, mystical spring. The faithful folk believed that with the first breath of the Holy Babe earth budded anew. The hazel bushes near the crib dripped with pollen-dusty catkins; the hosts of birds returned to the icy land they had forsaken, and sang as if it were May; and out of the iron ground the wild flowers burst in strange profusion.

All this, and much more, the unquestioning hearts of the mediæval peasants found it easy to accept, and so the rigours of mid-winter were made more bearable. For them the flight of imagination was unhindered by any doubt. So strong was it, in fact, that even to-day, all these centuries later, some hints of that mystical Spring of the Nativity still linger here and there in country tales and superstitions, in the names of flowers, and in the legends of birds and animals.

Do you know why, for instance, the wood of the ash tree burns so easily even when it is green? Because long ago, in ancient Bethlehem, when Mary asked Joseph to light a fire and fetch water to wash her new-born Babe, it was the ash tree that in some mysterious way communicated to Joseph its wish to serve the Lord. "And ever since that time it has retained its gaseous power; and when the sap of all other trees of the wood prevents their kindling, the ash will not refuse the ministry of its consolation to benighted traveller or homeless wanderer, for the more freshly it is cut, the more sprightly will be its flame."

And do you know why, in some parts of the country, you will still hear a certain wild flower, that trails among the grasses, called Our Lady's Bedstraw? It is because that lowly flower wove itself into a halo which presently took the prophetic form of a crown of thorns; and ever since that time its golden hue reflects the glory that emanated from the Divine Child.

And again: the Christmas Rose, braving the bitter winds of December, do you know the legend of that? When the shepherds tramped into Bethlehem, guided by a star, they brought with them gifts, one a snow-white lamb, another a pair of doves, and yet another honey and late autumn fruits. But there was a poor shepherd girl with them who had no gift to offer; and as she saw the shepherds kneeling at Mary's feet, she wept for her lack.

"Why do you weep?" asked a voice.

She looked up and saw it was the Archangel Gabriel.

"Because I have nothing to give the dear Jesus," she replied.

And thereupon the Archangel touched the barren ground with his staff; and wherever he touched it there sprang up those lovely, waxen flowers that ever since have gladdened our darkest days of mid-winter.

Such was the kind of legends accepted in simple faith by the Mediævals, and who shall say how sweet was the consolation they provided? To-day we profess to be in need of no such consolation. It is our boast that we prefer to look things in the face, see life as it really is, and so forth. Well, except for the boasting, there is nothing wrong with such an attitude. Perhaps it was time that we went in for a little austerity. Anyway, the bare tree in mid-winter has a beauty entirely comparable with its leafy summer counterpart, and a newly ploughed field i December, bare as the bac! of your hand, is　e seeing eye every

Illustration by C. F. Tunnicliffe

1942

bit as pleasing as acres of ripening wheat in August.

And so, rather than indulge our nostalgia for the vanished nightingales, we pay more attention than usual to those faithful birds that still remain with us to cheer our chilly landscape. And nobody can say that in this respect we are poor.

Here, at the edge of the wood, for instance, where the plough lies heeled over on the headland, idle now till the weather breaks, a charm of goldfinches has just darted away from the thistle bed. As they flew up, the frosty sunlight picked out the bright bars on their wings, like gold dust put on with a painter's brush. And now the robin and wren, "God Almighty's cock and hen," for a moment seem to have the woodside all to themselves. Pugnacious, perky little birds, both of them! Perhaps that is why the cottager is so fond of them that on no account will he harm them; not because of the holy rhymes and tender legends that still cling to their names, but because they brighten our English winter with their pluck and beauty, and because he sees in them something of his own enforced hardihood. He likes the way the robin comes close up to his spade when he is digging.

As for the wren, why, its very tail is a permanent exclamation mark apostrophising life. And when it suddenly pauses in its grub-hunting, mounting a twig to sing, its song is so loud and piercing you wonder that so tiny a body can sustain so great a noise. To hear the wren braving the cold with such an explosive burst of song is a wonder indeed. But then have we even the ghost of an idea of the strength and tenacity of birds? We are proud of our ingenuity that can invent engines to fling an aeroplane around the world in a matter of hours; but when all is said, what is this in comparison with the power of the corn-kernel heart of a bird that crosses the ocean?

And if it is miracle you want, take a look at those starlings that are "hosting" just now in the corner of the wood. They seem like things possessed. Closer than locusts they sit on the boughs of the trees, thousands upon thousands of them, blackening the twigs, each giving out a squeaky cry like two pieces of wet glass being rubbed together. They come in from all quarters, in brigades. There is never a moment's cessation in that enormous din; and then, sharp as the crack of a gun, it stops—you can almost *hear* the silence—and as one they leave the trees, wheeling through the sky with a precision that has no counterpart in the best-drilled actions of men. The rush of wings is pertecostal.

Yes, if you so prefer, there is poetry enough in the facts. Mid-winter for us to-day isn't the grim business it was for our mediæval forbears, and so perhaps it is true that we don't so much need the consolations of fancy. And yet . . .

As I went down the lane this morning, I noticed a small boy perched precariously in a holly tree. He wanted one particular twig, thick with berries; but it was hard to reach. I gave him a shoulder to stand on and a stick to hook the coveted sprig, asking him what he was going to do with it.

"Stick it in the Christmas pudding," he answered. "Mum says it ain't worth calling a pudding this year; but still, we must have berries to stick in it, else it wouldn't be Christmas."

It seems that the consolations of fancy are an urgent necessity for children, anyway. And, round about Christmas, isn't there still a bit of the child in every one of us?

1944

Party— PICK-UP TREATMENTS

By Susan Drake

Half an Hour for Beauty. If you've been clever enough to fit in hair-do, facial and manicure, your pick-up treatment won't take long—just half an hour. Off with your clothes and into a dressing-gown, pin up your curls and slip on a hair-net, previously moistened with brilliantine. Cream off your make-up, pat skin food on face and throat and, moving pillow from head to foot of bed, lie down flat with the feet raised, pads of cotton-wool soaked in eye lotion over your closed eyelids.

When ten minutes have flown, get up, and, standing in a few inches of hot water, rub down with alternate sponges of hot and cold water. This is twice as reviving as a full bath, and four times as quick. When you are dry and powdered, apply that hoarded perfume, use your fragrant mouth-wash and slide quickly into your party clothes.

Make-up next. Remember to carry your powder-base down over your throat and try covering the eyelids with it, too. Use a holly-red rouge and lipstick to match the Christmas decorations, outlining your lips and filling in with colour more carefully than usual. Pat on plenty of powder, brush off the surplus, then emphasise eyebrows and lashes, moistening the mascara brush with brilliantine for extra shine. Massage a greaseless cream into your hands, and you're ready!

An Hour for Your Hair. Perhaps you had to skip the appointment with your hairdresser, and your hair is a sight, but the day can still be saved. Retire to your room with setting lotion or a spirity hair tonic, and all the hairpins you can beg, borrow or steal. Saturate the head with the tonic, and give the scalp a quick massage. Having made your parting, divide the hair into a series of small strands—the smaller the strand the tighter the curl—and twist each strand into a firm disc curl, each one facing towards the parting. Should your supply of pins or patience give out, roll the back hair in curlers.

WHEN you're shopping for Christmas, planning Christmas meals and organising Christmas festivities, don't forget the beauty question. Book a hairdressing appointment *now*; for this Christmas, if never before, the hairdressing salons will be thronged. Arrange for a super-manicure and a wizard facial—we'll tell you where to go—and let these be your Christmas presents to yourself. Above all, plan a peaceful hour when you can arrange hair and face, pretty up your hands, and generally conjure up the party spirit. No matter how good your Christmas fare, no matter how successful the presents, if your hair is wispy, your complexion doubtful, and you feel like sitting on your hands, you and your Christmas party will lose sparkle and swing.

to help you with your CHRISTMAS FARE

A Good, Dark Christmas Pudding·

2 oz. plain flour, ½ level teaspoon baking powder, ½ level teaspoon grated nutmeg, ¼ level teaspoon salt, ¼ level teaspoon cinnamon, 1 level teaspoon mixed spice, 2-4 oz. suet or fat, 3 oz. sugar, ½-1 lb. mixed dried fruit, 4 oz. breadcrumbs, 1 oz. marmalade, 2 eggs (fresh or dried), ¼ pint brandy, rum, ale, stout or milk.

Sift flour, baking powder, salt and spice together. Add the sugar, fruit and breadcrumbs and grated suet or melted fat. Mix with the marmalade, eggs and brandy, rum, or other liquid. Mix very thoroughly. Put in a greased basin, 2 pt. size. Cover with greased paper and steam for 4 hours. Remove the paper and cover with a fresh piece and a clean cloth. Store in a cool place. Steam 2 to 3 hours before serving.

A Delicious Stuffing

The flavour of this stuffing goes with any meat, rabbit or poultry. Stuff any suitable meat, or arrange balls round meat not suitable for stuffing. 4 oz. breadcrumbs, 2 oz. chopped onion, 4 oz. chopped celery, 4 tablespoons grated apple, 2 teaspoons sage, 2 teaspoons salt (all level), a little pepper.

Mix all ingredients together. If necessary, moisten with a little milk, reconstituted dried egg or melted fat. If to be served separately, form into balls and bake in greased pan, or round the joint about half an hour before it has finished cooking.

Rich Mock Cream

2 level tablespoons custard powder or cornflour, ½ pint milk, 1 oz. margarine, ½ oz. sugar, flavouring. Blend the custard powder with a little cold milk. Boil the rest of the milk in saucepan. Add it to the custard powder and return to pan. Stir over heat till well cooked. Put aside to cool. Cream margarine and sugar together very well; beat in the thick custard, add flavouring, and continue to beat till creamy. This makes about ½ pint of cream similar in texture to whipped cream.

Christmas Cake with Holly Leaf Icing

THE CAKE : 4 oz. sugar, 4 oz. margarine, 1 tablespoon syrup, 8 oz. flour, 2 level teaspoons baking powder, 1 level teaspoon cinnamon, 1 level teaspoon mixed spice, 2-4 eggs (reconstituted), 1 lb. mixed fruit, ½ teaspoon lemon substitute, pinch of salt, milk to mix (about 1/8 pint).

Cream sugar and margarine, add syrup. Mix flour, baking powder, salt and spices together. Add alternately with the egg to the creamed mixture and beat well. Add fruit and lemon substitute and enough milk to make a fairly soft dough. Line a 7-in. tin with greased paper, put in the mixture, and bake in a moderate oven for two hours.

HOLLY LEAF ICING : For this you will need : 4 oz. soya flour, 2 oz. margarine, 2 oz. sugar, 4 tablespoons water, almond essence to taste, few drops of green and red cookery colouring.

Melt margarine and water together, stir in the sugar, then the essence. Divide about a quarter of the resulting liquid into two cups; a little more in one than the other, and keep warm. Stir about three-quarters of the soya flour into the bulk of the liquid, turn out, knead the paste thoroughly, pat to about 1/8th thick, press on top of cake and neaten edges. Put a drop or two green colouring into cup holding most liquid, stir in flour and treat as for plain paste. Cut into leaf shapes, mark veins with knife, pinch round edges to form " prickles." Put red colouring into other cup, treat as before, form red paste into tiny balls. Arrange leaves and berries on top of cake in wreath shape or sprays, as you fancy.

ISSUED BY THE **MF** MINISTRY OF FOOD

(S135)

1945

Return

Cornflower-blue crêpe in a mixture of half wool and half rayon. The belt is embroidered in fuchsia, famille rose and delphinium-blue beads. Eleven coupons, costing approximately £22 19s. 6d. The belt, which may be bought separately, costs £3. A Brenner Sports model

Peter French blouse (above) in turquoise wool taffeta with long sleeves and a back fastening. Six coupons, costing approximately £6 6s. With it is worn a Lancelot skirt of black wool taffeta with a highish tucked waist at the back and tying with a bow in front. Six coupons, approximately £7 5s.

to Elegance

1945

THE London scene has changed, and once again the long dinner dress reigns supreme, giving to women that luxurious feeling of elegance and charm so long denied them.   If you cannot spare eleven coupons for a dress, choose a long black skirt, which takes only six.   With this you can wear a variety of blouses, long- or short-sleeved, pastel or brilliantly coloured, while a matching black one converts it into the complete dinner dress.

Rima's glamorous full skirt of black georgette has a satin top with a batik design in pink and shades of grey.   Eleven coupons, approximately thirty - seven guineas

Left : Peter French blouse with cape sleeves in a lovely range of pastel colours. Four coupons, approximately £5 10s.   The Lancelot skirt is in wool taffeta, cut with a flare and a detachable peplum. Six coupons, approximately £7 5s.

1946

Christmas in
The Bahnhofstrasse

*Snow covers the Bahnhof-
strasse, one of the most
' atmospheric ' shopping
streets in the world*

YOU can keep Fifth Avenue. You can
pocket the Rue de la Paix. The Bahnhofstrasse, for me, has always been the world's
loveliest, most ' atmospheric ' shopping street.
There it is, broad but not too broad, straight
but not too straight, running from the busy
neon-lit gaiety of the main station down to the
blue lake of Zürich. In winter the snow is
piled and banked under the plane-trees, a
white margin edging the befurred, festive
crowds. In summer the trees are grateful
shade as you wait for your blue-and-white
No. 10 tram. I prefer winter. And of all the
winter months, December, please !

The summer tourist throngs are gone.
(And what a summer it has been !) The winter
sports transients have not begun. (Only a
month or two to the first real post-war season.)
In December the Bahnhofstrasse is itself again.

The latest cars from America, the newest
from England, whip their chains on the frosty
tarmac. The handsome Swiss police wave
huge gauntlets from their operatic white
rostrums. There's that moment I love when
the snow turns to drizzle and the women, instantly unzipping coloured raincoats from
plastic wallets, stage a Cochran quick-change
in waterproof nylon. Imagine it for yourself.
And let me paint in the luscious brilliance of
the shops in the background—the fruit and
hothouse flowers, rainbow umbrellas, perfumes,
jewellery, silk stockings galore, *confiserie, pâ-
tisserie*. We are beginning to know what it is
ourselves to see a little more in the shops,
month by month. Can it be merely contrast
that gives the Bahnhofstrasse its glittering,
sumptuous air ?

Visiting Zürich earlier this year, after the
seven lean years, it took me only three weeks
of ardent, exclamatory window-gazing to

ILLUSTRATED BY TAGE WERNER

regain my sense of proportion. I remember in London the hopeless quest for a christening mug for my godson. In Switzerland, shopping on his behalf, I could judicially discriminate—just as I should—between the due virtues of marzipan Dumbos and celluloid ducks.

Switzerland played fairy godmother to British visitors all summer and, if you were among the lucky ones, perhaps you felt as I did, first happy, then shabby, then slightly annoyed. Pyramids of tins of pineapple and pears, figs and fruit salad create a feverish condition best described as *Matterhorn popeye*. Yet, surprisingly, this will be Switzerland's first Christmas of plenty. Last year they also faced docketed textiles, rationed shoes, a litre of milk, an egg for Monday's child. To be sure, there is a fuel shortage and food rationing is still in force, but it controls distribution rather than quantity.

My Swiss friends comfortably emphasise that the switchover to plenty came *abruptly*. " It took us by surprise," said Freda Jung, one of the four daughters of the eminent psychoanalyst. " The shops suddenly flooded. It will be the same in England. You'll see ! "

So perhaps, with this happy portent, we can Christmas-shop, after all, down the Bahnhof-strasse. Like so many streets, it begins with essentially little shops where you will be startled to find that the V.2 is a brand of cigarettes and the Spitfire a children's firework. But the plate-glass expanses rapidly widen and deepen, and we can stare at the shimmering silks (and even the *(continued overleaf)*

Many exquisite and elegant little tea-rooms have sprung up in Zürich

1946

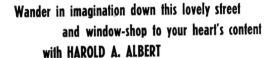

Wander in imagination down this lovely street and window-shop to your heart's content with HAROLD A. ALBERT

Through plate-glass expanses, Christmas shoppers stare at shimmering silks and rolls of chiffon

1946

Christmas in the Bahnhofstrasse

cotton sheets)' without too many twinges of conscience. Here is a bookshop with a lavish display of Warwick Deeping's *Isobel und Jess* and the latest Swiss best-seller, Alexander Frey's *Hotel Aquarium;* and you realise that Somerset Maugham, Priestley and the lovely art books of the Phaidon Press are among Britain's exports. Here is a dining-room ensemble, with everything ' original Englisch ' from the Belfast linen and Sheffield plate to the precious bottle of Worcester sauce, and you perceive that we have indeed been working our passage. It is not irrelevant that I saw the Old Vic principals and a Swiss chorus in *Peter Grimes* at the Zurich State Theatre.

Casually in a side-window is a pastel-blue, feather-weight portable sewing-machine, one of Switzerland's post-war surprises. Here is sheerest lingerie, a night-dress posed against background curtains of real chiffon. Here are unravelling rolls of Wilton carpet, spinning through a Dali tangle of tapes and scissors.

But we'll skip the taste and ingenuity of the window-dressing, shop by shop. One must mention the exquisite and elegant little tea-rooms that have sprung up in Zurich, new as to-morrow, although drawing their warmth and beauty from our own Georgian inspirations, not from the chromium age. We've forgotten what flowers and silk-shaded lamps can do to the heart. Inevitably, you'll reflect, we've seven years' catching-up to do in the fields of décor and design, not to stress the seven lost years in our knowledge of Continental literature and art, music and films.

We may have overtaken Picasso. But I admit that until I visited a vivid exhibition at the Kunsthaus I had never heard of Switzerland's Jean Jacques Lüscher, whose astonishing grasp of colour reinvigorates the kind of pictures I understand. Then there's Curt Oertel's stimulating film, *The Life of a Giant,* a picture that tells the life-story of Michelangelo merely by allowing the camera to dwell on details of architecture, sculpture and paintings, a masterpiece that scorns living actors, though it stirs the emotions. And I think we have surely not heard enough of Robert Hartung, a Swiss impresario who has rallied hundreds of Swiss artists to industry, persuading sculptors to design desks and painters to turn their attention to textiles—or wardrobes.

Similarly there are new social forces at work in Switzerland, triumphant as our National Trust, though they have blazed different trails. Switzerland is the land of private enterprise *par excellence,* just as Sweden is the land of socialistic experiment. And perhaps in our seven years of united effort we have forgotten the viewpoint of sturdy individualism, which the Swiss so aptly champion. Although Lucerne Canton has introduced £20 to £100 sliding-scale old-age pensions, the Swiss have no better-than-Beveridge plan. " You must remember, we have no social insecurity," I was told.

Not for nothing is Boucheron's, the jeweller's, one of the most impressive shops on the Bahnhofstrasse. The solid gold brooches and clasps, though exquisitely wrought, strike an English visitor as strangely barbaric, but the thrifty Swiss have seen the inflation of too many European currencies not to believe in gold as a touchstone. They work hard, these people—shop assistants are only just beginning to discuss a Saturday half-day—and the average Swiss holds more insurance than any other national. There are 3,200,000 savings accounts in a population of 4,000,000; and personal wealth at £625 per head, compared with £420 in the U.S.A., actually ranks as the world's highest.

However, the picture is not entirely material. Every shop in the Bahnhofstrasse carries its placard of a wistful Viennese child and the slogan, 'Zurich helps Vienna.' Every shop contributes its share to relief work, a new idea in township adoption that might be copied nearer home. One of my happiest memories of the Swiss year was a visit to the two hundred ailing London children, who were given a halcyon summer of mountain air and Alpine fun at Adelboden. In solid cash, at six francs a day per child, the cost of this hospitality to the Swiss Red Cross amounted to some £15,000. And the Swiss have given a similar convalescent holiday to thousands of children from France, Holland, Belgium, Poland and elsewhere—75,000 from Czechoslovakia alone.

Again, in a land where women are voteless, I was stirred by the astonishing success of a chain of non-profit restaurants and hotels, the *Alkoholfreies*, launched by a powerful women's movement, the Frauenverein. Just as we tend to think in terms of gardens and landscape, hence the National Trust, the Swiss tend to think in terms of cuisine and setting and have plumped for the *Alkoholfreies*, with their new standards for low-cost food in pleasant surroundings.

While we grumble at catering profits, who hasn't dreamed of an elegant little café in Hyde Park and longed to consign all our dreary tea-shops and cafés to limbo? Well, the Frauenverein has achieved the equivalent, gutting old-fashioned beer-halls, adorning fresh-painted—or fresh-panelled—walls with the works of young artists, laying warm carpets in place of cold lino . . . and they've made sweeping play with lamps, flowers and racks of current magazines. On the Rigiblick, Hampstead of Zurich, a derelict and ghostly hotel was taken over and pepped up with new interior lamps for winter and new terrace parasols for summer, and its non-tip, non-profit policy won a new public. Needless to say, special attention has been paid to staff conditions.

Yet, in Switzerland, as elsewhere, lack of materials has caused a housing shortage. To cope with the situation the city of Zurich has hurriedly built blocks of wooden barracks on its outskirts, where hundreds of young marrieds each enjoy a bedroom and separate kitchen—to give Mrs. Newly Wed a chance to win her pastry-board laurels—and communal dining- and living-quarters are shared. But the barracks are considered a distasteful last resource. Fortunately several thousand new houses have been built in Switzerland this year, and the traditional Christmas trees are found on the roof-tops as well as downstairs at the stove-side.

But there, we have finished our stroll down the Bahnhofstrasse. We have come past the stores and the glittering windows, the banks and insurance offices, to the dignified art shops at the end—and the final climax of deserted parks and gardens and snowy mountains, with the trees in their winter coats of coconut matting and the snow piling on the head of the naked bronze fisher-boy. . . .

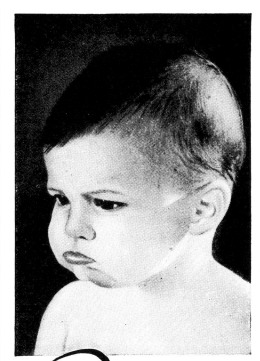

1946

1947

a garland of evergreens

HOW TO START A STORY
Lord Chesterfield

I knew a man who had a story about a gun, which he thought a good one and that he told very well. He tried all means in the world to turn the conversation upon guns ; but, if he failed in his attempt, he started in his chair and said he heard a gun fired ; but when the company assured him they heard no such thing, he answered, " Perhaps then I was mistaken ; but however, since we are talking of guns "—and then told his story, to the great indignation of the company.

Make an enemy of your temperament, and you will make the worst of life.

Arnold Bennett

ANTHONY TROLLOPE TO A YOUNG RELATIVE

Barchester Towers was written before you were born. Of course I forget every word of it! But I don't. There is not a passage in it I do not remember. I always have to pretend to forget when people talk to me about my own old books. It looks modest. But the writer never forgets. And when after thirty years he is told by someone that he has been pathetic, or witty, or even funny, he always feels like lending a five-pound note to that fellow.

MY LITTLE LOVER
Cecile Sauvage

My little lover, here you are
Upon the big bed with mamma.
You frolic and you jig and kick
And play me many a roguish trick,
And as you dribble your morning milk
You knead my neck with hand of silk;
O young joy of the spring-tide earth,
You find me fair and full of mirth ;
We love and we caress each other ;
How merrily do we together
Chuckle to see the dusty light
That dances here for your delight !
I kiss and hold you and surmise
Your happy future from your eyes.
Good-day, wee statue made of joy,
Of naked flesh and blood—my boy !
My little I, my bliss, my elf,
Squeezing your hand I touch myself.
O let me graze your cheek and sip
The bubbles from your pouting lip !
I feel you with a kiss, my son ;
No, do not stir, but lay upon
My breast your tired slumber and
You'll be like my numb sleeping hand,
My hand that seems another's, who,
Though I, is not I—I am you.

BEGGAR'S RHYME

**Christmas is coming, the geese are getting fat,
Please to put a penny in the old man's hat ;
If you haven't got a penny, a ha'penny will do,
If you haven't got a ha'penny, God bless you !**

THE BOOK OF COMMON PRAYER

Wine that maketh glad the heart of man : and oil to make him a cheerful countenance, and bread to strengthen man's heart.

LOVE'S LABOUR'S LOST

Shakespeare

At Christmas I no more desire a rose
Than wish a snow in May's new-fanged
winter ;
But like of each thing that in season grows.

DR. JOHNSON

Boswell: " Sir," said I, " the season of the London fog is upon us. Even as I came here to wait upon you, I bruised myself in suddenly encountering a tree. Cannot I persuade you to make a journey out of the metropolis with me? "

Johnson: " No, Sir, you cannot. If I choose to go, that's another matter. I am sick of this pother about the air of London. It is good enough for me, even if I cannot see the trees through the fog; and for a Scotchman I cannot see what difference it can make, since in his own country he is used to see no trees at all."

IN A DREAR-NIGHTED DECEMBER

John Keats

In a drear-nighted December,
Too happy, happy tree
Thy branches ne'er remember
Their green felicity.

TWELFTH NIGHT

Shakespeare

Contemplation makes a rare turkey-cock
of him :
Now he gets under his advanced plumes!

THE TWELVE DAYS OF CHRISTMAS

On the twelfth day of Christmas, my true
love sent to me
Twelve lords a-leaping, eleven ladies dancing,
Ten pipers piping, nine drummers drumming,
Eight maids a-milking, seven swans a-
swimming,
Six geese a-laying, five gold rings,
Four colly birds, three French hens, two
turtle doves,
And a partridge in a pear tree.

EPIGRAMS FROM OSCAR WILDE

When a man is old enough to do wrong he should be old enough to do right also.

Cheap editions of great books may be delightful, but cheap editions of great men are absolutely detestable.

I can believe anything, provided it is incredible.

Only dull people are brilliant at breakfast.

Women have a much better time than men in this world ; there are more things forbidden to them.

ALEXANDER BROME

Tell me not of a face that's fair,
    Nor lip and cheek that's red,
Nor of the tresses of her hair,
    Nor curls in order laid,
Nor of a rare seraphic voice
    That like an angel sings ;
Though if I were to take my choice
    I would have all these things ;
But if that thou will have me love,
    And it must be a she,
The only argument can move
    Is that she will love me.

The glories of your ladies be
    But metaphors of things,
And but resemble what we see
    Each common object brings.
Roses out-red their lips and cheeks,
    Lilies their whiteness stain ;
What fool is he that shadows seeks
    And may the substance gain?
Then if thou'lt have me love a lass,
    Let it be one that's kind :
Else I'm a servant to the glass
    That's with Canary lined.

1947

Read and enjoy afresh the well-remembered words of other days

1948

books for EVERYBODY

and every mood, recommended by our Book Critic

FOR EVERYBODY

First on the list this year, of course, is Winston Churchill's memoirs, *The Second World War, Vol. I, The Gathering Storm* (Cassell, 25s.). This historic record—if by hook or by crook you can get hold of a copy of it—will gain in interest and value as the years go by, and is unique in its appeal to all classes and types of reader.

Even for those of your friends who seem to have no time or taste for reading, as well as for those of whose subject preferences you are uncertain, and above all for those who love flowers, let me recommend the first volume in a new series published by Messrs. Batsford —*Garden Flowers*, with an introduction and notes on the plates by R. Gathorne-Hardy (6s. 6d.). This little book is adorned with plates by the famous Victorian artist, Mrs. Jane Loudon. They are a delight to the eye, and I would like to wager you will find no contemporary artist who can surpass her in accuracy and grace.

FOR HUSBAND, SON OR DAUGHTER

It is a long time since I have been to school, so that I am not aware how present-day history is taught. But whatever the curriculum may be, I suggest that Mr. John Harvey is a writer whose books should be included in the school library. Let me hasten to explain that *The Plantagenets* (Batsford, 18s.) is not a history book designed for schoolboys, but is a volume so incomparably more fascinating than any of the average and mediocre novels, that it will go far in inculcating a love for historical study. Mr. Harvey is

a sort of male version of Agnes Strickland, and records, as far as is possible, the personal lives of the Plantagenet Kings, with brief mention of their Queens. For the benefit of simple souls uncertain of dynastic intricacies, Plantagenets include the kings from Henry II to Richard III. Mr. Harvey unfolds their story—which is England's too — dramatically and so realistically that there are none of those dry-as-dust patches most of us fear in our historical reading. I must, however, add a postscript to this inadequate review. In his introduction the author has contributed an important note on kingship. His views are not cluttered up with the usual clichés about the malignant autocracy of the Crown. On the contrary, he points to the benefits of monarchy, and asks, " Where have the people so benefited under other forms of government? " This is a subject upon which I should have liked to see Mr. Harvey digress. The book is magnificently illustrated with photographs of our Kings and Queens taken mainly from various cathedrals and abbeys.

FOR THOSE WHO READ IN BED

Mr. Arthur Stanley has already edited a *Bedside Book* and a *Bedside Bible*. Now he has chosen Shakespeare. In his foreword to *The Bedside Shakespeare* (Gollancz, 6s.), he writes, " Among the great body of readers there must be many to whom Shakespeare is little more than a name, and many others to whom he is more, but who sometimes lack the time or the inclination to read throughout even one of the plays." I have no doubt this is true, and if Mr. Stanley awakens genuine

interest and extends the number of those who appreciate our greatest heritage in literature, then his little book will have more than served its purpose.

FOR CATHEDRAL-LOVERS

Winchester Publications Ltd. have inaugurated a new series of lavish quartos upon our cathedrals. The first two volumes are *The Glories of Salisbury Cathedral*, by Jeffrey Truby, and *The Glories of Norwich Cathedral*, by R. H. Mottram (21s. each). For both, the photographs, which are masterly, have been taken by A. W. Kerr. It is a pity the text was not fuller and that the books were not indexed. But, I repeat, they will be treasured by any recipient for their lovely photographs.

FOR FRIENDS ABROAD

From cathedrals we pass to a survey of the complete English countryside. *The English Counties* (Odhams, 12s. 6d.), is excellent value for the money! Miniature essays on each county and profuse illustrations will whet the appetite of all who love England It is an admirable " bird's-eye view." Equally valuable to our friends abroad is *The British Empire*, edited by Hector Bolitho (Batsford, 21s.). It is an immense compilation. I trust to goodness it will not become out of date! You might also like to give *A Book of Praise*, by Harold Burdekin (Dent, 8s. 6d)—a book of pictures, many of the English countryside, taken by a photographer who was killed in 1944. The book is not, however, a very good advertisement for us, as it was indifferently printed abroad.

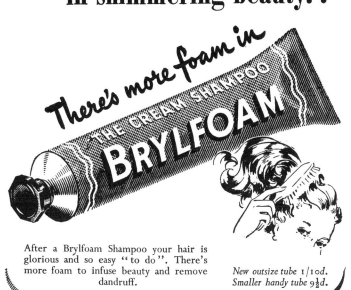
THROUGH OUR SHOP WINDOW

Three of our attractive books for children are illustrated on page 44. *Enid Blyton's Good Morning Book* is a new book for children from six to ten years who waken early eager for something to do till getting-up time. It is printed in clear type, with over thirty delightful stories, nature tales, picture stories, verses and puzzles. *Tales of Green Hedges* contains twenty-four Enid Blyton nature tales. Both books are illustrated, price 7s. 6d. each (7s. 10d. by post).

Good Housekeeping's Book of Fairy Stories contains twelve nursery tales chosen by our readers as their favourites. Older children will enjoy *A Gateway to Poetry*— an anthology arranged under subjects that appeal to children (6s. each, 6s. 4d. by post). An attractive edition of *Treasure Island* will delight the older boys, and two titles only are still available of Malcolm Saville's popular scrapbooks—the *Open Air Scrap-book* and the *Seaside Scrap-book*, price 7s. 6d. each (7s. 10d. by post).

Gifts that will delight children and their parents are the large nursery pictures "Bunnies' Market Day" and "Bunnies' Bedtime" (21 in. by 15½ in.), by Jennifer Rickard. Produced in lovely colours on heavy paper, these pictures will brighten any room where children live and play. They cost 7s. 6d. each (postage and packing 1s. extra, or 16s. for the two).

Books and pictures are obtainable at Good Housekeeping Shopping Centre, 30 Grosvenor Gardens, S.W.1.

1949

1950

The Stuffings and Sauces

These are the recipes you will want for those appetizing extras

Chestnut Stuffing

1 lb. chestnuts	1 oz. butter, melted
About ½ pint stock or milk	A little grated lemon rind
2 oz. ham or bacon	Salt and pepper
3–4 oz. breadcrumbs	Sugar
1 teaspoonful finely chopped parsley	1 egg

Make a slit in both ends of the chestnuts, so that the skin may be removed more easily, and boil them in water for about 10 minutes. Take a few at a time from the water and skin them. Put the shelled nuts into a pan with just enough stock or milk to cover, and simmer gently until tender, then mash the chestnuts or rub through a sieve. Pound with the finely chopped ham or bacon, then add the breadcrumbs, parsley, melted butter, and grated lemon rind; season with salt, pepper and sugar, and bind with the beaten egg.

Use for stuffing turkey, chicken, etc.

Sausage Stuffing

1 oz. dripping	1 teaspoonful chopped parsley
1 large onion	
1 lb. pork sausage-meat	4 tablespoonfuls fresh breadcrumbs
Seasoning	½ teaspoonful mixed herbs

Melt the dripping, chop the onion and mix with the sausage-meat. Lightly sauté the sausage-meat and onion in the dripping for a few minutes to give it a good flavour. Thoroughly mix in the other ingredients, and use as required.

Gooseberry Sauce

1-lb. bottle gooseberries	2 oz. sugar (if bottled in water)
1 oz. butter	Colouring (optional)

Cook the gooseberries and sugar until pulpy. Pass through a sieve and return to the rinsed-out pan. Reheat, and add the butter just before serving. A little colouring may be added, if required.

Bread Sauce

1 medium-sized onion	Salt
2 cloves	A few peppercorns
½ pint milk	½ oz. butter
3 oz. breadcrumbs	

Peel the onion and stick the cloves into it. Place in a saucepan with the milk, salt and peppercorns. Bring almost to boiling-point, and leave in a warm place for about 20 minutes in order to extract the flavour from the onion. Remove the peppercorns and add the butter and breadcrumbs. Mix well, and allow to cook very slowly for about 15 minutes, then remove the onion. (If liked, the onion may be removed before adding the breadcrumbs, but a better flavour is obtained by allowing the flavour of the onion to penetrate the breadcrumbs during cooking.)

Cranberry Sauce

1 tin cranberries	3 oz. sugar
Port wine (optional)	

Put the cranberries into a pan, and simmer gently until reduced to a pulp. Add the sugar, and a little port wine if liked.

Bacon Rolls

Remove the rind from some thinly-sliced streaky bacon, and cut the rashers in two or three lengths, depending on size. Roll up, and spear with a skewer. Cook in the oven or under a slow grill until crisp, turning at intervals to prevent uneven cooking. Allow 10 to 15 minutes in the oven, or 5 to 10 minutes under a slow grill.

Brandy Sauce

½ teaspoonful cornflour	1½ oz. sugar
½ pint milk	1 egg-yolk
2 to 3 tablespoonfuls brandy	

Blend the cornflour with a little of the milk. Boil the remainder of the milk and pour on to the cornflour, then return to the pan and boil for 5 minutes, stirring all the time. Add the sugar, cool slightly, then stir in the egg and brandy. Serve at once.

Hard Sauce or Brandy Butter

2 oz. fresh butter	1 dessertspoonful brandy
2 oz. caster sugar	Nutmeg

Beat the butter to a cream with a wooden spoon, add the sugar gradually, and flavour with brandy or rum. A stiffly-beaten egg-white may also be stirred into the mixture. Set the sauce in a cool place until wanted, and serve piled up in a fancy dish with a sprinkling of nutmeg on the top.

La Duchesse d'Abrantès visits M. le Duc

AN EPISODE BASED ON HISTORICAL FACT

1950

It is Paris in 1810, and Laure, Duchesse d'Abrantès, young, lovely and witty, is a magnetic figure at the Court of the Emperor Napoleon.

Her husband, a General of Napoleon's army in Spain, sends a message begging her to join him.

Her preparations for the adventure — for it is nothing less — are careful and lengthy.

At last she sets out on the long, fatiguing and at times perilous journey.

The roads are rough and hilly, the coach stuffy and uncomfortable. The young Duchesse, usually so vivacious, becomes jaded and fretful.

From time to time she has recourse to her treasured Jean Marie Farina Eau de Cologne, which, as always, quickly relieves her fatigue and restores her spirits.

Arrived at the Duke's headquarters, she steps out of her coach looking, to his delight, as fresh and radiant as if she were taking a walk in the Tuileries.

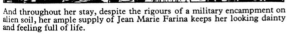

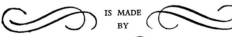

And throughout her stay, despite the rigours of a military encampment on alien soil, her ample supply of Jean Marie Farina keeps her looking dainty and feeling full of life.

Almost 150 years later . . .

Since its initial success at Napoleon's Court in 1806, Jean Marie Farina has held uninterrupted sway as the world's premier Eau de Cologne ; uninterrupted, but not undisputed—for no fewer than 39 lawsuits against imitators have been fought and won by its manufacturers, Roger & Gallet. You cannot be misled if you insist on seeing the name ROGER & GALLET on the label. If you have any difficulty, write to Roger & Gallet (London) Ltd., N.W.2.

JEAN MARIE FARINA
the true Eau de Cologne

IS MADE BY

ROGER & GALLET

Some Royal devotees of Jean Marie Farina

The Emperor NAPOLEON · *The Empress* JOSEPHINE

The Empress MARIE-LOUISE

The Emperor NAPOLEON III · CAROLINE, *Queen of Naples*

LOUISE, *Queen of the Belgians*

LOUIS-PHILIPPE I, *King of France*

ALFONSO XII, *King of Spain*

4/8, 8/3, 15/8, 30/-

1951

Now, take this glass

If you want to, taste all the orange squashes on the market, with or without gin . . . you'll find there's only one that gives you **Schwepperfection** *(that's a secret between Schweppes and ripe golden oranges)*

Schweppes Fruit Squashes

True-to-the-Fruit

Orange.Lemon.Grapefruit.Lime Juice Cordial (3/- per bottle)

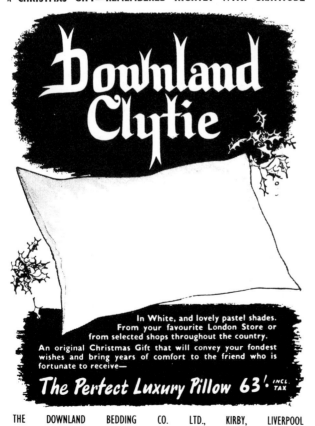

WHEN YOU'RE SERVING cocktails

1951

Remember this rule for cocktail savouries. They should appeal irresistibly to eye and appetite. These are planned to do just that

We do not propose here to give recipes for the cocktails, as these can be readily found in any good cookery book (our own *Good Housekeeping's Cocktails and Canapés* in the 1s. series, for example, or in the chapter on *Hot and Cold Drinks* in the revised edition of *Good Housekeeping's Cookery Book*). We intend instead to concentrate on showing how any cook who has imagination and a neat hand can build up a pleasing and seemingly lavish spread of cocktail snacks from quite simple ingredients. Some of these will have a pastry foundation, others be arranged on slim fingers or cut-outs of toasted or fried bread, or on biscuits, others set rakishly on cocktail sticks, and all intermixed with small dishes of tiny appetizers such as olives, cheese straws, potato crisps, salted almonds, peanuts, tiny silverskin onions and the like. If you are in doubt about quantities, remember that it is usual to allow an average of 4 or 5 small savouries per person.

Let us, for convenience, start with savouries with a pastry foundation, canapés, bouchées, etc. For these you can safely estimate that ½ lb. of cheese or shortbread pastry will be sufficient for about 30 small savouries if you roll it thinly. But with puff pastry, do not count on making more than 24 small bouchée cases from ½ lb.

With Cheese Pastry

Now here is a recipe for a rich cheese pastry which will make a good foundation for Caviare Boats, Miniature Cheese Horns, Anchovy Twists, or for some of your Cold Canapés.

RICH CHEESE PASTRY

3 oz. flour	Pinch of dry mustard
1½ oz. margarine	tard
Salt	2 oz. finely grated
Pinch of Cayenne	cheese
pepper	Egg yolk

Sieve the flour, rub in the fat, and mix in the remaining dry ingredients. Mix to a stiff dough with the egg yolk and knead slightly: use as directed in recipes that follow.

CAVIARE BOATS

Cheese pastry	Lemon juice
Caviare (or cod's roe)	Savoury butter
	Rice paper

Line some boat-shaped tins with thinly rolled cheese pastry and bake blind in a hot oven (450° F.) for 10–15 minutes. Mix the caviare or roe with some lemon juice, and when the boats are cold fill them with the mixture. Pipe a little savoury butter around the edge of each, and put a triangular "sail" of rice paper in each boat.

ANCHOVY TWISTS

Prepare 6 oz. cheese pastry and roll it out to a thickness of about ⅛ inch, then cut into strips about 2½ inches long and ½ inch wide. Prepare thin fillets of anchovy of the same length and place one on each strip of pastry, pinching the two together at the top slightly (use a little beaten egg if necessary to help them stick), then twist them several times; squeeze the two ends tightly together at the other end. Brush each over with a little beaten egg, and cook in a moderately hot oven (425° F.) until crisp and golden brown. This will take about 10-15 minutes.

MINIATURE CHEESE HORNS

Cheese pastry	Top of the milk
Cream cheese	Chopped parsley

Make some very small pastry horns and bake in a hot oven (400° F.) until crisp and golden. Allow to cool. Soften the cream cheese with a little top of the milk, if required, and pipe it through a potato star pipe into the pastry horns. Garnish with chopped parsley.

Cold Canapés

Canapés have a foundation of cheese pastry, or toasted or fried bread. Cut your foundation into a pleasing shape with a small fancy cutter, or into neat fingers. Get variety by arranging various toppings and garnishes on these bases, and a still more attractive appearance by adding final decorative touches.

To make your toppings adhere firmly to the bases, spread these with a little margarine or meat or fish paste. Then try any of the following as your topping:

SUGGESTIONS FOR TOPPINGS

Anchovies, sardines, prawns or shrimps, tongue, ham, liver and kidney, asparagus, cucumber, tomato, hard-boiled egg, olives, gherkins.

Chopped walnuts blended with cream cheese.

Minced ham and mayonnaise.

Sieved hard-boiled egg.

Flaked crabmeat and white sauce.

Lightly scrambled egg and finely chopped prawns.

Fried mushrooms (chopped finely) with white sauce.

Creamed kippers.

the choice

Careful planning is the key-note of Christmas catering. It pays, in the long run, to work out with paper and pencil the times when preparations for the various parts of the menu must be undertaken. Below we have tabulated information and ideas which will help you make your plans not only for the dinner itself, but also for other holiday meals. Here and on page 70 we give recipes for the more unusual dishes and accompaniments

1951

Recipes for the accompaniments:

ORANGE SAUCE

1 orange (preferably Seville)	Juice of ½ lemon
½ pint well-flavoured brown sauce	Cayenne pepper and salt
	¼ pint port wine

Grate the orange rind finely and add it to the sauce with the lemon juice and seasoning. Heat very gently until boiling and add the wine before serving.

OYSTER AND MUSHROOM STUFFING

1 rasher of bacon	1 dessertspoonful parsley
4 oz. mushrooms	
1½ doz. oysters	Salt and pepper
6 oz. breadcrumbs	1 egg
2 oz. suet	Milk
Grated rind of ½ lemon	

Cut the bacon into small pieces and chop the mushrooms. Beard the oysters and cut them into pieces. Mix all the dry ingredients together and add enough beaten egg and milk to moisten the stuffing and make it bind together.

As a variation, 1 pint of cooked mussels could be used instead.

CRANBERRY STUFFING

¼ lb. cranberries or small tin	Salt and pepper
2 oz. butter	¼ lb. finely chopped celery
2 oz. sugar	1 teaspoonful chopped parsley
6 oz. breadcrumbs	

Cook the cranberries in the butter for about 5 minutes, then stir in the sugar. Mix together the crumbs, seasoning, celery and parsley, and add to the cranberry mixture and cook together for 8–10 minutes.

	TIME FOR COOKING	STUFFING	USUAL EXTRAS
ROAST TURKEY	15 minutes per lb. for birds up to 14 lb. 10 minutes per lb. for birds of 14–20 lb.	Veal forcemeat at neck ; chestnut or sausage meat at parson's nose end.	Thin gravy. Bread sauce. Sausages. Bacon rolls or ham.
ROAST CHICKEN	1 hour. If very large, 1¼–1½ hours.	Veal forcemeat. Sausage meat.	Thin gravy. Bread sauce. Sausages. Bacon rolls or ham.
ROAST GOOSE	1½ hours for medium-sized bird. 2–2½ hours for large bird.	Sage and onion stuffing.	Gravy. Apple or gooseberry sauce.
ROAST DUCK	1–1½ hours.	Sage and onion stuffing.	Gravy. Orange salad. Apple or gooseberry sauce.
ROAST PORK	30 minutes per lb. and 30 minutes over.	Sage and onion stuffing.	Apple sauce. Thick gravy.
BOILED HAM (For Baked Ham see page 70)	30 minutes per lb. and 30 minutes over. (Soak 12 hours in cold water first.)	———	Served cold with turkey or chicken. Served hot with parsley sauce.

for dinner

Here and on the next eight pages: our summary of good food to serve at Christmas

1951

APPLE AND ONION STUFFING

4 large onions	2 teaspoonfuls sage
2 large cooking apples	1 teaspoonful grated lemon rind
6 oz. breadcrumbs	Seasoning

Slice the onions and cook until quite tender. Cook the apples separately until soft and pulpy. Drain the onions and mix in the apples. Add the breadcrumbs, sage, rind and seasoning.

CORN AND SAUSAGE FRITTERS

4 oz. flour	½ lb. sausage meat
Pinch baking powder	¼ lb. tinned sweet corn
Salt and pepper	
1 egg	

Mix together the dry ingredients, combine with the sausage meat, corn and egg yolk. Beat the egg white until stiff, then fold into the mixture. Melt some fat in a deep tin and heat in a hot oven until smoking hot, drop by spoonfuls into the hot fat and cook until golden brown. Drain well on a piece of paper before serving.

NUT AND PRUNE STUFFING

2 oz. margarine	6 oz. breadcrumbs
¼ lb. chopped walnuts	1 tablespoonful chopped parsley
½ lb. chopped stewed prunes	Seasoning
	1 egg

Melt the fat in a pan and lightly fry the nuts until golden brown. Add the remaining ingredients and mix well.

APPLE RINGS

2-3 large cooking apples	2 oz. syrup
½ pint water	Brown sugar
	Nutmeg

Peel and core the apples and cut into rings about ¾ inch in thickness. Poach the apple rings in the simmering water and syrup until half cooked. Then finish cooking by baking in the oven in a tin with smoking-hot dripping. Sprinkle with brown sugar or grated nutmeg before serving.

RICE STUFFING

1 large onion	Poultry giblets
1 oz. dripping	2 teaspoonfuls chopped parsley
4 oz. rice	Seasoning
½-¾ pint stock	

Chop the onion and fry lightly, add the rice and the stock and cook gently until the rice is tender and the stock absorbed. Chop the giblets and parsley and add to the rice with the seasoning. Put stuffing in the neck end of bird.

UNUSUAL EXTRAS AND STUFFINGS	VEGETABLES	IDEAS FOR LEFT-OVERS	COLD PARTY DISHES
Neck stuffed with oyster or mussel and mushroom stuffing. Cranberry sauce.	Roast or sauté potatoes. Brussels sprouts. Braised celery. Artichokes.	Blanquette of turkey (reheat in a savoury white or bechamel sauce). Turkey and mushroom cutlets.	Turkey vol-au-vents. Turkey slices (set in aspic and serve on pastry).
Nut and forcemeat. Rice stuffing.	Potato chips or croquettes. Green salad. Peas and diced carrots. Endive or cress salad.	Chicken pilaf (serve chicken in savoury rice). Chicken à la King. Chicken curry.	Stuffed boned chicken. Chicken mayonnaise.
Corn and sausage fritters (garnish with orange slices and orange sauce).	Sautéd chestnuts. Creamed potatoes. Braised red cabbage and apples.	Salmi of goose. Ragout of goose (garnish with croûtons of fried bread and serve with apple rings).	Goose-liver titbits. Goose and tomato mousse.
Turnips (small, whole) cooked and browned with duck. Orange sauce and green olives. Rice or mushroom stuffing.	Green peas. Roast or chip potatoes. Braised celery. Sprouts and chestnuts.	Cutlets of duck with green peas. Duck à la Verjus.	Darioles of duck.
Cranberry stuffing. Nut and prune stuffing. Apple and onion stuffing.	Mushrooms. Mashed or creamed potatoes. Brussels sprouts. Beans.	Pork and apple casserole. Ragout of pork with sage and onion dumplings.	Pork pie. Brawn (set hardboiled egg with chopped pork in jelly).
Cranberry sauce. Cider sauce. Red-currant jelly.	Baked parsnips. Beans. Sweet Corn.	Ham omelets. Croquettes.	Ham mousse. Ham in bridge rolls.

THE INSTITUTE: PRINCIPAL PHYLLIS L. GARBUTT, A.R.I.C.

1952

DARN WEARY WIVES
kill two birds with one stone!

A gift for HIM!

Wise women buy BYFORD "98" because they know that here is a gift that men really appreciate. Apart from the *extra comfort* of the pure botany wool, the smart appearance, the attractive shades, they know full well that . . .

and a blessing for YOU!

. . . never before has a sock been designed to *save so much darning*. And no wonder! With extra nylon above the heel, as well as normal nylon at heel and toe, BYFORD "98" socks are reinforced at every major rub-point of men's shoes — *to cut down darning to a minimum*. BYFORD "98" also wash without the slightest fear of shrinking.

buy him **Byford "98"**

In case of difficulty, write for name of nearest stockist and illustrated folder to Imacula Hosiery Ltd., The Sock Specialists, Dept. D, 27/29 Southgate Street, Leicester.

IMACULA HOSIERY LTD., LEICESTER

The loveliest gift . . . and so practical

From him to you — a watch so elegant, so accurate — to make your Christmas perfect.

Crusader
Dainty Swiss made wristlet watch in 9 ct. gold. Precision 17 jewelled lever movement. Fully guaranteed. **£24.9.4**

Yeoman
Attractive yet inexpensive Swiss made 15 jewelled lever wristlet watch. Fully guaranteed. **£7.17.6**

See these and other Crusader & Yeoman ladies' and men's models at your local Jewellers.

CRUSADER TIMEPIECES LTD., • VICTORIA ROAD, RUISLIP, MIDDX.

Family Book-shelf
Surveys the field of children's Christmas reading

Initial from Emett's *Nellie Come Home*

Let's start with the Annuals. If you want a really exquisite galaxy of fairy-tales, loved but not too-familiar classics, try **The Wind in the Wood**, by that expert, "B.B.," superbly illustrated in colour by D. J. Watkins-Pitchford, F.R.S.A., A.R.C.A. (Hollis & Carter, 18s.). For young radio or television fans, take your choice of the **B.B.C. Children's Hour Annual**, edited by May Jenkin (Burke, 9s. 6d.), or **Uncle Mac's Children's Hour Story Book** (Collins, 7s. 6d.)—both compiled by experts at finding good yarns and bright, knowledgable features to enthral boys and girls alike. **The Tip-Top Annual** (Epworth Press, 8s. 6d.), a bumper with nearly 200 pages, includes Bible stories in its well-assorted contents, and a number of unusually imaginative prayers and verses. **The Helen Hayward Christmas Book** (Hutchinson, 7s. 6d.) crowns an assortment of stories, things to do, etc., with a 1,000-prize competition; and for excellent value you can safely choose **The Treasure Book** (Collins, 4s. 6d.) for five-to-eight-year-olds, or **Collins Children's Annual** (Collins, 6s. 6d.) for the six-to-tens. The same firm offers, at 6s. each, two big books of Bible stories—**Bring Forth My People** and **The Lord of Kings**—by Lucy Diamond, printed in large type, each with four colour plates.

ANIMAL AND NATURE STORIES

This year's selection of animal and nature stories is particularly good. **Ray of the Rainbows**, by Mortimer Batten, illustrated by G. Vernon Stokes (Hollis & Carter, 16s.) takes rank not only among the best of the nature tales but also among the best of children's novels. It's about a young half-breed Indian boy, skilled hunter and trapper, living untamable in the woods—a grand character, created by an author expert in nature knowledge. **Grey Chieftain**, by Joseph Chipperfield, grandly illustrated by C. Gifford Ambler (Hutchinson, 10s. 6d.), and **Master Jim**, by Rutherford Montgomery (Faber & Faber, 8s. 6d.), both have animal heroes—the first a German police-dog who rises to film fame; and the second a lovable grizzly. **Brandy Tells His Story**, by Kenneth Hare-Scott (Peter Garnett, 6s.), is about a "waif" from the Battersea Dogs' Home, told, with a fine sensitivity and gentle humour, for rather younger children. For girls of eleven to fifteen who love horses, try **Jill Has Two Ponies**, by Ruby Ferguson (Hodder & Stoughton, 8s. 6d.), told in natural, happy style. **Animals Under the Rainbow**, by Aloysius Roche, with wood-engravings by Agnes Miller Parker (Hollis & Carter, 12s. 6d.), is a pleasant collection of tales of animals and saints.

CHILDREN'S NOVELS

Among children's novels, **Barbie**, by Kitty Barne (Dent, 9s. 6d.), is first-class—delightfully convincing characters, unhackneyed, credible plot about a child musician. **The Islanders Follow a Clue**, by Gaye Knowles (Heinemann, 8s. 6d.), is another good, believable tale, involving a runaway boy; and so is **John's Journey**, by Amelia Gay (Hodder & Stoughton, 9s. 6d.), about a

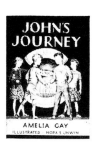

holiday spent in America and a little girl who disappeared. **Bill Brown, C.I.D.,** by Alan Brock (Dent, 9s. 6d.), should be marked for older boys, for its exciting, unhackneyed plot. The ever-popular if not very probable mixture of spies, crooks or hidden treasure furnish four other novels with exciting plots. **The Rubadub Mystery,** by Enid Blyton (Collins, 6s. 6d.), **The Buckinghams at Ravenswyke,** by Malcolm Saville (Evans, 8s. 6d.); and **The Necklet of Buddha,** by Monica Marsden, and **The Goose Green Mill Mystery,** by Norah Mylrea (both Hutchinson, 6s. each).

FOR THE VERY YOUNG

The very young and their elders can both rejoice this year that Her Majesty's Stationery Office has reprinted, at a modest 1s. 6d. a copy, Edward Lear's immortal **A Nonsense Alphabet** with his own illustrations. The incomparable Roland Emett, too, has been busy. If you've a small boy who'll go shares with you, buy him **Nellie Come Home,** an exciting train story (Faber & Faber, 12s. 6d.). **The Poetic Parrot,** by Margaret Mackay (Faber & Faber, 6s. 6d.), is Percy, a delightful creature who, escaping from the Zoo, goes about shouting rhymes of his own composing. As he puts it himself,
Fun, fun
For everyone.

NOTABLE NON-FICTION

Among notable non-fiction **Exploring Old Buildings,** by Evelyn V. Clark (Hollis & Carter, 16s.), subtitled "every child's guide to architecture," is for boys or girls interested in old churches, castles, etc. The illustrations are first-class. In **The Greatest Book Ever Written** (World's Work, 25s.) Fulton Oursler reverently retells the Old Testament story, presenting it as a linked-up, comprehensible, inspired whole. A fine gift for young people of enquiring mind. Teenagers just awakening to the beauty of art and literature will delight in **A Book of Beauty,** by John Hadfield (Hulton Press, 17s. 6d.), anthology of words and pictures designed as a reminder of the lovely things life holds.

For the slightly younger age group, there's a good historical biography, **William the Conqueror,** by Dorothy Margaret Stuart (Methuen, 10s. 6d.) ; and children with an eager curiosity about the ways of animals and about the wonders of the heavens will delight in Marie Neurath's **Let's Look at the Sky** and **The Wonder World of Animals** (Parrish, 6s. each), with their brightly coloured, fascinating diagrams. **John and Jennifer Go Travelling,** by Gee Denes and Elsie M. Harris (Nelson, 6s.), is about London and the Isle of Wight and trains and ships and 'planes, with fine photographic illustrations.

Finally a book of reference—**The Schoolgirl's Pocket Book** (Evans, 5s.)—contains information on every practical subject likely to interest a girl, from cooking, first-aid, nursing, camping to gardening and careers.
G. A. W.

Tailpiece from
The Wind in the Wood

1952

"Mummy says Hot OXO is a sure way to melt a man's heart."

OXO

FOR NOURISHMENT AND FLAVOUR

ENJOY THE STIMULATING PROPERTIES OF PRIME BEEF

3 REASONS WHY THIS — WILL GO FURTHER IN A COURTIER STOVE

- The Courtier Stove heats by radiation and convection, giving more warmth than an open fire.
- The fuel consumption of the Courtier Stove can be controlled—up to 10 hours' warmth from one stoking.
- The Courtier Stove burns any solid fuel, down to the last shovelful of slack. There is no waste.

From Ironmongers and Builders' Merchants, or write for illustrated Brochure No. 22/36.

THE **Courtier** STOVE

MITCHELL, RUSSELL & CO., LTD. · BONNYBRIDGE · SCOTLAND

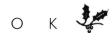

1952

A PAGE OF VERSE

NURSERY TERRORS

Night, in a ragged, cloudy cloak,
Fastened with old pale stars,
Goes riding by on the wind's wet wings,
While the rain in the withered branches sings
And the faces of mad, imagined Things
Peer in through the window bars.
With frenzied fingers of ivy leaves
She taps at the speckled pane,
Her trailing tendrils of curious dreams
Have strangled the moon with its own dim beams.
The curtains lift and a mad Thing screams
And the curtain falls again.
The clock has a dreadful hollow sound
That it never has by day;
The blown smoke writhes and the chimney gapes,
And the shadows assume impossible shapes,
Then a door that is fastened creaks and scrapes
And the morning is years away.

Helen Gow.

CHRISTMAS CAROL

How sweetly sleeps the Infant Lord
Our watch we keep, Presence adored !
When Thou wakest, smile, and see,
Love awaits to cherish Thee.

Blest soul Maria, gives Him birth:
Oh world behold !   Fair Light on earth;
Life of Love, His children see
How in His Image they may be.

Star in the East !   Thou Holy guide !
Lead us to where He doth abide:
May our hearts His Way enshrine,
Jesus, Christ, the Lord within.

Mary Harvard.

A GRACE FOR CHRISTMAS

For cloth of damask, white as snow,
For silver's softly muted glow,
    For crystal's brighter, diamond gleam,
For tapered candle's gentle beam,
    For holly's cheerful, crimson berry,
For children's faces, shining, merry,
    For all our loved ones gathered here,
For absent loved ones, far and near,
    For food to hearten us in eating,
For wine to gladden us in drinking,
    For love, for health, for happiness,
For joy and faith and hope of peace,
    For countless other gifts beside . . .
We thank Thee, Lord, this Christmastide.

Edna Franklyn.

FOOTSTEPS IN SNOW

Snowly, the countryside
Gleams in the eventide;
Swept with a purity,
Whitely, the meadows wide.

Swiftly, the chuckle brook
Flows with an icy look,
Passing the barrenness:
Tree leaves, the autumn took.

Softly, the stars behold,
Crossing the frozen fold,
Trail of a wanderer,
Darkly imprinted, cold.

Ian Healy.

AMORINA

Signor Amore
    (Once little Cupid)
Pricked himself with some
    Arrow-tips,
And so fell in love, and,
    Not being stupid,
Kissed Yuanita
    On both lips.

Then came a lovely
    Little bambino,
And they gave him a
    Lovely name:
Half Yuanita,
    Half Amorino,
Yuan-ino
    He became.

Young Yuanino,
    Being ambitious,
Looked for a wife, and
    So, ere long,
Found Amorina, and
    Found her delicious.
Soon he was singing this
    Sweet sad song :

" She is a darling,
    Sweet Amorina,
She is a marvel of
    Maidenhood.

She is a beauty
    (Haven't you seen her ?)—
And she is mine, that's
    Understood.

" Sometimes she loves me,
    My Amorina;
Sometimes she doesn't, but
    Oh, she should !
Sometimes she loves me,
    Dear Amorina :
Sometimes she doesn't, and
    Life's no good.

" When she loves me,
    No one is sweeter ;
When she doesn't, I
    Wish she would.
When she loves me,
    No one can beat her :
When she doesn't, I
    Almost could."

E. W. Dickes.

AND NOW FOR THE CHILDREN:

LET THEM
GO GAY

● *Our choice of gay,
amusing party-time clothes
for little girls*

1953

1 A bright tartan lining for a camel or navy wool hooded duffle-coat. Deeply snug and fun to wear and fasten, made in sizes 18 to 34 for ages 2 to 12. A Peter Pan coat obtainable from Shirley's, Oxford St., W.1, and Preston's, Leyton, from 57s. approx.

2 Winning heart-shaped grey wool pinafore that is oh so practical, given a festive touch by the crimson velvet pocket piping. Sizes 20 to 36 for ages 3 to 13. Minimode model. Price, 37s. 6d. to 63s. approx., from Selfridges, Oxford St., and Bladons, Hull.

3 A Christmas fairy dress in sugar pink or forget-me-not blue broderie Anglaise, cut with a circular skirt and boasting pearl buttons and velvet sash. Sizes 18 to 28 for ages 3 to 10. Horrockses Pirouette. Price, 50s. to 80s. approx., from Dickins & Jones, Regent St., or Elliston & Cavell, Oxford.

4 Fine rose-coloured needlecord dress, quilted at the shoulder, wrist and pocket. The white collar and flap are made of nylon for light-hearted laundering. Also in royal, nutbrown and green. Sizes 28 to 40, ages 4 to 14. Horrockses Pirouette. Price, 80s. 6d. to 97s. 6d., Graychild, South Molton St., W.1, and Mayfair Junior Miss, Winchester

1953

An expert helps you find the ideal complement to the feast

BY BON VIVEUR

Cook's Treasury

The old, grim, shortage days are over. We no longer face those painful alternatives, disagreeable, inky Algerian potions, or vintage wines at prices beyond our means. We can all afford gay and generous table wines once again. But we must exercise discretion in our choice.

Do not be afraid to set off on a wine-buying expedition because you know very little, but don't pretend you know more than you do. Choose a reliable wine merchant and trust his honesty and guidance.

What have you Planned for Christmas Dinner? You will want first wines which will make happy marriage with the soup and fish dishes, which will precede your chosen bird and the fruit and nuts which will follow after. So let us move to the table and, course by course, compile a guide to wine-buying which will enhance and flatter your fare.

With Soup. Consommés, those palate-clearing preludes to rich meals, delight in sherry as an accompaniment. Neither is a sprinkler amiss, containing a small quantity to shake into your clear golden cup. The average palate will respond contentedly to a dry medium Amontillado (approx. £1), which wine will also support those staunch, brown soups of winter. For the more sophisticated palate there is infinite pleasure in the partaking of dry Sercial Madeira, both as a before-dining aperitif and with the soup (between £1 and 24s.). This latter, like old Marc at the coffee stage, is enjoying a merited renaissance. We abstain from recommending the extra-dry sherries which we so much enjoy before we dine—the driest are too dry for these soups.

With Fish. You really should incline here towards dry-ish white wines, whether they are the vintage aristocrats or their more modest cousins. The sweeter whites come into their own *with* all sweets—which are of a frailer category than Christmas puddings! The fish wine choice is, nevertheless, so very wide that specific suggestions are practically invidious, but we will just cite a few examples to stimulate your sampling. For 7s. you can purchase a Graves; for 9s. 6d. a Graves Supérieur—both fairly dry, robust wines from Bordeaux. Burgundy will contribute much drier, somewhat more delicate Mâcon Blanc for 9s., Chablis from 9s. 6d. and the delightful Pouilly-Fuissé '49 or '50 for as little as 10s. 6d., an immensely popular choice. Bâtard-Montrachet '49 at 14s. 6d. and Chevalier-Montrachet '47 (23s. 6d.) will certainly enhance your status with friends and family alike. Nor should you overlook the merits of a fresh, young Alsatian (9s. 6d.), a Vouvray from the Loire if you incline towards the sweet-ish undertone (about 14s. 6d.), or, if well chilled, the very low-priced Clairette from the Languedoc selling at 6s. 6d.—a modest purchase of surprising alcoholic strength.

The Roast, Stuffed Bird needs a lusty companion, but here, too, we find many gradations. In the broadest possible terms you should choose red Bordeaux for the more feminine wine characteristics—hence the styling, " Queen of Wines "—Burgundy for more masculine power and depth—the " King of Wines "—or a Rhône wine if you desire the heaviest, stoutest party of the three!

Among this trio your modest outlay will be rewarded by a Château Loudenne, sturdy, heavy-ish for a Bordeaux (8s.), a Mouton-Cadet '47, less robust (9s. 6d.), or a Cos d'Estournel '49, gay and graceful, for 12s. Moving upwards in price thinking, you can rate 16s. wisely spent on a Château Calon-Ségur '45, or on those great wines of Châteaux Lafite, Margaux and Latour '43 (22s.) and Château Mouton-Rothschild '37 (27s. 6d.), all rich in classic claret characteristics. Forsaking Bordeaux for Burgundy, you can buy Beaujolais '49 for 8s., a wine to be drunk when young, please! A Beaune '47 or '49 for 11s., very generous but not too heady, a Vosne-Romanée '37 for 23s. 6d., and a Chambolle-Musigny '28 to invoke an ode or two from vinous poets (32s.).

Add in among the smaller fry one red Languedoc, Corbières Supérieures, a sturdy, peasant red wine of full value for 6s. 6d. Please exert care with its service and draw that cork in sufficient

1953

time for the wine to draw its breath. These youngsters need as much chance to show their prowess as the great old Kings and Queens of Burgundy and Bordeaux. The same also applies to the treatment of invigorating, sturdy Châteauneuf-du-Pape from the Rhône (13s. 6d.).

With the Pudding, Mincepies and Dessert to follow. A brown sherry and a Bual or Malmsey from Madeira are the only wines which you can choose to follow immediately before port. Port and nuts are indivisible from Christmas dinner, so we must plan accordingly.

You can buy an ordinary tawny or vintage port from around the 20s. mark, and hope, as we do, that funds or friends will enable you to drink a Loyal Toast in such wines as Cockburn or Croft's '35 or '27 (32s. 6d. and 36s.).

How is Our Spending Going? Here are two budgets, reasonably moderate, which allow for one bottle of each wine.

Under three pounds		£	s.	d.
As aperitif and with soup	Special Madeira or Dry Amontillado	1	0	0
With fish	Pouilly-Fuissé		10	6
With bird	Château Loudenne (Bordeaux) or Beaujolais '49 (Burgundy)		8	0
	Port	1	0	0
		2	18	6

Under five pounds				
With soup	Dry Madeira	1	4	0
With fish	Bâtard-Montrachet '49		14	6
With bird	Château Mouton-Rothschild '37	1	7	6
With dessert	Port. Cockburn's or Croft's '35	1	12	6
		4	18	6

The Cold Buffet will gracefully accommodate any of the above chosen wines. Your selection of fare can be such as to make you perfectly content with one wine only. If so, there is no better extra-indulgence suggestion than champagne, so let us see what we can safely drink among those which rate lower in price than the most exalted brands. Richard de Ayala can be bought for 21s. It requires careful chilling and is then very agreeable, and the same treatment should be meted out to Taittinger (22s. 6d.), Perrier-Jouët Special Reserve (27s. 6d.) or Ruinart (26s.). All these are, of course, non-vintage. But one such bottle still costs as much as several bottles of young, low-priced table-wines if you prefer variety! Non-vintage is, too, the unvarying rule with:

The Wassail Bowl. Mutter to yourself as you reach for an old china tureen and ladle, a plain earthenware vessel, or a fine silver punchbowl, " the *claret for mulling* must be young and unimportant, I am going to 'hot it up.'" Pour your chosen claret into a saucepan, add to one bottle a medium-sized orange stuck with cloves, an eggspoon of powdered cinnamon and the same of grated nutmeg, *sugar to taste* (there should be no ruling beyond your palate here), a tiny sprig of mace and a small bay leaf. Warm through *without boiling*.

When the wine is hot, stir in a claret glass of young brandy, pour into your chosen container, set the brew alight and stir continuously for a few moments to allow the peacock flames their pretty dance. Serve in warmed glasses.

Finally, let us resolve to create a fine excuse for indulging in a little wide wine spending when we invite rich old Uncle George (from whom we have expectations), or our employer. Only the best is good enough wine-bait for such important personages. Thus can we solace conscience when such labels catch our eye as Château Climens '37, Château Margaux '28, Meursault Genêvrières '47, Grands Echézeaux '29, Krug '47 and Cockburn's or Croft's '22—so little known and so hard to obtain in England!

In imagination we lift just such wines—in plain tulip-shaped glasses of course!—as we frame the toast: May no worse wine fates befall you in your prosperous New Year.

Sooner or later you'll hear it said...

In a cinema queue they talk of many things; it isn't all about Gable or Grable by any means — nor even Gregory Peck. I've noticed that, sooner or later, the men always get on to football, and the women work their way through clothes, children, houses — and FOOD! Like the lady in front of me at the Regal the other night.

I couldn't help hearing that she'd just bought a new twin-set; that little Gordon had worn out another pair of shoes; that the sitting room was draughty and that her husband had got home early, but it was all right because she had a few left-overs and with a couple of OXO Cubes she'd soon had a tasty hot meal ready.

And that's a funny thing! Wherever I go I'm bound to hear somebody say how valuable OXO Cubes are. I always use them for my gravies, stews and such — and what a difference they make.

Yes, every time, it's OXO Cubes for extra goodness!

Where there's cooking there's

1953

"THANK GOODNESS FOR A CUP OF HORNIMANS"

When the party is in full swing and the children at their happiest and noisiest, *that's* the moment for the delicious 'cup that cheers'. Like most really good things HORNIMANS is worth a little trouble to get. If you don't see it at your usual tea dealer's, please *ask*.

RICH & FRAGRANT —
The connoisseur's choice
DISTINCTIVE —
The family favourite

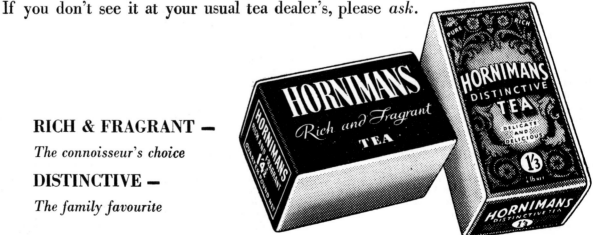

W. H. & F. J. HORNIMAN & CO. LTD. EST. 1826 · ORIGINATORS OF PACKET TE

BY MARGARET LEE RUNBECK

Where Does Christmas Happen?

1953

In our heads or in our hearts?   Yesterday, today or all the time?   Here's a brief guide to lead you to a three-dimensional Christmas

The house is full of it again. The streets are full of it, and shops and trees and churches all speak of it in different ways. Even strangers' faces are advertisements showing the transforming power of it. I've an old friend who always insists that as Christmas draws near everyone gets better looking. And then he goes on, " Even the really stingy ones think about somebody else at Christmas-time."

If there were nothing more to Christmas than each of us thinking about somebody else and trying to find some little object to express our affection, that would make it worth celebrating. But there is more to it. So very much more.

Christmas happens to us on three levels of experience. First, riding on the busy surface of the calendar, is the Christmas we're getting ready for right now. Next, we remember other Christmases, even more precious now than when they happened. And then, so still we may easily miss it, there is the deep private miracle that cannot be seen or shared or even made to come, for it is a divine event that can happen only in the heart.

The three levels of Christmas are like the three layers of our very selves: the physical, the mental and the spiritual. We have the whole of Christmas, as we have the whole of ourselves, when we accept each layer, and love it, and make it rich in meaning.

The top-layer Christmas is the shimmering, exciting one, compounded of surprises and sentiment and rapturous nonsense. It has lists and recipes and time-tables all twisted into it, plans scribbled, erased and

improved. We go about our daily business, and sometimes we even grumble over what a lot of work Christmas is. But underneath everything (even the grumbling and the work) we're wistful children, still believing in revised versions of Santa Claus. We know he doesn't exist, but we believe in him anyway, in one form or another. We know he's real because now we have found out that he is us, as recklessly generous as we dare to be, as flagrantly sentimental as we are.

So we believe in him, and we contract to pay his bills quite cheerfully through " January, February, June and July."

We have, in fact, two budgets—the long list of people we want to remember, and the short list of money we ought not to spend more than. When we talk about making both ends meet, we mean we're trying to fit the long budget of fondness within the short budget of funds. We know it can't be done, but it's fun trying; and it takes one into a realm of economics that boldly declares that loving is worth whatever you dare to spend on it.

And while you're running about, clicking off errands like a human taximeter, you're remembering other gifts and other Christmases: the gift from an original friend that provided your first painting lesson, then widened out to become a lifelong delight; the expensive wrist-watch that wasn't an engagement ring; the lovely, lumpy, home-made gifts your child creates each year. And the card your father always gave your mother, which said something like, " How could I give you anything now, when everything I have belongs to you? "—and the year she rebelled and announced two weeks before

Christmas, " Will, I expect a piece of jewellery this year. No more highfalutin laziness out of you." (He looked shocked, and then burst out laughing and said, " By golly, you're right! You've found me out "; and the bracelet he gave her she never took off.)

You remember hundreds of Christmas moments, and you laugh to yourself, or weep with the dearness of them. You take this Christmas on the run, and you live a score of other Christmases while you shop and wrap and bake and bedeck until the whole house—and the whole heart—is filled with gaiety.

And with something else. That comes to you silently, without warning, as quiet as a star rising in the sky. You know the pattern well, the Babe and the star, and the bright meaning shining down through the centuries. You know that the world began counting time from the rising of that star. And yet it cannot be said that the Babe and the star happened only once; they happened millions of times, and will happen millions of times again as long as the world lasts.

For that star rises across the sky of a human heart, and that Babe is born in a manger that only humility can know.

There are no mass-production miracles. They come intimately to one and to another until across the tired darkness of this world there is, from within, peace on earth, goodwill to men.

That is the miracle we famish for today. So let the star rise in you. Let the Babe be born, not at the gaudy inn, but in the quiet manger of your heart. Never mind when; never mind how. Only welcome it, and let it happen.

1954

Christmas is a happy thought

BY JULIA COPPARD

FROM the oldest to the youngest, there are always *some* people who don't seem to need anything. Imagination, plus the courage to be a little outlandish, may suggest the best answer of all. Real thoughtfulness often prompts the best ideas—but above all, don't "play safe."

Beginning with the elderly, who are often a problem; don't fall back, this year, on yet another handkerchief sachet or sock suspenders. To Grandmother, give a leather album containing photographs of all her children and grandchildren, with a personal message from each. Present her a lorgnette, or a ticket to the opera. Give her a lacy woollen stole in a gay colour woven with gilt thread. She'll probably love a canary in a fancy cage of gilt or wicker.

For Grandfather, choose a pair of "cad's braces" in bright red or yellow. Give him a sun-ray lamp, or book him a course of sun-ray treatments. A stylish present is a silver-knobbed cane; or a pair of antique onyx cuff-links.

Give someone who lives alone an Abyssinian kitten, together with detailed instructions for feeding and care. Or give them a window-box that will exactly fit the sill of their favourite window, ready planted for the spring. Or a box of writing paper, die-stamped with address and telephone number.

Give a hostess a collection of frivolous aprons in organdie, taffeta or tulle. Or a pile of guest towels, all different colours. She'll probably appreciate a set of Russian tea glasses in silver holders. Give her half-a-dozen boxes of candles, in various sizes and vivid bold colours.

Give a busy man six free car washes at the local garage; or a pair of tickets to a show that he has not managed to find time to book for. Give a waffle iron to a bachelor who enjoys cooking. Give any cooking enthusiast a box planted with herbs for the kitchen window-sill—parsley, mint, chives. Give a favourite uncle an antique paper-weight, or a complete set of his favourite author. Give anyone studious a set of reference books: dictionary, book of quotations, and Roget's *Thesaurus*.

A teen-age girl is sure to appreciate six pairs of jersey gloves, each pair a different colour. Or give her a pair of antique ear-rings. She may love a sophisticated nylon bed-jacket, or a shortie night-dress in red flannel. A teen-age boy will probably welcome a subscription to a jazz or film club, or a

1954

Give an art-lover a lithograph by a contemporary artist, or a facsimile reproduction of an old master. Give a nature-lover a set of bird or flower prints. Give someone with time on their hands a huge lump of clay and a manual of pottery-making. Flatter an animal-lover with a sleeping-basket, feeding-bowl or collar-and-lead for their favourite pet. Give someone with a special hobby a subscription to the appropriate technical journal. A gift that is sure to be popular with a budding photographer is a light meter. Give someone on a diet packets of health foods—starch-reduced rolls and cereals, and low-calorie soft drinks. Give your mother a bunch of flowers on the first of every month throughout the year (you can arrange it with the local florist). Give a hard-working schoolboy several dozen pencils with his name on them.

Give a young married couple sheet or towel sets in the brightest colours you can find. Or give them a large witchball to hang in the drawing-room window. Give someone who lives far away a dozen stamped envelopes with your name and address on them. Give a pretty girl a small travelling case to carry her party clothes for evenings out straight from the office. Give a gay young man an old snuff box (filled, of course). Give a very new baby girl her very first piece of jewellery, to keep until she is old enough to wear it. For a new baby boy, put down half-a-dozen bottles of vintage port or claret. Give a car-owner a foot muff for cold driving days.

Give a whole family an old door-knocker, or give them a huge box of Cox's Orange Pippins. If there's a chance of snow, give the younger members a racing toboggan. Most families would welcome a portable gramophone, or a compendium of well-known games. Give the boys of the family a football, and football boots in the appropriate sizes; give the girls sets of dolls' clothes, with diminutive suitcases to pack them in. Make a mother and small daughter matching nightdresses; give a father and young son identical dressing-gowns.

Take a deep breath, and give yourself a pat on the back !

course of driving lessons at a good school. Or give him a course of lessons in ballroom dancing, if he is approaching the social stage.

Give a housewife a picture for her kitchen wall (reproductions of the bolder moderns look very well). Or a set of colour-matched kitchen utensils on their own rack. If she has no help, pay for a weekly char for six months (you can deposit the money with a domestic-help agency). For the mother of young children, arrange for a weekly baby-sitter, at a time that suits her convenience. Give any woman who is house-bound an appointment at a hairdresser or beauty parlour, and arrange to cope while she is away from home.

For a small child, choose a set of pottery plate, bowl and mug decorated with his or her own name. Give a feminine little girl a heart-shaped pincushion with her name marked in pins (the kind with coloured heads). Give a tough little boy a course of boxing lessons. Give a family of children a tank of tropical fish. Give a small gardener his own wheelbarrow and set of tools. For a baby, choose a set of toys for the bath (including a funnel and sprinkler). For a pre-school child, provide a sand-pit or a garden swing.

A schoolgirl or schoolboy who is artistic will certainly value a set of oil paints, some pieces of hardboard to paint on, and an easel. The athletic youngster will be grateful for winter tennis coaching, or fencing lessons. The studious child will treasure a really good atlas or a set of draughtsman's instruments. Give any schoolchild his own wooden junk box, painted with his name and securely padlocked against the rest of the family.

The Christmas present that no-one but

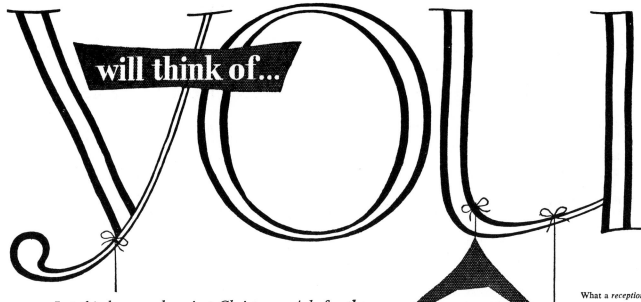

will think of...

Let this be your happiest Christmas. Ask for the thing you really want most of all. When it's made by 'ENGLISH ELECTRIC' you know you will have many happy New Years too. It really is a treat to be the proud owner of any or all of the 'ENGLISH ELECTRIC' "Better Living" appliances. **Suggest it to him now!**

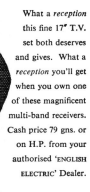

What a *reception* this fine 17" T.V. set both deserves and gives. What a *reception* you'll get when you own one of these magnificent multi-band receivers. Cash price 79 gns. or on H.P. from your authorised 'ENGLISH ELECTRIC' Dealer.

There's nothing like a good *Mixer* at any Christmas party—with speeds graduated from sponge to fruitcake and two non-slip mixing bowls—5 and 2 pint. Price £19.17.5. Juicer and Mincer attachments extra. And look! You can talk turkey *and* keep it hot if you have one of these decorative and highly efficient Plate Warmers. Beautifully finished in chromium and polished glass —yours for £12.12.0.

It's a gift. This Refrigerator has nearly 3½ cu. ft. of storage space. Takes up next to no room in the kitchen. Table-top strengthened for use as an extra working surface. The hermetically-sealed 'ENGLISH ELECTRIC' refrigerating unit is guaranteed for 5 years. Price 63 gns. Your Dealer will be pleased to arrange terms.

ENGLISH ELECTRIC

BRINGING YOU BETTER LIVING

The **ENGLISH ELECTRIC** Company Limited, Domestic Appliance and Television Division, East Lancashire Road, Liverpool 10

Gifts that taste good can look good as well

1955

MAKE THEM AT HOME—PACK THEM IN THESE

■Fill a narrow-necked pottery ornament with peaches in brandy or pickled plums from your store cupboard. Corks can be bought from your chemist. Low bowls with lids are fine for lemon curd or cottage cheese.

■Fill wooden or pottery bowls with fruit nestling in brightly coloured shredded Cellophane.

■Gifts which are spared the hazards of posting early for Christmas and can be delivered by hand present less of a problem.

■The bread basket in our photograph was made by junior schoolchildren, filled with fresh rolls and twists ribbon-tied, it would be welcomed in any home, especially if a box of butter pats could be included. For these, try some of the novel wooden moulds now in the shops. Fill cut-glass tumblers with jellied consommé, or wine-glasses with port wine jelly, and if you are giving a set of dessert glasses, why not deliver them ready for the table—containing a trifle or cold soufflé? (No perishable foods should be kept more than 24 hours in containers.)

■You may have some glass jars of unusual shape, bought originally filled with galantine or tongue. Re-fill these, as in the illustration. Or give a container which can be used again: for instance, plastic refrigerator boxes are inexpensive,

and, having lids, protect the food inside. Do not cover these for too long, though, before they are to be used.

■Lined clay or glazed pottery casseroles, containing a terrine mixture would be useful, especially the individual size for people living alone. An egg-cup set could well carry potted shrimps or meats.

■For sweets, we suggest attractive transparent celluloid boxes, but fudge or other unwrapped sweets could fill a small ginger jar.

■Biscuits can be packed in brightly painted store tins or glass jars, or in a biscuit barrel. An assortment of small cakes or savouries would pack easily into a three-tiered cake-tin.

■The small Christmas cake you made from the family mixing would look nicest in a round box. Send a little brandy butter too: the butter can be piped into an unusual shaped shallow dish, or send it in a waxed carton; as a final touch to the dish in our picture we added a sprig of marzipan holly.

■Most foods can be packed in a gift container, but for the exceptions, such as a raised pie or large roast bird, use waxed cartons or paper, or aluminium foil.

BUY THEM IN TOWN—WRAP THEM YOURSELF

■Look for special blends of tea, China and Indian, and perhaps select a tea-caddy. Coffee beans, freshly roasted, are a good gift for a friend who has a hand or electrically operated grinder. Take care to buy the right type of beans for the Espresso coffee fan.

■Among unusual items in the shops we note jars of mustard which would grace any table. For a selection of small things to pack together, there are tubes of mustard, mayonnaise ready with piping nozzle, smoked salmon and candied chestnut spread. Tiny 2-oz. bottles of red pepper sauce (good with salads) have sprinkler tops.

■Brandy sauce is available in bottles, also fruit salad. The numerous shallow jars of fish and vegetable concoctions, garnished with stuffed olives and truffles, also make colourful gifts. Many pickles are contained in unusual glass bottles.

■From Denmark come small containers of blue cheese. From nearer home, we found attractive, glazed pottery crocks of

Stilton. There is also a blend of cheese, butter and wine, wrapped in aluminium foil and packed in neat wooden boxes.

■While searching for the out-of-the-ordinary, don't forget old favourites, marrons glacés, crystallized fruits, Gentleman's relish and pâté de foie gras—now available from 12s. 6d. Bottles of chicken breasts or turtle soup, all these and many more are available.

■To wrap your gifts there is a much wider selection of papers this year; some we liked particularly were in bold stripes of red or green on white and pink or silver on white. Use glossy wrapping ribbon in bunches to form rosettes and have a supply of gold, as well as green-leaved holly sprays, for tucking into the final knots.

■Coloured Cellophane adds a magic touch. Match real ribbon to the paper and don't be afraid to stray from the conventional red and green. Orange-spotted yellow ribbon looks gay with orange and gold-lined white paper, black-and-white check ribbon is smart and a little formal.

SHOPPING GUIDE

For people living in or near London, here are a few suggestions where to buy specialities as well as wrappings:

Wrappings and boxes: From all large stores; some operate a packing service and for a small charge will transform your gift in a few moments. One of the boxes in our picture was packed by The Army and Navy Stores.

The boxes themselves came from a wide selection at F. G. Kettle, 23 New Oxford St., W.C.1.

Pottery, fabrics and novelties: Primavera, 149 Sloane St., S.W.1.

Kitchen Equipment: Mme Cadec Ltd., 27 Greek St., W.1; Leon Jaeggi and Sons Ltd., 29 Dean St., W.1.

Glassware: Finmar Ltd., 20 Kingly St., W.1.

Specialities: There are so many wonderful provision stores in Old Compton St. that it is difficult to select just one, but look in on Parmigiani Figlio in neighbouring Frith St., W.1.

For spices and all the requirements of Eastern cookery, visit the Bombay Emporium, 70 Grafton Way, W.1.

Chocolates: Bendick's (Mayfair) Ltd. have a branch at 184 Kensington Church St., W.8.

Use ATORA
FOR CHRISTMAS PUDDINGS
just like Grandma used to make

1955

Do you remember Grandma making the Christmas Pudding in the old days? The assembling of the "sugar and spice, and all things nice"—the fragrance of the peel and the nutmeg? And, of course, her favourite suet—ATORA. Yes, even in her day this best of all beef suet made light of the work, ready shredded to save time and trouble, ready to pour straight from the packet. And Grandma also knew that these fine ATORA shreds would mix evenly with all the other ingredients, blending them together into that wonderful flavour only found in the old-fashioned home-made pudding.
So do as Grandma did—make your puddings with ATORA—and make them in good time to mature.

FOLLOW THIS RECIPE: *Christmas Pudding (sufficient for 4 Puddings); ½-lb. ATORA, 1-lb. Raisins, ½-lb. Currants, ½-lb. Sultanas, ¼-lb. Candied Peel, 6-ozs. Sugar, 6-ozs. Self-raising Flour, 1-oz. Sweet Almonds, rind and juice of ½ Lemon, 3 Eggs, ½-lb. Breadcrumbs, ¼ Nutmeg, a pinch of Salt, Milk sufficient to make right consistency, 4-5 tablespoons Rum.*

Clean currants, stone raisins, put all the dry ingredients into a basin, blanch and chop almonds, add eggs, well-beaten, grated rind of lemon, and the juice strained. Mix all thoroughly, put into greased basins, filling them only two-thirds full. Cover tightly with greased paper and steam, preferably in a proper steamer, for six hours. Re-steam for 2-4 hours on Christmas Day.

HUGON'S
ATORA
SHREDDED BEEF SUET

HUGON & COMPANY LTD., MANCHESTER 11

Do you say Grace?

Is yours a home where it is the custom? If today's pace of living has, alas, led many of us to neglect this small and pleasant act of Christian good manners, surely Christmas is the most fitting of all times to start. As much for homes where the offering of Grace is a favourite tradition as for the many where it might easily become one, we give on this page five specially chosen for this issue by THE REV. ROBERT W. A. COLEMAN

★ ★ ★ ★ ★ ★ ★ ★ ★ ★ ★ ★ ★ ★ ★ ★ ★ ★

O Thou, who kindly dost provide
For every creature's want!
We bless Thee, God of Nature wide,
For all Thy goodness lent:
And if it please Thee, heavenly Guide,
May never worse be sent;
But whether granted or denied,
Lord, bless us with content!

ROBERT BURNS

Blessed Lord, we pray Thee
To be present at our table,
Hallowing Thy gifts to our use;
That eating to satisfy our needs
We may remember those who lack.

ST. FRANCIS PRAYER BOOK

We thank Thee, Lord, that Thou dost give
The food and drink by which we live
We pray that we may grateful be
And give our lives again to Thee. Amen

ANON

God blesse our meale,
God guide our waies,
God give us grace
Our Lord to please.
Lord, long preserve in peace and health
Our gracious Queene Elizabeth. Amen

GEORGE BELL, OF EXETER (1565)

Dear Father God;
We will fold our hands as we remember Your love;
We will close our eyes as we quickly think of You;
We will bow our heads as we come to speak to You;
And in our hearts we softly say,
"Thank You, dear Father God, for this good meal."

ANON

The Charming Visit

1956

A story for children certainly, but really for

every sensible person who believes in

magic at this time of the year

BY HELEN CLARE

Wearing the lampshade

14gns

lightly powdered with snow

WHEN Michael Carmichael wrote from school to say he would like to bring home a prince for Christmas, his parents could see no reasonable ground for objection. Mrs. Carmichael, however, had never before entertained a prince and awaited his coming nervously. But when he arrived her fears vanished. Prince Dabra (whose nationality it would be safer not to divulge) was a small, dark, solemn boy, completely dwarfed by Michael, who was a tall fifteen, and even by Arabella Carmichael, who was three years younger.

Nevertheless he clearly had the poise and decision proper to a potentate, for no sooner was he settled in London than he asked if he might be taken upon a shopping expedition. Also, he was evidently used to taking the lead, for when they arrived at Swanlake & Peabody's, he made straight for the glass doors. These, surprisingly enough, opened of their own accord; Arabella gave her brother a startled glance as they hurried through behind him, but Mrs. Carmichael, tall and willowy and looking anxious (for the responsibility of shepherding a prince through London was weighing upon her) noticed nothing.

Prince Dabra marched ahead into the shop, said:

" Lampshades? " in a tone of authority to a surprised assistant, and, scarcely waiting to listen to her instructions, proceeded up the stairs, the Carmichaels following in his wake. He had found out from Arabella that Mrs. Carmichael would like a new lampshade, but, faced with the acres of lampshades that the shop provided, he seemed for a minute at a loss. He soon recovered himself, chose a confection in pink satin and pearls, which Mrs. Carmichael pretended not to see, and was turning away with it in his hand.

" But he hasn't paid," whispered the outraged assistant.

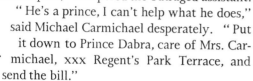

" He's a prince, I can't help what he does," said Michael Carmichael desperately. " Put it down to Prince Dabra, care of Mrs. Carmichael, xxx Regent's Park Terrace, and send the bill."

" And his initials? " asked the assistant.

" A. K.," said the Prince, a little impatiently. " You know, Abra K." And a distant look came upon his face as he watched the assistant writing. Arabella and Michael watched too : for as quickly as she wrote, the writing erased itself, a word at a time.

" Excuse me, sir," said the lady blushing, and hurried away. The Prince took the chance of her absence to proceed to the sports department.

" You stay here," said Mrs. Carmichael.

" No, no," said her son, " we must follow him." And the whole family did so. Prince Dabra chose some golf clubs for Mr. Carmichael, a pair of skis for Michael Carmichael, and some new skates for Arabella, while distracted Carmichaels shouted at the assistants, " Prince Dabra . . . you know, Abra K. . . . care of Mrs. Carmichael, xxx Regent's Park Terrace, send the bill. . . ."

" At least," remarked Michael, as they tore up and down stairs following the Prince, " we cannot be accused of concealing our identity."

They caught up with their young friend as he was ordering a box of Turkish delight, some crystallized

Startled assistants saw snow covering up the counters

1956

fruits, a jar of ginger, three boxes of chocolates, two tins of sweet biscuits and a Christmas cake. He loaded these lesser things on to his panting slaves.

" How hot it is in here," complained Arabella.

The Prince looked surprised : he had remained cool throughout. And pointing to the ceiling he remarked :

" Ah ! Your English climate invade even your English shops, no? " Before Arabella's delighted gaze, the whole department became a whirling pattern of white flakes. It was snowing : it was fast covering up the counters.

" Charming ! " sighed the Prince.

But Michael saw the look of terror on the faces of the assistants, and said urgently: " Where next, Dabra? "

The lift twirled the passengers to a standstill; stepped manfully out

ILLUSTRATED BY REX MORETON

1956

"A taxi," gasped

Mrs. Carmichael

The Charming Visit

The Prince, who was by now wearing Mrs. Carmichael's lampshade lightly powdered with snow, walked towards a crowded lift and pushed himself, his golf clubs, his skis and his skates inside, followed by three Carmichaels weighed down with parcels. The attendant gave a fascinated glance at the snow, pushed the button and the lift began to descend. Descend? It began to revolve, slowly, upon its axis, but with each turn it gained speed. The faces of its occupants, as each realized the nature of the motion, were a joy to Arabella and a horror to her mother.

"We shall all be butter," exploded a peppery old gentleman, "if this goes on much longer!"

But the lift twirled to a halt and the passengers, their cheeks various shades of green, stepped manfully out.

NEXT the Prince announced that he would like to go in an English underground to try the escalator.

"No, I think a taxi," said Mrs. Carmichael, feeling wilted and faint. She had suddenly realized that there was a connection between her young guest and these strange happenings. He was not to be trusted on an escalator. The Prince was as docile as a puppy, and the taxi set off.

But docility in princes is known to be dangerous.

At Marble Arch the lights turned against them, the taxi came to a halt behind others, and Michael saw once more that significant distant look replace the docility on Dabra's face. If he should tinker with the lights!

Even as he thought it, every stream of traffic, all see-

It rose, and with the help of **a delighted driver, circled**

ing green, began to move together and became jammed tightly in the middle of the road and round the Arch. Drivers swore and shouted, hooters hooted, shop doors opened, police appeared, pedestrians wildly waved their arms in all directions.

"Your English traffic, yes?" smiled the Prince. "So inconvenient, no?"

And the taxi rose like a helicopter above the seething street, circled, with the delighted help of the driver, round the Arch, and hummed off across the roofs towards Baker Street, followed by the cries of wonder which had replaced the hooting. It did not touch down again until it arrived at Regent's Park.

Mr. Carmichael was at their door to meet them.

"My dear," he whispered, "the Prince's guardian is here."

"What a blessing," replied his wife.

The Prince's guardian explained sorrowfully that he must take the Prince home at once.

"If I do not," he said, "it will cause an intertribal incident."

"Heaven forbid," said Mr. Carmichael.

"How we shall miss him," said his wife, "such company for Michael, so full of ideas. The tickets, the journey . . . ?"

"All is arranged," said the guardian, and, presenting each Carmichael with his expensive present, the Prince said good-bye.

Michael ran upstairs to see the last (until next term) of "old Dabra," and stopped dead on the landing. Two figures sailed past the window sitting solemnly cross-legged upon. . . . What? It was almost dark, it was foggy, it was beginning to snow. It was in fact, as Arabella said, joining him, very Christmassy. Altogether it was difficult to see. Mrs. Carmichael's Persian rug indeed, which lay in the hall near the telephone, was never seen again. It was not a large rug, but it might, perhaps, have held two. THE END

Two figures sailed past **the window sitting solemnly** *cross-legged upon . . . what?*

1956

I don't know what they'll think— *their* place is always so comfortably warm

The gayest party chatter will never disguise the fact that your house is not as warm as it ought to be. And there is no escaping the quick shudder as your guests hurry across a cold hall. They expect you to have a civilised heating system and, of course, lots of hot water.

Proper heating these days need not mean hard work or heavy expense. What you want is a 'Potterton' Boiler which will do the whole job absolutely automatically. And because of its accurate controls and high efficiency it will give you the maximum possible amount of heat from every shillingsworth of fuel.

Whether you are planning a new house or trying to make an old one habitable, you would be well-advised to find out what the 'Potterton' people can do for you. Why not drop them a line now—or, if you prefer, ask your husband's secretary to ring Miss Meredith at Vandyke 7202.

There is a wide range of 'Potterton' Boilers, both oil-fired and gas-fired, capable of supplying all the hot water and central heating demands of any size of house. When you are in town drop into the Company's new showroom at 84 Regent Street, W.1 and see how good the boilers look.

POTTERTON BOILERS
OIL-FIRED OR GAS-FIRED
The Key to comfort

POTTERTON DIVISION, Thomas De La Rue & Co. Ltd., 20/30 Buckhold Road, London S.W.18.

MANKOWITZ MENAGERIE No. 10

Spirits for Christmas

1956

BY WOLF MANKOWITZ

ILLUSTRATED BY NORMAN THELWELL

SINCE we were tired of giving one another pairs of slippers, miniature motor-cars, hot-water bottles in the shape of cowboys and bears, and boxes of crystallized fruit, last year my wife and I called a family council to discuss the project of a joint Christmas present of —as they say—lasting value.

"The idea," I explained to my three sons, "is for us to pool our present-money which we all collect from me, and buy one great bumper present for the entire family."

My wife knew at once what would make us all happy. A new vacuum-cleaner, she pointed out, was a benefit to the entire community, since the old one was inclined to shoot the dust out instead of sucking it in.

"An excellent suggestion," I said. "We shall put it to the vote. Gentlemen," I addressed the boys, "if you want to squander our present-money on a noisy, hygienic, mechanical object which is neither consumable nor available for disorganized games, please raise your right arms."

Not an arm moved.

"My love," I said to my wife, "I can't tell you how sorry I am that the council does not see fit to support your superb plan."

She sighed. "It's a pity," she said, "because I've already bought a new vacuum-cleaner, thinking to save you money."

The new vacuum-cleaner, it seemed, was actually at that moment hiding in a cupboard coyly waiting to be switched on for Christmas.

The Baby Ogre being now able to express himself in a combined secret language of Esperanto, Urdu and pidgin English, made a long statement in an imperious manner, concluding by shaking a clenched fist above his head. This I interpreted as meaning that he was in favour of anything I suggested.

"Thank you for your solidarity," I told him. "I hope the rest of you will take example from this honest child who not only knows but respects his own father."

We then considered the not unexpected scheme of the Miser—that we should take our present-money, sell the house, realize on all

movables, and set up as confectioners. He was prepared to undertake the entire risk of testing our products and would work a day and night shift simultaneously at half-pay, starting from now.

It took a box of liquorice Allsorts to soothe him. "Just to rehearse," I suggested, "why don't you take those delicious lumps of liquorice upstairs and gorge yourself into a coma?" Then, since the Director was being strong and silent throughout the discussion I took the floor myself.

"You will all appreciate," I said, "that a great deal of thought and consideration has gone into the proposition which I am about to make to you. I trust, therefore, that you will not waste further time in meaningless discussion, but will at once accept a scheme which, not only of benefit to the entire family, will, I am certain, prove of lasting value." I paused for my wife to sneer encouragingly, and the Director to pretend not to have heard me speak. "Very well then," I continued, "assured of your support, I come triumphantly to the point. I suggest that you send me to the Bournemouth Health Hydro for a Christmas fortnight of comfortable starvation and recuperation."

I do not care to remember the open jeering which greeted my suggestion. Even the Baby Ogre burbled cynically. Undeterred, I went on to explain how, thoroughly rested, my use to the entire family would be greatly increased.

I could be tied up more vigorously, I could be tripped up more often, clubbed, beaten, tricked and man-handled to much greater effect if my powers of resistance were improved. "Think of the barracuda," I implored. "Fish him with the rod and you get a fight. Trail him with the line and you get a worn-out, helpless fish, hardly worth the trouble." But the Director, attracting attention by carefully catching his foot in the telephone wire and pulling the instrument off its perch, took the floor.

"What we need this Christmas," he announced, "and we are sick and tired of not having one every time it's Christmas, is a ghost." This, then, was why we decided to have a ghost for Christmas.

For a few days I noticed that my sons were studying me very closely. They seemed concerned about my health, and a little depressed that the chill weather had a tonic effect on me. "Look, my loving lads," I said, "I am devoted to you one and all three, but I don't intend being your ghost for Christmas. Of course," I continued, struck by a brilliant idea, "I wouldn't really mind—it's simply that you don't need me."

Then, inspired, I explained to them that the litter of three golden hamsters which had been devoured recently by their gourmet parents in the zoo division of our house, had, it was reliably reported, been seen in the still hours. "Actually," I lied, "only last night I saw a quantity of small ghosts scuttle across the floor. A group of scientific ghost-hunters like yourselves should be able to trap them."

I am deeply sorry I am so brilliant in my handling of boys. I spent the most abysmal Christmas ever; for no spectacular toy I suggested deterred my sons from hunting those baby hamster ghosts. The house was rigged with booby-traps and the still night disturbed by creeping children noisily whispering, "It went that way." In the middle of Christmas dinner the Miser leapt from his seat, his eyes staring from his head, and screamed, "Look there! Thix of them with pink eyes." As I slept in the afternoon, turkeyly, voluptuously, a small child shouted in my ear, "They're climbing out of your mouth, Dad." For months the entire house crawled with ghostly infant hamsters. They had the bright and eager features of my sons, and even less respect for my exhausted privacy. Even when an end came to these revels, there was still that vacuum-cleaner wailing like a disconsolate phantom all over the house—demanding to be paid for.

Christmas is a good time to take
stock of the year.   Seated round the friendly Yule log
(or radiator) work out with your family your

FAMILY RATING

(You can score plus or minus 1, 2 or 3—or 0—for each question)

1957

Start as you mean to go on

Quarrels
to be answered by Mother

HAS THE FAMILY quarrelled on the average: once a week only (*score* **1**); only on wet Sundays (*score* **2**); practically never (*score* **3**)? _____

. . . resorted to bad language (*score* **– 1**); disturbed the cat (*score* **– 2**); scored a bull's-eye with the best china (*score* **– 3**)? _____

. . . been described by slight acquaintances as a united family (**1**); been commended by your daily help (**2**); been referred to flatteringly in your parish magazine (**3**)? _____

Have you: argued mildly doing this test (**– 1**); torn the paper up (**– 2**); come to blows (**– 3**)? _____

□

Bruce Roberts

Holidays
to be answered by Father

Did you go somewhere with: a pier (**1**); a casino (**2**); a yacht squadron (**3**)? _____

Did you see: your bank manager (**–1**); a minor film star (**–2**); King Farouk (**–3**)? _____

Did it look: much like anywhere else (**1**); picturesque (**2**); like the travel brochure picture (**3**)? _____

Did you return: thankful to be back (**–1**); hoping the food poisoning/rheumatism would pass off soon (**–2**); planning to sue the hotel (**–3**)? _____

□

Mother
to be answered by Father

HAS SHE sewn on 15 buttons (**1**); darned 30 socks (**2**); invented three new dishes (**3**)? _____

. . . acquired a backache from her work (**– 1**); hired an incomprehensible foreign girl to do it (**– 2**); got you to do some (**– 3**)? _____

. . . joined a bridge club (**1**); bought herself a sack (**2**); tried a blue rinse (**3**)? _____

Do you think she: is a brilliant conversationalist (**–1**); tends to go on rather too long nowadays (**–2**); just jaws away (**–3**)? _____

□

Be ruthlessly precise here

Father
to be answered by the children

HAS HE tried hard (**1**); shown willingness to learn (**2**); made good progress in the year (**3**)? _____

. . . clumped heavily about the house (**–1**); talked about when he was a boy (**–2**); got your homework wrong (**–3**)? _____

. . . driven the car sensibly (**1**); taken the dog for walks (**2**); paid your pocket money allowance promptly (**3**)? _____

. . . attempted to rebuke you (**–1**); openly disagreed with you (**–2**); frankly disregarded your advice (**–3**)? _____

□

You should have scored about 8 by now

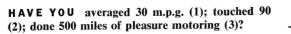

The Car

to be answered by Father

HAVE YOU averaged 30 m.p.g. (1); touched 90 (2); done 500 miles of pleasure motoring (3)? _____

. . . scratched the paint (−1); crumpled a wing (−2); demolished a gate-post (−3)? _____

. . . found that rattle (1); taught your wife to drive (2); discovered a new place to park (3)? _____

. . . had a breakdown (−1); a smash (−2); are you doing this in hospital (−3)? _____

You needn't be too honest here

Recreation and Health

FATHER, have you walked 20 miles in a day (1); played four rounds of golf or six sets of tennis (2); scored a century or won a tournament (3)? _____

. . . have you noticed: your trouser-belt shrinking (−1); the stairs adding a step or two (−2); the policemen looking *very* young these days (−3)? _____

MOTHER, have you been to: 20 films (1); 10 matinées (2); one opera (3)? _____

. . . have you been: addressed as " Ma " by a bus conductor (−1); asked if you remember Marie Lloyd (−2); helped across the road (−3)? _____

House and Garden

to be answered by Mother

HAVE YOU given the house a spring clean (1); bought a new carpet (2); avoided buying a TV set (3)? _____

. . . suffered from: chimney on fire (−1); dry rot (−2); demolition order (−3)? _____

Has the family worked: 40 hours in the garden (1); 80 hours (2); 100 hours (3)? _____

Have the neighbours got your: lawn-mower (−1); hose (−2); gardener (−3)? _____

The Children

FATHER, have they: remembered your birthday (1); let you choose the TV programmes (2); listened with respect to your remarks (3)? _____

. . . do you think they: are typical members of the younger generation (−1); ought to be sent to a strict boarding school (−2); to sea (−3)? _____

MOTHER, have they: gone to bed when told (1); cleaned their teeth (2); emulated George Washington (3)? _____

. . . have they been ordinarily noisy (−1); terribly noisy (−2); hideously noisy (−3)? _____

1957

Fortune and Misfortune

to be answered by Father

HAVE YOU had: a vote of thanks (1); a decoration (2); a legacy (3)? _____

. . . been to court (−1); not come out again (−2); are you still behind bars (−3)? _____

. . . had: a new position (1); a rise in salary (2); a bit of luck with the Inland Revenue (3)? _____

Are you: behind with the rent (−1); reading the Sits. Vac. (−2); making a detour round your bank (−3)? _____

YOUR FAMILY TOTAL IS

IF YOUR RATING IS

−54 to −16   *We would rather not comment*
−15 to −1   *Next year may be better*
0 to 15   *A moderately happy family*
16 to 40   *A very happy family*
41 to 54   *Too good to be true: deduct* 20

1958

Allies in Wonderland

'The time has come', the Walrus said,
  'To say a thing or two :
Of hops—and crops—and Butter-Scotch
  And what is Good for You—
And whether toffee's nice to drink—
  Or stout is made to chew'.

'O, Walrus', said the Carpenter,
  'It's very plain to see
You've got the story wrong-way-round,
  Here's what it ought to be :
Callard & Bowser now have joined
  The Guinness family'.

To Alice said the Carpenter :
  (She'd heard the news with glee)
'Callard & Bowser's good for you,
  Guinness is good for me'.
And Alice said, 'I'm glad they met—
  'Twas very meet', said she.

Issued jointly by

GUINNESS and CALLARD & BOWSER

*Guinness, brewers of stout since 1759, seven years ago acquired control of Callard & Bowser,
makers of fine Butter-Scotch and other confectionery since 1837.*

G.E.2978.O

Good Housekeeping presents

THESE
NOTABLE
TIMES

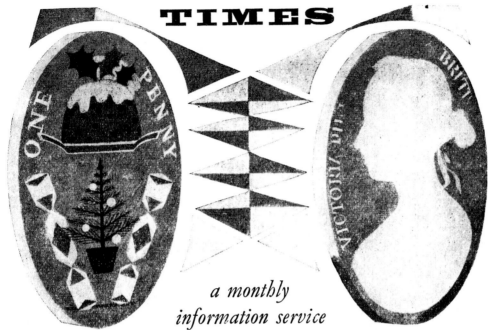

1958

*a monthly
information service
of useful, topical and fascinating facts*

SAVING BUNS FOR CHRISTMAS HAMPERS

How much is a bun penny worth? To an increasing number of old-age pensioners it has begun to mean a very happy Christmas. "Bun" coins—they show Queen Victoria wearing her hair in a bun—are being collected in various public houses in order to provide Christmas hampers and a party for old people.

There is nothing new about pub charities. They are a tradition of the licensing trade and are well supported. They range from the ordinary penny-in-the-slot box to coins stuck on the ceiling, or mirrors, or piled up in pyramids on the bar. It is up to the individual landlord how he collects and for what he collects, and although no actual figure is available, it is estimated that the money collected through pubs for charity runs into many thousands of pounds each year.

The "Peter Parish Bun Coin Collection Association" began some years ago. A B.B.C. engineer, Peter Parish, noticed two bun pennies in his change when he bought a pint at his local, the Chester Arms, Albany St., N.W.1. He began collecting them, and the habit soon spread to his friends. At Christmas 1951, he made up Christmas parcels for five old people.

Parish died in 1952, but some of his friends carried out one of his last wishes by forming an official association to continue the charity he had founded. It is now run by a group of business men under the chairmanship of Miss J. Mason of the Chester Arms. All help is voluntary and out-of-pocket expenses are met by the committee. In its first year the Association collected £5. Now they have collected over £4,000 in all and they expect that their 1958 figure will be around £1,500.

"Collecting the coins is our biggest problem now," says Miss Mason. The scheme which began in such a small way has spread to over eighty pubs in the London area, and others all over the country. There has been no deliberate attempt to publicize it, but the idea has an obvious appeal, and two short gossip paragraphs alone in national papers brought many new collectors recently.

The coins are put back into circulation by the Association, usually through big chain stores. This in itself is beginning to be a problem, as the bun coins were minted between 1860 and 1894 and are officially being called in by the Bank of England. So far, however, the Association has been able to continue limiting itself to bun coins and they are firm about the limit. Donations in other currency are not accepted.

Where does the money go? "Not a penny is deducted for expenses," stresses Miss Mason. "And we reckon to spend the lot each year. The idea is to give old people all they need to have a really good Christmas." In practice, this means a hamper—average cost £3 each—containing a chicken, Christmas pudding, sausages, soup, fruit, biscuits, tea, sugar, a half bottle of whisky, cigarettes, and also £1 in cash to cover vegetables and other extras. Volunteers with cars deliver the hampers on Christmas Eve, and also drive round 200 old-age pensioners to and from the big Christmas party which the Association gives each year.

The pensioners are mostly nominated by collectors and people concerned with the scheme. "We try to find people who are over seventy and depend entirely on their old-age pensions to support them," says Miss Mason. "Most of them are living alone or have no younger relatives with them—we have a few husbands and wives. And we do try always to choose people who have enjoyed a drink in their younger days and can't afford one now."

This is typical of the scheme. So far, even though it has spread widely, it retains a casual and spontaneous air. No suggestion of "good works" has chilled the genial "drinks all round" generosity which began it. And the hampers and the parties are received in the same spirit. Last year, 400 hampers were sent out, and 360 letters of thanks were received—many of them from old people who could scarcely write.

This is one of them: "Dear Madam. Thank you so much for the party. Thank you so much for the hamper. Thank you so much for the Xmas. Thank you so much."

1958

What it means to be

A PEER FOR LIFE

BECAUSE women are being admitted to the Lords for the first time, Life Peerages have the appearance of novelty, but in fact they are not new in English history.

Previous to the new Act of April 1958, no fewer than twenty-nine life peers had been created by various kings—and some of them have been women. For example, Melesina de Schulenberg, a natural daughter of George I, was made Baroness Aldborough and Countess Walsingham for life; another of the Schulenberg ladies was made Duchess of Kendal and Duchess of Munster—also a lifetime ennoblement.

Indeed, in former days, not only were peerages made for life, but they were also taken back quite easily. There is the case of Roger Stafford, heir to the ancient barony of Stafford. Charles I disliked him so much, and made his life such a misery, that he was obliged to resign the honour.

WHY THE ACT?

It is not because the sovereign lacked the power to create new peers for life that the new Act was passed. It was so as to make the House of Lords a more representative assembly than it has been in the past. What happened was that during the later seventeenth century and in the eighteenth century, the House of Lords was made a closed shop by its members. In 1678, the Lords passed a resolution that no man could extinguish a hereditary honour created by the Crown. Therefore, in our own times, when Wedgwood Benn and Hailsham tried to renounce their peerages, they were unable to do so.

Likewise, the Lords objected to the presence of life peers. It was only in 1876, when the congestion of legal business before the House of Lords became a scandal (see Dickens's *Bleak House*), that the House of Lords allowed the Crown to create some Lords of Appeal in Ordinary as life peers. There are usually a dozen of these in the House at one time.

NO SECOND-CLASS NOBILITY

Does a life peerage differ from a hereditary one, other than being for life only? Not at all. A life peerage is in no sense a second-class nobility. All the reference books from which the precedents of law are taken declare that the sovereign may create a man or woman noble for life.

A life peer is styled the same as a hereditary peer of the same degree. The new peers and peeresses created under the Act are all barons and baronesses, and are therefore styled the Rt. Hon. Lord—or Rt. Hon. Lady. The children bear the title of Hon. as in the case of hereditary barons. Even when the life peer dies, the widow and children still have their titles recognized under the Warrant.

The children of life peeresses have the same style as those of hereditary peeresses. Only the husbands of life peeresses are left out, and receive no honour or title. Here again, it is just a matter of following precedent, because unless she is Queen Regnant and he the Prince Consort, a man does not usually receive an honour through his wife. The precedence of life peers and peeresses will be the same as those to the honour born.

ROBES AND REGALIA

The robes of peers and peeresses will be the same as for hereditary peers. The mantle of a baron is of crimson velvet, edged with miniver pure, and powdered with two bars of ermine. The mantle of a baroness is the same as that of a baron, but edged with miniver pure, two inches in breadth and the train three feet on the ground. There is a baron's coronet, which is a plain circle of silver gilt, surmounted by six silver balls at equal distance; a cap of crimson velvet, turned up ermine, on which there is a golden tassel.

A life baron will be entitled to these garments for such state occasions as the opening of Parliament. In fact, it is very doubtful whether any of them will take advantage of the privilege, since these robes are very costly. For entrance into Parliament when they take their seats, they will probably follow custom as in many other cases, and hire the robes for the occasion.

The ceremony of a lady taking her seat will be the only item which is entirely new, and a special ceremony has been prepared for that. That ladies are present at all in this most exclusive of men's clubs is unlikely to be regarded as a precedent elsewhere.

EVEN WITH HOLLY,

it's " vive la différence "

Have you ever noticed, at Christmas time, that the traditional holly trees are not all alike? That some of them have only shiny green leaves and no vivid berries? If yours is one of these, and if it's a generally healthy tree, one of two things could be the reason. One, it could be a male tree, and if it is, it isn't going to produce berries now or ever. Two, it could be a female tree, and lonesome. For unless there's a male tree within pollen-blowing, or carrying, distance, there won't be any berries.

The reason for this is that hollies, like humans, are unisexual. (They are not the only trees with this characteristic, but they are the most widely known.) There must be a male tree close enough to the female so that bees and insects, as well as normal air currents, can carry pollen from the male, or staminate, flower to the female, or pistillate. In rare instances, pollination has taken place when trees were several miles apart, but experts advise plantings within several hundred feet.

Holly comes in over 300 species, such as the English, American, Chinese and Japanese. When planting a pair of trees, you should choose the same species, as hollies rarely cross-pollinate. It is not necessary that the male be of the same age, or growth, as the female.

JAEGER
for giving and for getting

1958

HER Jaeger Dressing Gown, warm and soft as a kitten, just 6½ gns in exclusive Jaeger colours

HIS Jaeger Dressing Gown, all-wool, braided with cavalry splendour 7 gns in many Jaeger colours

GO TO YOUR NEAREST JAEGER

Enquiries to Jaeger House (Dept. G.H.), Regent Street, London W.1.

1959

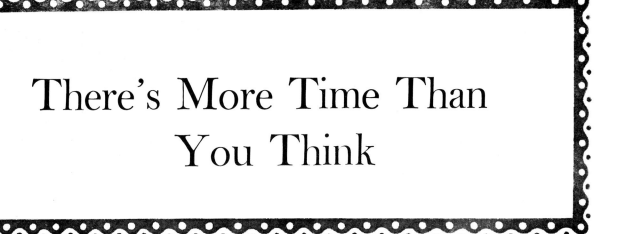

There's More Time Than You Think

1959

HAVE you ever said to yourself: " How I wish time would stand still . . . ! " We have all done that sometimes, just breathed a soft sigh and wished that life would hold on, just for an hour, a day, a week so that we could catch up and do all the things we have always wanted to do, the personal things, the constructive things.

Just now as the old year flashes by and the new one stretches in front of us, untouched and unused, let's try to make the time we need by saving it like a miser and planning how to use what we have saved.

Let us think of the things which would make our life richer and much more amusing. For instance, are you so sure that you could not:

.. **LEARN TO SPEAK FRENCH PROPERLY.** Enough to get by in cocktail party conversation, find your way about Paris or even merely know that you can. One hour a week would be fine.

.. **TAKE A HOLIDAY BY YOURSELF.** Urge your husband to go away golfing or fishing and then go away too, on your own, to an hotel, to be cossetted and waited upon. So good for the soul. Let's budget for three days.

.. **TAKE UP TENNIS AGAIN.** That's something to get you out of doors and out of yourself, besides being fun and good exercise. Twelve hours would cover that one.

.. **READ ABOUT FINANCE.** Why not learn a little more about how money works? You don't need much of it to be an investor nowadays, its an absorbing subject and you might even make a little profit now and again. Don't count this half-an-hour a day. You could do it in the bath or while you are having lunch.

.. **GO BACK TO SCHOOL.** It's quite an idea with all the evening classes there are nowadays: dressmaking, lampshade making, upholstery and—if you are that way minded—art appreciation or haute cuisine. Surely worth an hour a week.

.. **REPLAN THE GARDEN ON PAPER.** Of course you say that every year. But most years the seasons march on and leave you far behind. So plan the sequences of the beds, order the seeds and plants in good time. This could take three hours of discussion with your husband.

.. **VOLUNTEER TO HELP.** You may well be a helper already, but if not, ask the Red Cross, St. John or the W.V.S. if you could spend an hour a week in the service of your community. They'll be delighted.

.. **LEARN FLOWER ARRANGEMENTS.** That's an art every woman should know but it's got to be learnt. There is more to it than you think. And while you are about it, learn the Japanese way. A pair of blossoms and a graceful twig can look like something from a professional florist, and save you money too. It's worth six hours to master the principle.

.. **MAKE AN ADDRESS BOOK.** You have had your Christmas cards and all those festive season contacts. Now is the time to keep a tag on those elusive names, addresses and telephone numbers. It will save you so much frustration during the year and will only take you an hour.

.. **HAVE A TURKISH BATH ONCE A MONTH.** Relax, luxuriate in that lovely hot steam, feel your skin come alive again after the pummelling and the loofahing. Three hours a month.

.. **KEEP YOUR FEET PRETTY.** Cream them, powder them, look after them as you do your hands and you'll reap rich rewards in comfort and be proud of them on the beach next year. Five minutes a day.

.. **TEACH YOUR CHILDREN IMPORTANT THINGS.** We get so immersed *ourselves* in the material necessities that we often forget to open up new inspirational horizons for *them*. Talk to them, take them out for a specific purpose. Two hours a week.

.. **VISIT MORE GALLERIES AND EXHIBITIONS.** Make a date to go with a friend (it will be less easy to back out that way) then talk about what you have seen. You don't have to be an expert to learn something new and exciting every time. Two hours a month.

.. **STUDY RECIPE BOOKS.** Not half an hour before a meal, but study them in odd moments just for pleasure and ideas. Look out for two or three culinary masterpieces to add an inspired, professional touch to your meal planning. A quarter of an hour a week.

.. **READ THE BIBLE AGAIN.** How many times have you said that? It's vital to know the basis on which so much of our civilization stands. You'll never regret it. One hour a week.

Now there you are. There is a plan for making your next year vital, interesting and busy to a purpose. Do you know how long that will take you? 485 hours out of the 5,840 waking hours you'll have in 1960. One hour in every twelve. The price for all this luxury of skills and pleasures isn't too high. Finally, remember sometimes to do just nothing at all. It's the finest, sanity-saving relaxation you could want.

BY AUDREY CONDRY

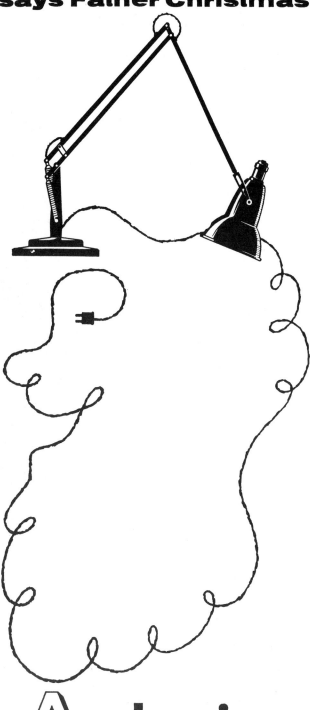
*Each month the Family Centre will discuss a
topic of particular interest to parents of*

The Under-fives

HOW LATE SHOULD
THEY STAY UP?

IT is natural to relax the normal
household routine to some extent at
Christmas time. That, after all, is what
makes the sense of a special occasion.
The children's friends and family ones
come visiting and invitations to go out
are accepted. Indulgent grannies come
to stay, and beg an extra hour for the
little ones. "After all," they say, "Christ-
mas comes but once a year." But does all this mean that, right through
the holiday period, small children's regular bedtime can happily be
forgotten, and that they will adapt themselves to more excitement and
later hours, and enjoy them?

The answer is that, even during the party season, the youngest members of the family need a recognizable pattern in their daily lives, and the
time they go to bed is a most important part of that pattern. Older
children, who are normally strong and resilient, can be given a fair
amount of latitude and be trusted to make up arrears of rest, but the
under-fives must depend on their parents to see that their life flows
evenly. The very atmosphere of excitement makes it more necessary than
ever that toddlers' minds and bodies should not be kept at full stretch for
too long.

Broadly speaking, the under-fives need an average of about twelve
hours' sleep at night and, if they are to spend a well balanced day (which
more often than not starts at crack of dawn), they should generally be
ready for bed by 6.30 to 7 p.m. In these early years, the children put all
of themselves into what they are doing; they are hardly still for a minute,
their tongues are constantly on the go, they are at the mercy of their
feelings, and all this output of energy should be made up by enough rest.

NOT only their bouncing health, but their serenity too, is built on the
sound foundation of a regular daily pattern of life, and this also
needs to be even more carefully safeguarded when there is a lot of excitement afoot. If, when mother says it's time for bed, father says, "Oh, let
them stay up a bit longer," or if, night after night, they wring conces-
sions by dawdling and pleading, then bedtime becomes an issue, and the
children grow querulous and demanding. If it is cheerfully taken for
granted that each child, according to his age, has a usual appointed bedtime, then the question of hardship doesn't arise. Never let a toddler get
thoroughly over-tired. Always let a relaxed bedtime be the last episode
in a happy day, an event to be looked forward to and enjoyed in its own
right.

It is against this background of ordered life that occasional adjustments can be made which really do give the sense of a special treat. The
young parents themselves have a claim to consideration. They need, and
deserve, a few uninterrupted hours after the children are safely tucked
up for the night, and it is hard for them always to feel completely house-
bound by a baby's six o'clock bedtime. So sometimes, perhaps, they can
take the baby to a friend's house in his carry-cot, put him to sleep in it at
the usual time, and bring him home later on without being disturbed.
Toddlers are not quite so accommodating, but again it can be quite
practicable to put a three-year-old to sleep in a friend's bedroom through
the evening while his parents enjoy a sociable chat, and then transfer him
almost without waking him, to his pram or the back of the car.

AT home, too, general rules can be applied flexibly and with common
sense, so long as they are not abandoned altogether. So long as the
smallest children are not getting over-tired and over-excited, let them
finish their share in that exciting game of Snap, or permit the extra half-
hour's story-telling, especially if the rest of the family will give a hand
with the bathing and suppers later on. Children love the high-lights of
festivities and family occasions, and their enjoyment will be the greater
if these happen against a background of ordered life to which their
minds and bodies are healthily accustomed.

THE WRITING MORTIMERS

1960

The angel on top of the Mortimer Christmas-tree is now ten years old. John made it, and it is still miraculously intact. A " large, familiar dish of macaroni cheese " is as much expected and enjoyed by the Mortimer family at Christmas dinner as the succulent duck with all its trimmings.

Some people may preserve their angels for a longer time, but not, I think, of the Christmas-tree kind. Some people may have macaroni cheese for supper, but I don't know any other English family that serves it, triumphantly, on Christmas day.

But then, the Mortimers are not all that usual. John, who is a lawyer and novelist and playwright (his plays include the 1960 success, *The Wrong Side of the Park*) and his wife, Penelope, who is a busy and established author, are most of all time-giving and loving parents to six children. In order of descent, they are twenty-year-old Madelon (" named after a French marching song "); Caroline, eighteen; Julie, fifteen; Deborah, eleven; Sally, ten; and Jeremy, five (the last four are in our picture). When all these are gathered together there is naturally a divergence of opinion on such matters as food—and Christmas.

They all love the real Christmas-tree, with real candles, and that is one reason why the head of the house became an excellent angel-maker. Although he's never dressed up in a white beard, he is a very successful Christmas dad, and apart from angel-making he is an excellent present-wrapper, champagne-provider and stocking-filler.

Three of the children have " a very boring taste in food, with a passion for white macaroni cheese ". And so it has its honoured place at Christmas dinner. " Fortunately," adds Penelope, " they all like Christmas pud and can daze themselves with brandy butter."

What, I asked, were the general family likes and dislikes in food? " Debby likes snails," John remarked, as he moved from his armchair to mix us some drinks. " We all like steak-and-kidney pudding and good beef casserole that cooks very slowly for a couple of days," Penelope volunteered, " and Spanish lamb—a shoulder or a leg—cooked in the casserole with white wine and a lot of garlic.

" Our work," she observed, " necessitates a fair amount of entertaining, so I hit on the idea of a dining-kitchen where I could be with my guests during that carefree time over a hot stove, made carefree, too," she grinned, " by careful menu planning. But I made a mistake. You *can't* make it appear as though it's easy as pie when you're teetering about on high heels with your guests watching you. I'd go back, any day, to the principle of privacy in the kitchen—except when it's dear old friends for a meal."

Their nice dining-kitchen will suit admirably this Christmas, however, for the Christmas holiday is very much a family time. " We have a children's party and, as a rule, one of our own on New Year's Eve. That, we hope, fixes everyone," John put in.

I asked what they felt about conjurers and magicians and things for the children's party. " Oh, we're emphatic-ally sold on ' canned entertainment '," said Penelope. " Children below four and over fourteen can be left to their own devices, but in between you need all the help you can get or pay for."

We were all voluble on the subject of Christmas decorations. " Theoretically, I loathe them," Penelope said. " They droop, trail, collect dust, make the whole house look like the morning after when it's still the evening before. But I can never resist doing macabre things with an old dressmaker's dummy that spends its normal life in the attic. I clothe it from the dressing-up box and it stands in an alcove in the hall which, until blissful January sixth, is papered with Christmas cards. (' We don't send any,' John murmured.)

" Last year, we wigged it with long nylon hair on a lobster-pot head with a light inside. Sounds horrible, I know, but it adds much excitement to going upstairs in the dark."

The children love nailing up evergreens and making immense paper chains. They can do what they like in the nursery and their bedrooms, and it's a marvellous competition during the first week of holidays. " They even read books on how to do it and produce large, angelic mobiles and keep dashing out for paper clips and gum," John said with a little bit of pride. " The purpose and pleasure of this is that they do it all themselves—and it's easy to admire."

The Mortimers are great with the gifts. " We are basically eight givers," Penelope said. " If eight people give presents to seven people it comes to. . . ." I'm still doing the multiplication.

" Beyond that there are grandparents and aunts, goldfish and canaries (all generous), and the heroes of the year—continually Pat Smythe and Sir Laurence Olivier, and currently also Adam Faith and Pop-eye—who provide diaries and pencil-sharpeners for people, cuttle-bone and fish food for animals," Penelope went on.

" John and I wrap them all on Christmas Eve. It's strenuous. We stagger on with it, fortified by champagne, into the early hours."

John smiled: " People who ask us to parties on December twenty-fourth think we have no Christmas spirit, I suppose." And then he made some rather unquotable observations about the Season of the Year. (He is not a man for organized jollity, but as a child he spent Christmas very much alone in the company of grown-ups; and his sympathy for children at this time is very real.)

We laughed and were rather sophisticated, then Penelope said: " I, too, dislike it intensely. If it weren't for the children I—we—would be far away, toasting toes in the sun. But in spite of commercialization and the general panic and disruption of it all, still has a magic for and with children, if you can reach it under the chaos."

As you may have realized already, these busy, professional Mortimers do not ever really lose sight of the magic under the chaos. That is why visiting their house is essentially being at home. And home also means Happy Christmas, to them and, surely, to us all.

12 tokens and vouchers

1960

CHOSEN BY MOLLIE BARGER

1 Comprehensive Vouchers. A gift voucher is heaven to receive because you have the joy of opening it on Christmas morning and the joy of buying anything you like with it on one of those dull January days when Christmas seems months away. Harrods, Knightsbridge, SW 1, and many other large stores sell them for any amount.

2 Chance of a Lifetime. Send them a voucher for premium bonds and let them enjoy a regular slice of optimism. £1 upwards from any post office. Youngsters will like savings stamps to spend or to add to their hoard.

3 A Good Book. Book tokens are a perennial joy to receive—and to spend. Available from booksellers and general stores in a wide price range.

4 Treat Her to a Facial. Give her something that she will never buy for herself—a course of beauty treatments. Elizabeth Arden, 25 Old Bond St, W 1, offers vouchers for treatments costing one guinea upwards available in many stores throughout the country, and other beauty salons have similar schemes.

5 The Music goes Round and Around. For music-lovers, gramophone-record tokens are welcome gifts. These can be bought from any large store or record shop in a wide price range.

6 Say It with Flowers. Fill their house with flowers for a week, or a month or a year, through a flower gift voucher obtainable from any florist belonging to Interflora.

7 The Play's the Thing. Gifts for parents are always a problem. They seem to have everything. Solve it by sending them a season ticket for the local theatre or concert hall, and they will bless you weekly.

8 Hair Styles Unlimited. Women of all ages will specially appreciate a voucher that will take care of their hairdressing expenses for a week or a month, or even a year if you feel generous. Most salons de coiffure will be glad to supply a voucher. Cost—anything from the price of one shampoo and set to a year's supply of weekly hair-dos.

9 Passport to Pleasure. What better gift can you offer than a holiday? The Erna Low Travel Service, 47 Old Brompton Rd, SW 7, offers gift vouchers for Christmas or weekend house parties, winter sports or summer holidays. These vouchers are in denominations of £5 and they will be pleased to bank the vouchers for anyone who is saving up for a holiday. The Manager of the Post Order Department of Thomas Cook & Son, Ltd, Berkeley St, W 1, will also issue vouchers for any sum of money for any service offered by them—trains, planes, cruises, hotels, etc.

10 For Bibliophiles. A subscription to the Times Book Club, 42 Wigmore St, W 1, will delight book-collectors. For eight guineas they can have one novel a month for a year. Non-fiction costs ten guineas and a mixture nine. Half-yearly subscriptions are half price.

11 Good Housekeeping All the Year Round. A subscription to Good Housekeeping costs only £1 17s. 6d. per annum, post paid, to any address in the UK or abroad. All you need to do is to write to The Belgrave Library, 22 Armoury Way, London, SW 18, giving the name and address of your friend and enclosing remittance.

12 A Gorgeous Feast. This is a splendid idea for your favourite young couple. Give them a voucher for The Guinea and the Piggy, where they can feast at one of London's newest restaurants, eating as much as they like of 120 hot and cold luxury dishes for one guinea each. Only drinks are extra. 20-21 Leicester Sq., WC 2

We present with pleasure the youngest-ever contributor to Good Housekeeping

ILLUSTRATED BY BILL BANKS

O NCE upon a time there was a little girl called Evelyn. One day her Mummy sent her to Brixton to buy a pair of sandals, and gave her a penny to pay for them. On the way she met a fairy, who was crying.

"Why are you crying?" said Evelyn.

"Because I saw a little boy who is very ill and his Mummy has no money to buy him some sweets. Have you got a penny?" said the fairy.

Evelyn gave the fairy her penny and went to the shop.

The man in the shop would not give her any sandals, not even one, without the money, so she went home.

Evelyn knew that her Mummy would be very cross, and she cried and told her what had happened.

"That's no use," said her Mummy. "You'll have to take some more money and get the sandals."

This time Evelyn took a shilling, but before she reached the shop she met an elf.

"Can you give me a shilling?" said the elf. "There is a little girl near here whose Mummy had smallpox and needs a bottle of cough mixture to make her quite better."

Evelyn gave the elf the shilling and went to the shop.

Still the man would not give her any sandals, and she had to go home without them. Her Mummy was very cross. "This time I will give you a lot of money, and if you come back without the sandals I will make you go to school with your feet quite naked," she said.

Evelyn reached the shop without meeting anybody, and bought her sandals.

On the way home she met an angel, who was hobbling. Evelyn looked at the angel's poor, scratched feet and felt very sorry for her.

"My sister says if I don't get some sandals soon my feet will have to be cut right off," said the angel.

So Evelyn gave her new sandals to the angel, and went to school with her feet quite, quite naked.

BY EVELYN STANLEY, age 6½

BERNARD BLATCH

PEOPLE WITHOUT CHRISTMAS

1962

THE fires are high, the lights shine more brightly than ever, the voices of children echo in the stillness of the night and from Poland to Patagonia the warm glow of Christmas settles upon the Christian world.

For us Christians, Christmas is at the centre of our lives, a feast for all, a thanksgiving, a remembrance of the day when the Son of God came down among us; above all it is the expression of an ideal of peace and goodness, of sincerity and charity which is the foundation stone of the Christian spirit.

At Christmas the good are loved yet more, the bad absolved, forgiven, and we gain a new hope for a life in which we believe man may be brother to man. We think, we *know* that this is how humanity should live its span on earth. We are convinced that we know the way and therein lies the supreme arrogance of man. Not long ago a great Muslim teacher in India, Raihana Behn, told a visitor: "When you first find the road to God, you think your road is the only road to him. But if you follow it with devotion, one day you come to a great open plain and find that there are many roads to God and many people following them from North and South, East and West. And then comes a day when you are suddenly caught up to the blue vault of heaven and you suddenly see that all the roads are one road. . . ."

How then do other people see our Christmas ideals? How do they see their brother? Do they know the meaning of charity? Have they, in fact, a Christmas of their own, a Christmas by some other name but with the same meaning and symbolism?

Many, many questions so soon answered when one looks into other religions. Of the world's eleven living religions,* there isn't one which fails to emphasize man's essential need for charity and goodness.

Did you perhaps think that the Christian idea of "love thy neighbour" was unique?

See what one of the sacred books of Buddhism says: "For hatred does not cease by hatred at any time, hatred ceases by love. . . . Let a man overcome anger by love, let him overcome evil by good; let him overcome the greedy by liberality, the liar by truth. . . ."

And what did Mohammed say about it? "Say not, if people do good to us we will do good to them and if people oppress you, you will oppress them. But resolve that if people do good to you, you will do good to them and if they oppress you, oppress them not again. . . ."

They may be without Christmas, but they, too, know the meaning of joyful charity. These Japanese children, for instance, also receive presents: magnificent traditional dolls for the girls, high-flying kites for the boys

BY RENÉ LECLER

One might so easily forget that the famous phrase "Thou shalt love thy neighbour as thyself" first appeared in Judaism's *Leviticus*. We may have already forgotten the words of the prophet Malachi: "Have we not all one father? Hath not one God created us all?"

Studying the religions of our neighbours, even perfunctorily as most of us would, and looking at the gentle, age-old customs which have grown around these religions and the feasts which symbolize them, leaves one in no doubt that those others, the people without Christmas, also know man's innate striving for love and charity.

It is not difficult to find it in Hinduism, a colourful, warm religion which personifies every aspect of God and teems with legends of the God-life coming down to mingle with men. Among the best loved of these is the story of Krishna, the Lord of Love, who is said to have been born and spent his boyhood in the country between New Delhi and Agra—a country which to the devout Hindu bears the imprint still of the feet of a holy child, just as Palestine does to the Christian.

No religion has more festivals and feasts than Hinduism but the one which corresponds most closely to our Christmas in its philosophy is the late autumn feast of *Deepavali*, or Feast of Lights. Like Christmas, it heralds the advent of winter and lays emphasis on the warmth and light within the spirit of man. A few days before *Deepavali*, Hindus whitewash their houses and renovate their furniture. During the feast, everyone, dressed in their best clothes, visits relations and gifts are given and received, particularly gifts from brothers to sisters.

In the evening rows of earthen lamps are lit on every house front and the children celebrate with crackers, squibs and fireworks. Modern Hinduism puts the spirit of giving into practice. In Poona, near a home for forgotten, neglected little girls, the local Hindu men are reminded during the Feast of Lights that these children are their little sisters whose hope for the future could be transformed by a gift.

This spirit of wider generosity is much emphasized by Vinoba Bhave, perhaps the most influential and deeply revered of modern Hindu teachers. At his call, many landowners have given one-tenth of their land to the poor and many homes have started the custom of setting aside a bowl into which the youngest child is instructed daily to place a handful of grain. "Don't tell him why he does it," Bhave says. "Then one day he will ask you himself and you will explain that it is to form a daily habit of remembering the poor and the hungry."

* Christianity, Confucianism, Islam, Hinduism, Buddhism, Taoism, Shintoism, Judaism, Sikhism, Jainism, Zoroastrianism.

1962

Hinduism is a colourful religion filled with the spirit of giving of which Indian children are the main beneficiaries

No family is ever more united than the Jewish one and Jewish children take a large part in the family ceremonial

For Egyptian children, the birthday of the Prophet means one thing: the arrival of the traditional sugar dolls

1954

The Christmas Shopper's Guide to Socks

100% SPUN NYLON
Looks and feels like wool. Cosy but very hard-wearing, resists shrinking.

100% CRIMPED NYLON
Very new. Very resilient. Dull crepe finish. Two sizes provide perfect fit for every foot.

100% CONTINUOUS FILAMENT NYLON
Light and silky, perfect for evening dress.

WOOL & NYLON BLENDS
Up to 50% nylon, blended with the wool. For extra wear.

nothing like nylon socks
for Christmas stockings

For all the men that every woman thinks of at Christmas. For men who live by themselves—and like it even better with no-darning nylon socks. For men who have everything (100% crimped nylon socks are newer than *that*, and very handsome). For men whose wives (you perhaps?) would love the time and money saved, the leisure gained with easy-washing, less-mending, shrink-resistant nylon.

For all sizes of present: one pair would be a blessing, three pairs boundless luxury.

WOOL SPLICED WITH NYLON
Nylon reinforces rub-points at the toe and heel for longer wear. High-splicing above the heels gives added strength.

Nothing like for socks

BRITISH NYLON SPINNERS LTD., PONTYPOOL, MON.

Good Housekeeping

DECEMBER 1931

1/- nett

Double Christmas Number
New Novel by O. Douglas

Virginia Woolf - Marguerite Steen - Coningsby Dawson

Good Housekeeping

December 1932

1s. NETT

CHRISTMAS NUMBER

D.K.Broster - Vicki Baum - Francis Brett Young
I.A.R.Wylie - Kate O'Brien - Walter de la Mare

Good Housekeeping

DECEMBER 1934

Christmas Number

New Novel by Joanna Cannan

1/- NETT

Beverley Nichols ~ Susan Ertz - Warwick Deeping
Maude Royden ~ Kathleen Norris ~ Temple Bailey

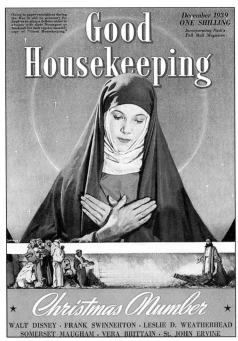

Good Housekeeping

December 1939
ONE SHILLING

Christmas Number

WALT DISNEY - FRANK SWINNERTON - LESLIE D. WEATHERHEAD
SOMERSET MAUGHAM - VERA BRITTAIN - ST. JOHN ERVINE

Good Housekeeping

Christmas Number

1/6

PEARL BUCK - HENRY WILLIAMSON - HOWARD SPRING
LORNA REA - DOROTHY WHIPPLE - LORD DUNSANY
Christmas Play for home acting by A. A. MILNE

Good Housekeeping

Christmas Number

1/6 Specially written story by Eleanor Farjeon

F. H. GRISEWOOD - WALTER KARIG - MARJORIE HESSELL TILTMAN
CHRISTMAS CATERING BY THE INSTITUTE

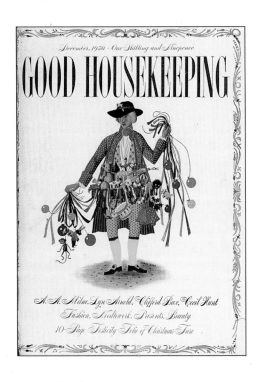

December, 1950 - One Shilling and Ninepence

GOOD HOUSEKEEPING

A. A. Milne, Lyn Arnold, Clifford Bax, Cecil Hunt
Fashion, Needlework, Presents, Beauty
10-Page Festivity Folio of Christmas Fare

DECEMBER 1956 2/-

Good Housekeeping

CHRISTMAS NUMBER

DECEMBER 1957 - 2s.

Good Housekeeping

CHRISTMAS NUMBER